20th Century Phillies by the Numbers

You can't tell the players without a scorecard

Celebrating the 100th Anniversary of the first Phillies NL Pennant – 1915
A fan's recollections

Ted Taylor

Ted Taylor

20th Century Phillies By The Numbers
You can't tell the players without a scorecard

© Ted Taylor, 2015
All Rights Reserved
Printed in the United States of America

This is a work of research and recollection. The facts, as near as possible, are accurate, the recollections are only as good as the writer can recall them.

To order additional copies of this book contact:
TTA LLC, P. O. Box 273, Abington PA 19001 or the publisher.
tedtaylorinc@comcast.net

Published by
The Educational Publisher
Biblio Publishing
BiblioPublishing.com
1313 Chesapeake Ave.
Columbus, OH 43212
ISBN: 978-1-62249-242-8

Research, Philadelphia Phillies National League baseball club
Recollection, The memories of "The Glenside Kid" (Ted Taylor)

Cover adapted by Cynthia M. Taylor
Photos come from the author's extensive baseball card collection, pictures in Public Domain, scrapbooks and other stuff he came across.

Critic John Shiffert's review of Ted's "Ultimate Philadelphia Athletics Reference Book"...

To the uninitiated, reviewing a reference book, like reading a reference book, might seem as exciting as either watching paint dry or spectating a long-distance bike race (which typically seems to involve 99 percent of the contestants riding in one huge pack for 99 percent of the race, after which everyone sprints like mad for the finish.) However, that's not the case with Henry R. "Ted" Taylor's most recent reference work on "his" team, the Philadelphia Athletics. Following on the heels of his equally entertaining "The Philadelphia Athletics by the Numbers," this next chapter in Taylor's campaign to keep alive the memory of the City of Brotherly Love's most interesting professional sports franchise, "The Ultimate Philadelphia Athletics Reference Book" (Xlibris Corp., ISBN 978-1-4500-2571-3, 457 pages, $23.99, www.Xlibris.com) is another example of how yeoman research, combined with a true love of your subject, can produce a compendium as interesting as its namesake.

Briefly recapping Taylor's credentials in terms of his status to both write and subsequently entitle such a book... **for the past 35 years or so, Taylor has been as important a name in Philadelphia baseball as**

Ted Taylor

Larry Shenk, Bill Giles, Whitey Ashburn, Harry Kalas, Ruly Carpenter, Allen Lewis, Jayson Stark or anyone else you care to list who hasn't officially worn a uniform. A nationally- respected authority on baseball cards and memorabilia, a former college (Ursinus and Spring Garden) baseball coach, a widely-read baseball columnist, an even more widely-read author, the co-founder of the first Philadelphia area baseball card show, the owner of the first Philadelphia area baseball card store, the host of a nationally-syndicated collectibles radio show, an expert witness in the anti-trust lawsuit against Topps, a vice president of two baseball card companies, the founding president of the Philadelphia Athletics Historical Society... well, you get the picture. Ted Taylor has been involved in Philly area baseball in just about every way possible, and that includes as an infielder at Millersville State (as it says on his baseball card), and, prior to that, on the sandlots of Cheltenham Township, where he'd sometimes let a young kid named R. Jackson into the game.

So, yes, Ted Taylor is well-qualified to discuss the subject at hand, the team he rooted passionately for up until the time they left town, when he was 13 years old. That was 56 years ago. And yet, the Philadelphia Athletics still live on, even in the minds of those of us who are too young to remember them directly as a franchise that reached the absolute pinnacle of major league baseball not once, but twice, and that also fielded awful teams featuring the likes of Squiz Pillion, Steve Gerkin, Bruno Haas and Lynn "Line Drive" Nelson.

Books by Ted Taylor

Card Collecting/Food

Baseball Cards – 300 All-Time Stars

The Official Baseball Card Collecting Handbook

100 Years & 100 Recipes
(The Story of Ralph's Italian Restaurant)

The Philadelphia Athletics Trilogy

The Philadelphia Athletics by the Numbers

The Ultimate Philadelphia Athletics Reference Book, 1901-1954

The Duke of Milwaukee, the Life & Times of Al Simmons

Autobiographical Novel

The Glenside Kid

Textbooks

Ted Taylor

Introduction to Mass Communications, 4th edition
Introduction to Public Relations, 4th edition
Creative Writing, 4th edition

Checklist Book

Phillies Baseball Card & Memorabilia Checklist Book (1979)

This Book is dedicated to my wife Cindy

*Also to My Mom (Helen)
& Two Dads (Jack & Ernie)...
Who taught me to love baseball*

*Also to Del Ennis and the Phillies,
they always tried*

Ted Taylor

Sometimes the Good Guys win..

Baseball was special
To a little kid like me
I loved the things it taught us
In the land where we are free.

My parents both loved sports,
They passed that to their son
When my English Dad played soccer
The good guys always won.

Our hometown had two baseball teams
The Phils last won in '15 and the A's in '31
As a kid neither one was all that hot -
And good guys seldom won.

And then in Nineteen Fifty
Lightning Struck our town,
Whitey, Del and Robbie saw to it -
That the good guys won the crown.

They won the NL flag that year
And we were keeping score,
But DiMaggio and his pals said "you're done" -
And our good guys won no more.

Ted Taylor

It was 1980, 30 years later
I was there for the last game of ball,
When Pete and Tugger closed the deal -
The good guys won it all.

Baseball is America
We try and try and try
And sometimes it goes our way -
And sometimes we only cry.

But teamwork is what it teaches,
A lesson sound and true
For a longtime little kid like me
I say "Baseball I love you".

- Ted Taylor

Contents

Prologue - xiii
Chapter 1 – Pick a number, any number 1
Chapter 2 – The Phillies and the A's 11
Chapter 3 – Phillies Hall of Famers 21
Chapter 4 – The "Skippers" 37
Chapter 5 – Phillies in the Post Season 51
Chapter 6 – Player Profiles (A-J) 77
Chapter 7 – Player Profiles (K-Z) 123
Chapter 8 – Unlisted Numbers 179
Chapter 9 – The Front Office 187
Chapter 10 – About the Phils 205
Chapter 11 – Strictly by the numbers 209
Chapter 12 – The Lineup Evolve 229
Chapter 13 – Player Awards 247
Chapter 14 – The Phils Trade That Changed 253
    Baseball
Chapter 15 – They Took My Team Away 261
Chapter 16 – The Phillies new stadium was 267
    almost in the suburbs
Chapter 17 – Cy Williams, Dick Allen, ... 271
    Del Ennis, Why the Hall Not?
Chapter 18 – Philadelphia's Third 277
    Big League Team
About the Author 297
Postscript 301

Center Lineup Page from 1950 Phils Scorecard Vs. Brooklyn Dodgers

Prologue

This book, it took almost four years of writing and research, is being released in 2015 in homage to and in celebration of the first pennant won by the Philadelphia Phillies – exactly 100 years ago. And it's not like they've won a lot of them. The other four of the five won in the 20th Century came in my lifetime (1950, 1980, 1983, 1993). **I write this book in the persona of "The Glenside Kid" and my reflections of growing up in the mid-20th Century. In my 2011 autobiographical novel I looked at the world through my own eyes – I reflect on the Phillies and baseball, in this book, with those very same eyes.**

As a young boy I had two teams to root for (until I was 14). The American League Athletics, the National League Phillies. There was always a ball game in town – 154 of them. When going to Shibe Park the first thing most fans did upon entering the stadium was to buy a scorecard – after all, you couldn't tell who the players were without one. I would diligently score each game – as if that really meant anything – and it was important to me to get it right. Ball player's numbers always fascinated me. Why was Richie Ashburn, an outfielder, #1 on the Phillies while Eddie Joost, a shortstop, wore that number for the A's? At some point I must have realized that numbers were more of a personal preference thing than what they were originally

Ted Taylor

intended to be, the positions in the batting order (it's why Babe Ruth wore #3 and Lou Gehrig #4).

As founding President of the Philadelphia Athletics Historical Society (in 1995) I took my lifelong fascination with uniform numbers to the next level and began researching all the numbers worn by the A's players between 1931 and 1954. It was a task that would take me many years to complete (though I must admit I did it "off and on" and got a lot of help from my friends).

But in 2009 the time had come and I published *The Philadelphia Athletics by the numbers – Let's give Skeeter #2*. The book was a success and led to the seminal work of my research career (up to that time), the 457-page *Ultimate Philadelphia Athletics Research Book – 1901-1954*.

While doing book signings (at such places at Citizen's Bank Park, Barnes & Noble, numerous book shops and sports-collectibles events) the same question kept popping up "when are you going to do a 'Phillies by the numbers' book? And my answer was, always, "The Phillies are a work in progress, the A's were finished". But, soon, even I didn't believe that.

After much soul-searching I decided to do a definitive Phillies by the numbers book, but limit it to the 20th Century, actually the period from 1932, when they first wore numbers, to 1999 the last year of the 100-year-window. The players that I'll focus on in this work will mostly be the ones that wore a numbered jersey – the

20th Century Phillies by the Numbers

group from 1900-to-1932 will get some space, but no in-depth, individual mention. It was a monster-sized task and one that, at times, I thought I'd never finish. The A's numbers book spanned 1931-54, the Phillies covered 1932 to 1999 – almost three times as many years, and a like number more players.

That's a lot of research – and much of it quite daunting. As with the Athletics, players came and went, that happens to bad teams and the Phillies had their share of clunkers. Some of the players came and went so fast that no one ever bothered recording their uniform digits. One pinch-running appearance, one at-bat, one-third of an inning on the mound and the player qualifies. There are, indeed, players from the era of numbers that won't have a number in this book.

Another thing we noticed was that - especially between 1932 and 1950 - players didn't seem all that focused on what number they would wear. Maybe, like when I played for the Glenside Midgets back in the 1950's, it was more about what uniform jersey fit best rather than what the number was on the back.

Hall of Famer Chuck Klein wore so many different numbers that when it came time to retire his number they had no idea of which one to retire. I got a call, many years ago; from Phillies PR Director, Larry Shenk (and fellow Millersville U. alumnus) asking if I knew what number Klein wore. My research turned up the fact that the Hall of Famer wore a lot of different numbers, six to be exact – and they couldn't come up with one he was really identified with, so they didn't

Ted Taylor

retire any of his, they just put his name up as being a "retired" number. Oddly enough during his career he wore two numbers that were retired for someone else (#1, #36). (I guess that means no one named Chuck Klein can ever play for them again. They did the same for Grover Cleveland Alexander, but he played in the era before numbers were even worn.)

Another Hall of Famer, Robin Roberts, ended up with #36 because, when he was recalled in mid-season 1948, the guy who was released to make room for the Michigan Stater wore that number and, when they met in the locker room, one coming, one going, the departing hurler (Nick Strincevich) tossed him the jersey and said "I hope you have more luck with this than I did."

And that's pretty much what we found. No rhyme, no reason for numbers. In this book, you'll find all the players from 1932 to 1999 in rough alpha/year order and what number(s) they wore. And lots of them wore several. There's even a well-used, often published, photo of Richie Ashburn wearing, what appears to be, number 9 on his back (taken in 1948 at Spring Training) – yet no record exists that he ever wore that number in a real (or even exhibition) game. Best guess is that a photographer needed a photo of the rookie outfielder, grabbed a jersey, tossed it to Whitey, and took the shot. Infielder Emil Verban wore #9 in 1948. I wish I'd have asked Rich that on one of the several occasions I was with him.

20th Century Phillies by the Numbers

A book just about numbers, while valuable as a research piece, lacks a certain amount of soul. Parts of this book will be from the perspective of "The Glenside Kid" (me) who, as a fan, hobbyist, sportswriter/columnist (*Daily News, Sports Collector's Digest, Montgomery Media*), show promoter, radio sportscaster and card company executive, was lucky enough to meet and spend time with many of my idols.

This book, therefore, will be unlike most research books because when I have a story to tell or a recollection to share of something I've heard or known about a player, I will weave it in to the body of this work. Since many liked the way "The Glenside Kid' approached growing up, hopefully you'll like the way he enjoyed baseball growing up (and as a grown up), too.

I have also included a chapter (18) on the Negro League Philadelphia Stars. I regret that I never saw them, knowing that I missed seeing some of the great players of the sport. As many as I could, I have listed players and brief bios of many of them, 1934-52.

Sit back, grab a bag of popcorn and a coke or, maybe, a beer, and let's go to the ballgame – remember, you can't tell the players without a scorecard.

The Glenside Kid….

Chapter 1
Pick a Number, any number

The Phillies first wore uniform numbers (along with the rest of the National League) sometime in June, 1932. The American League teams had been alternately using, then not using, numbers for a few years but started requiring them in 1931. In Philadelphia Connie Mack's American League team would only wear them on the road until 1937 – when they wore them at home, too. In his own bizarre way of thinking Mr. Mack (always thrifty) felt that numbers would eliminate the need for a scorecard and, hence, reduce revenue. Clearly it was the other way around.

It is reported that the 1883 Cincinnati Red Stockings were the first team to wear numbers and wore them on  their sleeves to help fans identify the players. The idea didn't take hold and they soon abandoned the practice. In 1911 the Cleveland Indians used letters to designate players, i.e., "Now batting #A Nap Lajoie" (a one-time Phillie, pictured, left in his T-206 card from that era.). This idea was so confusing that they quickly dropped it. In 1916 the Indians tried numbers on their sleeves, starting in mid-July, but only on their

Ted Taylor

home uniforms. It is said they also tried the idea again in 1917, though no real evidence of that exists.

The popular baseball publication of the early part of the 20th Century *Sporting Life* wrote an editorial in 1916 advocating the use of uniform numbers. They pointed out that football teams were wearing them and their use would be helpful to the fans.

The 1923 St. Louis Cardinals wore numbers on their home uniforms only (on the sleeves) and also did so in 1924, again just on their home whites. This apparently lasted another season or two but was deemed a failure when none of the fans seemed to take notice.

The 1929 Yankees wore numbers on both their home and away jerseys, as did the Cleveland Indians and on May 13, 1929 when the Yankees visited Cleveland it marked the first time that both teams took the field wearing uniform numbers.

By 1930 the Washington Senators were also wearing numbers but, inexplicably, the Indians gave up on the idea, after beginning the season with numbers.

In 1931 American League President Ernest S. Barnard decreed that all teams in his loop should wear numbers. He suggested the numbering be as follows: The "regulars", i.e., the starting fielders wear numbers 1 thru 7. Catchers should wear 8-11, pitchers 12-24 and the utility players wear the rest. The use of #13,

20th Century Phillies by the Numbers

Barnard suggested, be left to the discretion of each team.

When the '32 National League season began, only the Boston Braves wore digits on their jerseys. It wasn't until June until all the teams wore them following a special owners meeting. (As a result of that, some players seeing action that season pre-June, never had a number.)

Trying to come up with Phillies numbers, especially in the early days, was a challenge. First you'd get the season-end stats, then you'd try to find numbers to match against those players in the usual spots and, failing that, you got creative. Some few, mostly obscure, players defied the odds and will appear, later, in the "unlisted numbers' section.

Only 20 men ever wore #1 for the Phils, now retired in honor of Richie Ashburn. The first to wear it was an outfielder named Kiddo Davis (1932), the last, another outfielder, Jose Cardenal (1978-79) right before it was retired. One man, Mitch Williams, wore #99 (1993), another, Omar

Ted Taylor

Olivares, wore #00 (1995). Every number between 1 and 62 was worn at least once. No one ever wore #63, but pitcher Gary Wagner wore #64 in 1965.

Multiple numbers were common. Hall of Famer Chuck Klein wore the following – 1, 3, 8, 26, 29 and 36. Ironically two of the numbers would be retired but not for him. Other multiple wearers included Bobby Wine (1, 7, 13, 42); John Boozer, a pitcher (19, 21, 28, 29, 42), Benny Culp, a catcher (2, 20, 23, 25, 29, 31); Bob Dernier, outfielder (22, 24, 29, 30); Frank Hoerst, pitcher (8, 11, 14, 22, 34); Andy Karl, pitcher (3, 6, 11, 23, 28, 33, 44); Hans Lobert, coach and manager (1, 2, 25, 50); Danny Litwhiler, outfielder (4, 7, 11, 28, 31); Hal Marnie, infielder (7, 9, 15, 18, 24); Brad Moore, pitcher (37, 38, 46, 48); Ron Northey, outfielder (4, 14, 26, 30, 33); Lou Possehl, pitcher (12, 16, 29, 37, 39, 41); Steve Ridzik, pitcher (20, 27, 37, 42); Andy Seminick, catcher and coach (2, 15, 21, 24, 48); Rick Wise, pitcher (18, 28, 38, 62) and the two men who wore more numbers, seven, than any other Phillie were Granny Hamner, Whiz Kids era infielder and onetime pitcher (1, 2, 6, 17, 21, 33, 37); and the beloved John Vuckovich, infielder and coach (3, 7, 18, 22, 26, 28, 30).

Retired Numbers

The Phillies have retired five numbers, yet honored seven players. The numbers, 1, 14, 20, 32 and 36 – plus Chuck Klein (who wore many) and Grover Cleveland Alexander (who never wore any). They also (along with the rest of baseball) retired Jackie

20th Century Phillies by the Numbers

Robinson's #42. I get then symbolism, but don't particularly like the idea because no one who ever wore #42 for the Phillies deserved to have the uniform retired. Hugh "Losing Pitcher" Mulcahy wore it in 1937, Pitchers Ron Reed (eight seasons), Jack Meyer and Don Carman (seven each) wore it the longest.

But before we go any further let me state that I take issue with their retirement of #14. Not that the number shouldn't be retired but that they did so to honor Jim Bunning – and not Del Ennis, the man who owned the number for a lot of productive seasons. This is not new, my unhappiness with this retirement has been voiced in my *Philadelphia Daily News* columns, my internet blog at *TedSilary.com* and in letters and e-mails (mostly ignored) to the Phillies.

Jim Bunning was in my opinion not a great pitcher – he was a better-than-average, really pretty good, pitcher. He pitched for the Phillies 1964-67 and then, again, in the twi-light of his career 1970-71. In his first tour he won 19 games three times, 17 once. In his second tour he won 15 more. That's 89 wins. Who retires a number a pitcher wore and then won just 89 games? Other Phillies pitchers have done more than that – Chris Short won 132, Curt Simmons won 115 for example. Bunning's career numbers with the Tigers, Phillies and Pirates show just 224 wins (pretty low for the Hall), against 184 losses, a no-hitter in each league, and a 3.27 ERA. Go figure.

What did the Phillies win while Bunning was the acknowledged ace of their staff? Nothing, that's what.

Ted Taylor

They got close in 1964, but close only counts in horseshoes and hand grenades. Is it possible that they retired his number because he pitched a perfect game on Father's Day in 1964? That being the case, it's only a matter of time (now that he's retired) that Roy Halladay's number gets retired (and he's a better pitcher by any standard). I personally have doubts they'll do it.

If they had a burning desire to retire #14, then they should have done it for homegrown star Del Ennis. **(Pictured left on his 1951 Bowman Baseball Card, #4)** Born and raised in the Olney section of the city, Del was the power in the Phillies lineup for over a decade (1946-56). The Whiz Kids don't win the 1950 pennant without Del's .311 batting average, his 31 homers and league leading 126 RBI's. His career stats are pretty good too. In 14 seasons (Cards, Reds, White Sox) he batted .286 with 288 homeruns and 1,284 RBI's. There are players in the Hall of Fame that wish they had those numbers.

Perhaps if Pete Rose, the catalyst for the 1980 World's Championship, hadn't shot himself in the foot with his arrogance and gambling forays he, too, could be considered (though he wore Phils #14 only 1979-83) for number retirement. In fact how innovative would it

20th Century Phillies by the Numbers

be to retire #14 for all three of them? (The Yankees did it with #8, retired it for both Bill Dickey and Yogi Berra.)

The official Phillies party-line (heard ad nauseum) is that only Hall of Famers get their numbers retired. To me, that's just nonsense and disrespects the fans that supported the Phillies throughout Del Ennis's long run here.

No argument on Ashburn's #1, though it says here that doesn't happen unless he becomes a longtime Phillies sportscaster and part of the baseball landscape in town for over five decades. Ashburn had the misfortune to be a centerfielder in the era of Willie Mays, Mickey Mantle and Duke Snider, all playing the same position at the same time – and with the added benefit of the New York media to promote them. (Ashburn, though, accumulated more hits than any of that trio during the 50's decade.) Hobbyist Jim Donahue (from Upper Darby) deserves a lot of credit for Ashburn's induction. In fact Jim's "Why the Hall Not?" campaign mobilized fans and sportswriters to get the Veteran's Committee in Cooperstown to acknowledge that Ashburn had a darn fine career. I was privileged to be part of that effort and broke the story about Donahue's campaign first in my *Daily News* and also *Sports Collector's Digest* columns.

Retiring Mike Schmidt's #20 was a no-brainer. Many would argue that Dayton, Ohio native Mike was the best third baseman ever. Few remember that in Mike's rookie year (1963) he batted just .196 with 18 homers in 132 games. But his long 18-year stint with the Phils

Ted Taylor

produced 548 homeruns, a lifetime .267 batting average and 1,595 RBI's, not to mention numerous Gold Gloves.

Just the name "Lefty" is all most Phillies fans need to hear to recall the marvelous Steve Carlton, whose number 32 is also retired. The man could flat out pitch and his years with the Phils (1972-86) he won 20-or-more games four times (27 in 1972) and he was a complete game machine finishing 254 of the 709 games he started in his career (1965-88). Lifetime he is 329-244 with a 3.22 ERA.

Then there's Robin Roberts who inherited #36 in mid-season 1948 from journeyman Nick Strincevich and held on to it until 1961. Robbie was the ace of the staff when they won the 1950 NL pennant (in fact he was on the mound for that game) – and many other years too. He won 20 or more games six times and completed more than half the games he started (305 against 609 starts). Career totals show 286 wins, 245 losses and a 3.41 ERA (sadly hanging on much too long trying to get to 300 wins, he was pitching at Double-A Reading when he finally hung up his spikes).

CITY SERIES
ATHLETICS
vs.
PHILLIES

SHIBE PARK
OFFICIAL SCORE CARD AND PROGRAM

PRICE TEN CENTS

Ted Taylor

Brief History – In 1903 the A's & Phils played 12 games (some in season, some post season). The A's won 7, the Phils 5. The last games were in 1954 and the Phils took two out of three. Junior Baseball Federation and/or the Police Athletic League were the usual beneficiaries. The pre-season games were usually played on the weekend prior to the start of the regular season. The A's won the series 22 times, the Phillies won 16 times and there were 9 times that the series was tied.

Chapter 2
The Phillies and the A's

The Phillies were transplanted to the Quaker City from Worcester, Massachusetts and began their first season in town on May 1, 1883 when they hosted the Providence Grays. A crowd of just 1,200 was on hand at Recreation Park, 24th and Columbia Avenues. The team lost their opener 4-3 and it was all downhill from there. They ended up 17-81, dead last, and 46 games out of first place. Bob Ferguson and Blondie Purcell were the managers. Ferguson quit after winning four of the first 17 games, Purcell managed just 13 wins out of the remaining contests. (The City Series program pictured at left was from 1947, the Phillies won 7-3. (They played four games and split them that season.) Bill McCahan started for the A's, newly signed rookie Curt Simmons was on the mound for the Phillies.)

The Phillies were such a disaster after that one season that a lot of people never expected to see them again. But they returned in 1884 and guided by Hall of Famer Harry Wright they went 39-73 and finished sixth. In 1885, under Wright, they topped .500, winning 56 of 100 contests and finishing third.

The 1889 Phillies, pictured below, went 63-64 but finished fourth, it was manager Harry Wright's sixth

Ted Taylor

season (he was skipper for 12). Ed Delahanty batted .293, Sam Thompson .296 and Charlie Buffinton won 28 games.

When the American League was formed in 1901 Philadelphia was seen as prime territory and the first thing the new A's skipper, Connie Mack, did was raid the Phillies roster and sign future Hall of Famer Nap Lajoie (he'd hit .422, 14 homers and have 125 RBI's for the A's) and pitchers Chick Fraser (who would win 20 games for Mr. Mack), Bill Bernhart (would win 17) and Whitey Platt (who'd also win 17).

On opening day 1901 the A's drew 15,000 fans to Columbia Park, while the Phils managed just 779 to Baker Bowl. The A's would outdraw the Phillies annually until 1915 when the Phils won their first NL pennant.

20th Century Phillies by the Numbers

Ironically the Phillies finished second in 1901 (83-57) and one wonders if they'd have won it all had they not lost the four players to Mack's A's. The Phils drew 234,937 fans that year showing that Philadelphia was capable of supporting two teams – and would attempt do so for the next 53 years.

In fairness to the long-suffering Philadelphia fans, both the A's and Phillies were pretty dreadful over many of those seasons (yes, the A's won nine AL pennants – 1902, 1905, 1910, 1911, 1913, 1914, 1929, 1930, 1931 and five World's Championships – 1910, 1911, 1913, 1929, 1930 - and the Phillies won just two pennants 1915, 1950 – ("The Whiz Kids", pictured above) - but mostly they were bad.

After the first few years at Recreation Park the Phillies played their games at Baker Bowl (1887-1938, with a year at Columbia Park in 1903 as the Bowl was renovated), located at Broad and Lehigh, and the A's

Ted Taylor

played, from 1909 on, at Shibe Park, just down the street at 21st & Lehigh – which was a showcase of modern baseball architecture for many years. The Phillies moved in to Shibe Park, essentially became tenants of the A's, and in 1938 after years of neglected maintenance caught up to them at Baker Bowl and part of the stands collapsed. Connie Mack welcomed them, and said he thought they'd be a better team at Shibe Park, but they weren't. In fact for five straight years after the move to Shibe the Phils finished last and lost more than 100 games-a-season.

A long-ago story speaks of the famous Lifebuoy Soap sign on the right field wall at Baker. The sign said "The Phillies use Lifebuoy Soap". One night someone snuck in to the park and painted, directly below that statement "And they still stink!"

It's June 1955 and Phillies bonus baby shortstop Ted "Killer" Kazanski comes in to the dugout and is immediately met by an usher seeking his signature on some baseballs. Pitcher Dave Cole (#44) is in the background. Note the advertising signs now that the ballpark is under the Phils ownership. ("The Glenside Kid", age 14, took this picture prior to the Phillies-Milwaukee Braves game.)

Ironically, in their half-century of sharing the same city the two teams never met in post season play. The closest they got was a year apart when the 1914 A's won the American League and 1915 when the Phillies took the National. Both clubs lost, badly, in the World Series.

It's 1951 and new Philadelphia Athletics manager Jimmie Dykes, second from right, watches a ball tossed to Mr. Mack by an unknown person prior to the start of the first City series game in which the A's would play for a manager other than Connie Mack. Pictured, left to right, are the unknown thrower, Phillies President Bob Carpenter, Phillies

Ted Taylor

manager Eddie Sawyer, Dykes and A's President/owner Connie Mack.

But for many years as far back, at least, to 1911 the Phillies and A's began the season with a "City Series" with the proceeds going to one charity or another. That year a 24-year-old rookie with just two years of pro experience took the mound for the Phillies and held the defending World Champion A's hitless for five innings. It was clear to everyone that the Phillies had something special in Grover Cleveland Alexander, the quiet hurler from Nebraska.

More than 50 players were affiliated with both Philadelphia clubs – a few of them qualify for the trivia question "Who began their big league career with one team in the same city as they finished with another?" Among them, of course would be Babe Ruth, began with the Red Sox ended with the Braves; Hank Aaron, began in Milwaukee with the Braves, ended there with the Brewers; even Yogi Berra who started with the Yankees and saw action in four games at the end with the Mets.

The Philadelphians would include Jimmie Foxx (started with the A's, ended with the Phillies), also Bobby Shantz, Bill Nicholson, Nap Lajoie and even Chief Bender (if you disallow a one-game, one inning appearance in 1925 when he was a coach for the White Sox). Billy DeMars played for the A's at the start of his career and was a longtime Phillies coach at the end of it, Eddie Collins Jr. played for the A's, was assistant GM of the Phillies and Mayo Smith was an

A's outfielder and Phillies manager (though not his last stop).

Here's the whole list of players and officials that were affiliated with both clubs:

Dick Barrett, Stan Baumgartner, Bender, Joe Bowman, Frank Bruggy, Collins Jr., Lave Cross, Monte Cross, DeMars, George Earnshaw, Nick Etten, Dana Fillingim, Lou Finney, Elmer Flick, Chick Fraser, Foxx, Dave Fultz, Phil Geier, Kid Gleason, Joe Dolan, Bill Duggleby, Vern Kennedy, Nap Lajoie, Billy Lauder, Bevo LeBourveau, Walt Masters, Eddie Mayo, Stuffy McInnis, John McPherson, Fred Mitchell, Morgan Murphy, Nicholson, Herb Pennock, Johnny Gray, Rollie Hemsley, Ed Huesser, Bill Kelly, Cy Perkins, Dave Philley, Vic Power, Ken Richardson, Shantz, Dave Shean, Mayo Smith, Stan Sperry, Tuck Stainback, Elmer Valo **(pictured left on his 1954 Topps baseball card)**, Hal Wagner and Tom Zachary.

The Glenside Kid Remembers...

Elmer Valo was bad news for fans of the teams he played for – at least the cities they played in. He played for the Philadelphia A's (1954) and they moved to Kansas City. He played for the Brooklyn Dodgers (1957) and they moved to Los Angeles, then he played for the Washington Senators (1960) and they moved to

Ted Taylor

Minnesota. We were really worried in 1961 when the Phillies signed him for a second tour (he was a Phil in 1956, too). I got to know Elmer in the late 60's when I was baseball coach at Ursinus College in Collegeville, PA and he was scouting for the Phillies. Valo attended several of our games because he was interested in one of my outfielders, Harvey Pond, and my third baseman Steve Long. The Phillies did not sign either.

WPEN 950 — Philadelphia's Sports Station

BROADCASTING ALL THE
PHILLIES GAMES
HOME AND AWAY

With GENE KELLY

Play-by-play all Phillies games, colorfully reported by Gene Kelly, vivid new Voice of the Phillies!

PLUS TOP SPORTING EVENTS

"HERE COME THE PHILLIES"
A "must" program for sports fans featuring interviews with the players, coaches and managers of the Phillies and other major league clubs. Monday through Saturday at 6:30 P. M.
EVERY NITE AT 6:30 P.M.

BOXING EVERY MONDAY NITE
The best fights, from everywhere, excitingly described. Tune to WPEN "Fight of the Week".
EVERY MONDAY NITE AT 10 P.M.

- TEMPLE BASKETBALL
- PENN BASKETBALL
- WARRIORS BASKETBALL
- EAGLES FOOTBALL
- VILLANOVA FOOTBALL AND BASKETBALL
- NOTRE DAME FOOTBALL
- ST. JOSEPH BASKETBALL

BOXING - FOOTBALL - BASKETBALL - BASEBALL

THE SUN RAY DRUG STATION

Ted Taylor

The Phillies Broadcasts, 1950

Big Gene Kelly did the play-by-play on WPEN radio assisted by Bill Brundage. On TV the calls were by 26-year-old Bill Campbell

Phillies announcers over the years provided life and drama to the games. I am proud to say that I knew several of them. Big Gene Kelly was a friend, as was Bill Campbell. Others included Hall of Famer Byrum Saam, Andy Musser, Chris Wheeler and a series of talented announcers leading up to today's crews. I also got to work with Jim Donahue's "Why the Hall Not" committee that orchestrated Rich Ashburn's Hall of Fame selection and no one will ever forget, Ashburn's longtime partner, the immortal Harry Kalas.

Chapter 3
Phillies Hall of Famers

There are 38 men in the Hall of Fame that once wore Phillies colors; however most of them earned their Cooperstown stripes while actually wearing the uniforms of other teams. If the Phils had some of them in their prime – Jimmie Foxx, Lloyd Waner, Joe Morgan, Hack Wilson, Tony Perez, Ryne Sandberg - the team history might have been quite different.

In alpha order – and the Phillies numbers they wore - are:

George "Sparky" Anderson, 2b (#2, 45) – Anderson, a good-field, no-hit, second baseman came to the Phillies from the Dodgers organization. Played in 152 games for the '59 Phils, batted .218 and never played again in the majors. He was inducted in to the Hall after a successful career as a manager with the Reds (1970-78) and Tigers (1979-92).

Grover Cleveland Alexander, p (no #) – 190-91 with the Phillies (373-208 career). A member of the Hall's third induction class. Alexander also sparkled as a pitcher for the Cubs and Cardinals. He won 31 games (against 10 losses) for the Phils first NL pennant winner in 1915. When inducted in to the Hall of Fame in 1939 he was working as a janitor. His post-baseball life was not pleasant.

Richie Ashburn, of (#1) – One of the most beloved sports personalities in Philadelphia history. Ashburn was a fixture in the Phillies outfield from 1948-59 and then returned in 1963 as a broadcaster – a spot he held until his untimely passing. Named the MVP of the New York Mets in 1962 Ashburn retired at season's end. He often said it was no great accomplishment in being named the best player on the worst team ever. His 15 big league seasons produced a .308 lifetime batting average – including two batting titles. He stroked 2,574 hits mostly for the Phillies, but also for the Cubs and Mets. He batted over .300 nine times (and hit .297 another time).

Dave Bancroft, ss (no #) – A hard-assed player, they called him "Beauty" but it had nothing to do with how he looked. A Phillie from 1915 to 1920, he spent 16 years in the majors also playing with the Giants, Boston Bees and the Dodgers. He was a .279 lifetime batter.

Chief Bender, p (no #) – Most of his career was with the A's – and he was still with them as a coach when he passed in the early 50's. When the A's lost the 1914

20th Century Phillies by the Numbers

World Series, badly, to the Braves Connie Mack broke up the team and many of his stars, Bender included, were gone. Rumors persist that the A's threw the series, not so much for gambling gains as the Black Sox would do a few years later, but to protest Mr. Mack's penchant for thrift. In his 16-year-career the full-blooded Crow Indian won 210, lost 127 and was 6-4 in five World's Series.

Dan Brouthers, 1b (no #) – Dan's career spanned 1879 to 1904. His tenure with the Phillies lasted one season – 57 games, .344 batting average – and that was 1896, his last year before a two game cameo for the Giants in 1904. Lifetime .342 hitter.

Jim Bunning, p (#14) – On Father's Day 1964, at Shea Stadium, Bunning needed just 90 pitches to record a perfect game against the lowly Mets. He had an earlier no-hitter as a member of the Tigers. He was the ace of Gene Mauch's staff when the team squandered a big lead and lost the pennant on the last day of the season. In 17 years Bunning went 224-184 (he won 89 games as a Phillie).

Steve Carlton, p (#32) – All you need to say is "Lefty" and everyone knows that you are talking about Steve Carlton. A menacing slider that reduced good hitters to tears, Carlton carried the Phillies for many years. Ironically the Philly fans, never happy, moaned loud and long when the locals traded favorite Rick Wise for Carlton. Before long, though, the moaners get very quiet. Steve's career lasted 24 seasons (the last four a tragedy as he tried to hang on) winning 329, losing 244. He was a five-time 20-game-winner, winning 27 in his first Phils campaign in 1972.

Earle Combs, coach (#31) – A Yankee immortal, spent one year as a Phillies coach (1954). "The Kentucky Colonel" played peerless outfield with the Yankees from 1924 until 1935. In those dozen years, he batted .325 – and had a .350 mark in four World Series.

Roger Connor, 1b (no #) – In 1892 Connor played in 155 games for the Phillies and batted .292. He broke in with Toronto NL in 1880, also played with the Giants, the New York team of the Player's League, and the Cardinals before retiring in 1897. Lifetime .317 hitter.

Ed Delahanty, of (no #) – A great player, but best remembered for falling off a train in 1903 as it crossed Niagara Falls. Needless to say no one ever found him. Most of Ed's 16-year-career was as a Phillie, though he played a year in the Player's League (Cleveland) and his last two with Washington (42 games before his demise in 1903). Lifetime .346 hitter between 1888 and 1903.

Hugh Duffy, manager (no #) – Managed the Phils for three years (1904-06) and had one plus .500 season. Also skipper of Milwaukee (AL) in 1901, White Sox (1910-11) and Red Sox (1921-22). Made the Hall based on lifetime .324 mark (1888-1906). Won the NL homerun crown with Boston in 1897, stroking 11 of them.

Johnny Evers, 2b (no #) – Tinker & Chance didn't make it here. Evers was one of the legendary Cubbie trio that got in to the Hall of Fame, some say, on the strength of a poem. His one year with the Phils was 1917 and he appeared in 56 games and batted .224. His playing career, 1902-1917 (with cameos in 1922 and 1929) produced a less-than-immortal .270 batting average.

Elmer Flick, of (no #) – Broke in with the Phils in 1898, was lured to the A's (then to Cleveland in 1902). He spent most of his career in Cleveland where he fashioned a lifetime .313 batting average. Won the batting title in 1905.

Jimmie Foxx, 1b-3b-p (#4) – By the time "Old Double X" got back to Philadelphia his career was all but in the rear view mirror. Still, because of World War II, his signing made sense for the Phils. Called the right-handed Babe Ruth during his years with the A's and Red Sox, Foxx was one of the most feared hitters ever. Like Alexander, his post career life was not a happy one. In the film "A League of their own" Tom Hanks plays a Foxx-like character as a usually drunk, uncaring, lout. Foxx's daughter, Nanci Foxx Canaday, told me that he was nothing like that

Ted Taylor

during the year he managed in the AAGBL – and she should know, she was the bat girl. Foxx's magnificent career (20 years) reflected a .325 batting average, 534 homeruns, 1,921 RBI's. Batted over .300 14 rimes! The man could flat out play. After his playing days ended he, literally, begged Connie Mack for a coaching post with the A's (such as he had given Bender, Mickey Cochrane and Al Simmons) and Mack refused, some say, because of his penchant for drink.

Billy Hamilton, of (no #) – Sliding Billy played six of his 14 years with the Phillies (1890-1895) and then finished up with Boston NL in 1901. He stole 915 bases during his career and won the title four times. In 1889 with Kansas City of the American Association he swiped 117 and didn't even win the crown. Imagine. As a hitter he fashioned a .344 average, meaning he was always on base, always ready to steal another.

Bucky Harris, manager (#24) – Gained fame as the "Boy Wonder" manager of the Washington Senators in the 1920's (winning the pennant in 1924 and 1925). Managed a lot of other places (Detroit twice, Senators three times, Yankees, Phils and Red Sox) and fashioned a 2157-2218 record. Won World Series with 1924 Washington and 1947 Yankees – who canned him a year later despite a 94-60 record, go figure. Bucky was a pretty good second baseman during his playing career (1919-1931) and had a lifetime .274 mark.

Ferguson Jenkins, p (#30, 46) – The only Phillie to ever play for the Harlem Globetrotters, the locals badly misjudged his talent and sent him to the Cubs for a fishcake – where he earned hall of Fame stature. Later he spent two years with the Red Sox and then was an ace with the Texas Rangers. He finished up with the Cubs in 1983. Only two of his 284 wins came with the Phillies. He lost 226 along the way (one as a Phil). He won 20 or more seven times.

Hughie Jennings, ss (no #) – Anyone with the nickname 'EE-Yah" belongs in the Hall of Fame on general principles. Managed for 15 years, won World's Championships in 1907-08-09. Was the skipper of the Tigers 1907-1920 and the Giants in 1924. As a player, his Phillies visit covered two seasons (1901-02). He batted .275 and .277 playing in limited games as an infielder. Played from 1891 to 1918.

Tim Keefe, p (no #) – The righty spent the last three years of his 14 year career (1880-93) with the Phillies (32-29). Career shows 342 wins, 225 losses. He won 41 games for New York AA (1883) and 37 the following year for the same club. He won 32, 42, 35, 35 and 28 with the New York Nationals the next five years running.

Chuck Klein, of (#1, 3, 26, 29, 36) – He came, he went and when he was a Phillie he was as good a player as there was. Broke in with the Phils in 1928 was traded to the Cubs in 1934, traded back to the Phils in 1936, He was traded to the Pirates in 1939 and then was back on the Phils in 1940. In 1933 he and his A's counterpart, Jimmie Foxx, each won the Triple Crown. Klein last played for the Phils in 1944 (4 games), Foxx was with the Phils in 1945 for one season. Lifetime .320 hitter in 17 seasons. He stroked an even 300 homers and drove in 1,202 runs. Post baseball life was not good to him (mistreating him as it did Foxx), he ran a bar in Northeast Philly for a few years, moved out of the area to be with family, and he died at age 54.

Chuck Klein, outfielder, Phillies

Larry "Nap" Lajoie, 2b (no #) – Stolen from the Phils by the 1901 A's, all he did was bat .422 for the AL newcomers – he also stroked 14 homers, drove in 125. Contracts were simply pieces of paper in those days and the upstart AL had no qualms about raiding the senior circuit for talent. Nap's career covered 21 seasons (1896 to 1916). He batted .338 and hit 83 homers (14 of them for the '01 A's). Most of his career was spent with Cleveland to whom Connie Mack traded him in 1902 (after one game) to avoid having to return him to the Phillies. Whenever the Indians traveled to the Quaker City for games Lajoie got the time off (often spending it in Atlantic City). A Philadelphia judge had ruled that if he played in the city it must be for the Phillies.

Bob Lemon, coach (#2) – A great hurler (and a pretty darn good hitter, too) with Cleveland, Lemon was pitching coach here. Broke in with the Tribe in 1941 as an infielder and after he became a fulltime pitcher was often used as a pinch-hitter and fashioned a .232

20th Century Phillies by the Numbers

batting mark, with 37 homers, during his 15 year Cleveland tenure. As one of Cleveland's top hurlers he won 20 or more seven times and finished with a 207-128 record. He spent eight years as a big league skipper with the Kansas City A's (1970-72), White Sox (1977-78) and the Yankees (1978-82). He won the World's Championship with the '78 Yankees, the AL pennant with them in 1980.

Pedro Martinez, pitcher (#45) – Pedro joined the Phillies in mid-season 2009 and appeared in just nine games for them (winning 5, losing 1). He also dropped two decisions in the World's Series that year versus the New York Yankees. He retired and though there were constant rumors of a comeback, it never happened. Elected to the Hall of Fame (Class of 2015) in January, this native of the Dominican Republic broke in with the Dodgers in 1992 (10-6) but had his best seasons with the Red Sox (117-37), Expos (55-33) and the Mets (32-23). He had 409 career starts, a lifetime ERA of 2.93, and appeared in a total of 476 contests.

Tim McCarver, c (#6, 11) – A solid catcher in the big leagues for 21 years (1959-80), and known for a period as Steve Carlton's personal catcher. One season my wife and I had a 16-game-plan and, as luck would have it, Carlton started almost every one of them. Had anyone asked me, I'd have said Tim was the Phils regular catcher. He played in 1,909 games, batted .271. Broke in with the Cardinals, also played with the Expos and Red Sox. McCarver was inducted in to the Hall as a broadcaster. He started his broadcast career in Philadelphia on the radio and with PRSIM TV casts of the Phillies.

Tom McCarthy, of (no #) – No relation to the Phils play-by-play announcer of the same name, McCarthy played for 12 seasons (1884-1896) and two of them were with Philadelphia (1886-87). Lifetime he batted .292.

Joe Morgan, 2b (#8) – Joined Pete Rose and Tony Perez as "Big Red Machine" ex-patriots on the '83 NL pennant winner". Joe broke in with Houston (1963) and finished up with the Oakland A's in 1984. In his 22 years, Morgan batted .271. In his lone Phils year he saw action in 123 games, batted .230 and popped 16 (of his 268 career) homers. Spent many years announcing nationally broadcast games.

Dolan "Kid" Nichols, p (no #) – Appeared in just 21 Phillies games at the tail end of his great career (1890-1906). As a Phillie he was 10-7, but overall he logged a 361-208 record. The Kid won 30-or-more games seven times. Imagine. Most of his career was to the benefit of the Boston NL club. He also logged some time with the Cardinals (seven games).

Tony Perez, 1b (#24, 37) – A member of the 1983 pennant-winning "Wheeze Kids", Perez was brought in to back up Pete Rose at first and as a pinch hitter. He played in 91 games, batted .241 and kicked in six homers. Broke in with the Reds and a good piece of his Hall of Fame career was spent as a member of the legendary "Big Red Machine" (1964-76, 1984-86). He also played with the Montreal Expos and Boston Red Sox. Career 23 years, .279 batting average and 379 homers. Briefly managed the Florida Marlins.

Eppa Jeptha Rixey, p (no #) – Broke in with the Phillies in 1912 – came to them right off the University of Virginia campus - and stayed with the club until 1921 when he was dealt to the Cincinnati Reds – and was the mainstay of the Cincy staff until he retired in 1933. At 6'5 Rixey was one of the tallest hurlers of his era. In 1932 at the age of 41 hurled 27 consecutive scoreless innings – over seven games (two complete shutouts and five relief appearances). Career shows 266 wins, 251 losses. He had 39 lifetime shutouts and won 20 or more four times, lost 20 or more twice.

Robin Roberts (#36) – Robbie, with all due respect to Grover Cleveland Alexander, is likely the greatest pitcher in Phillies history. He certainly was a great human being. His career with the locals ended with a 1-10 record in 1961 when Gene Mauch suggested that Roberts "pitched like Betsy Ross". In his 19 years Robbie won 286, lost 245. He won 20-or-more games six times (28 in 1952). He also pitched for Baltimore (1962-65), and both Houston and the Cubs near the end of his career.

Ryne Sandberg, 2b (#24) – Dealt to the Cubs (with Larry Bowa) in the, what many consider the worst deal in Phillies history (though the one that sent Ferguson

Ted Taylor

Jenkins away wasn't real good either). The trade brought the immortal Ivan DeJesus to the Phils. Sandberg put up Hall of Fame numbers in Wrigley Field for 11 years (1982-92). Lifetime .289 hitter. Returned to the Phillies organization as their AAA manager and, in 2013, their third base coach. Replaced Charlie Manuel as Phils manager in mid-2013.

Mike Schmidt, 3b (#22, 20) – The man could flat out hit and played third base as good as anyone ever. Mike was never really appreciated by Phillies fans – until he was gone. Broke with the varsity in 13 contests in 1972 and the jury was out on him after he hit a meager .196 in 132 games the next year. But once he got going he really got going – in 18 seasons he stroked 548 homers, drove in 1,595 runs and hit .267.

Casey Stengel, of (no #) – Stengel, a Hall of Famer as a manager, was a pretty good, if sometimes goofy, big league outfielder. Was with the Phils in 1920 and part of 1921, but his career began with Brooklyn in 1912 and ended with the Braves in 1925. In 14 seasons he batted .284. A pedestrian manager for many years (1934-43 with the Dodgers first, then the Braves), Stengel became a genius when the Yankees hired him in 1949 and he won nine pennants and seven World's Championships. It is easy to be a genius when you have players like Mickey Mantle, Joe DiMaggio, Yogi Berra, Phil Rizzuto and Whitey Ford. When he wore out his welcome with the Yankees ("too old" they said) he became the first manager of the newly minted Mets and, again, reverted to pedestrian (1962-65). As a skipper he's 1905-1842 in 25 seasons.

20th Century Phillies by the Numbers

Sam Thompson, of (no #) – Big Sam (6'2, 207) was a Phillies slugger (in the days when there were few) playing with them 1889-1898. He broke in with Detroit in 1885 and made a cameo return with the Bengals in 1906. For his 15 year career Sam batted .331 with 128 homers. As a Phillie he won two homerun titles with 20 in 1889 and 18 in 1895.

Lloyd Waner, of (#34) – "Little Poison" (brother of "Big Poison", Paul) spent just one of his 18 big league seasons with the Phillies. In 1942 he played in 100 games, batted .261. He retired after the season, but then due to a World War II shortage of decent players came back in 1944 and played with Brooklyn and the Pirates (with whom he spent most of his years) though in just 34 games. He played in 23 more in 1945 for the Bucs and retired for good. Lifetime, he batted .316.

Hack Wilson, of (#34) – Hack played just the last seven games of his 12 year career with the Phillies in 1934. He batted .100. Broke in with the Giants in 1923, moved over to the Cubs in 1926 and ended with the Dodgers (except for the last seven games). Lifetime he batted .307 with 244 homers (and four HR championships). He smacked 56 round-trippers for the '30 Cubs. He stood just 5'6, weighed 190.

Ted Taylor

Harry Wright, manager (no #) – Harry played just two big league games (one each, 1876, 1877), but spent 18 years as a big league skipper (12 with the Phils), winning 1000, losing 825 (27 ties, one no-contest). He won three pennants along the way. Manager from 1876 to 1893. Died in Atlantic City NJ in 1895.

Note: While they never donned a uniform, three other men closely associated with the Phillies are also in the Hall of Fame. Two of them are broadcasters, one a sportswriter. Byrum Saam came to Philadelphia to do the Athletics and, soon, was doing both ball clubs. In the 1960's Harry Kalas came to Philadelphia as the Phils primary play-by-play man and soon he and partner Rich Ashburn formed one of the best duos in the nation. Sportswriter Allen Lewis, who covered the Phils for both the Bulletin and Inquirer is also enshrined.

This ad for 1951 Bowman Baseball cards (Phils vs. Cardinals scorecard) has puzzled collectors since it was published. The ad clearly states 340 subjects but the complete set ended up being 324 cards. Pictured are 1950 Bowman cards.

Chapter 4 – The "Skippers"

The first Phillies manager of the 20th Century was Bill Shettsline – he actually started as skipper in 1898 and managed the club until 1902. The last manager of the century was Terry Francona, who piloted the club from 1997 to 2001 – and later went on to very successfully manage the Boston Red Sox.

The first Phils manager to wear a numbered uniform was Burt Shotton (1928-33) who donned #'s 26 and 27. Ironically, later in his career, while managing Brooklyn, Shotton did a Connie Mack and refused to wear a uniform, managing, instead, in street clothes. Fate intervened in another way; too, Burt was manager of the Dodgers in 1950 when Dick Sisler's homerun carried the Phillies to the pennant. It also carried Shotton to the unemployment office.

Following Shotton was long-time Phils catcher Jimmy Wilson (1934-38) who wore #12. Hans Lobert, a coach under Wilson and Doc Prothro, managed the club in 1938 (before Prothro) and 1942 (after him). As a skipper Hans wore #25, 1 and 2.

Ted Taylor

The first Phils skipper to win a pennant in the 20th Century would be Pat Moran (1915). It would be 35 years and 14 managers later until another one of them won a pennant, and that would be Eddie Sawyer in 1950. Sawyer, a Yankee farmhand as a player (he never made it to the majors) replaced Ben Chapman in 1948 (Dusty Cooke, a coach, actually managed the team for 13 games, winning six before Sawyer arrived from Triple-A Toronto, the Phils top farm club. Chapman wore #7 and Sawyer wore it for the balance of 1948 too. In 1949 he assumed his familiar number 24. Lightning struck for the '50 Whiz Kids and they won the NL title. By 1952 the team was clearly going nowhere and veteran big league skipper Steve O'Neill came on to replace him.

There would be 30 more years and ten managers from the Whiz Kids until the 1980 Phils won the first World's Championship in their long history – and a former marginal big league hurler, Dallas Green, was the pilot. Green wore #46, the digits he wore for several seasons as a pitcher. Big and gruff, he was the complete opposite of the mild-mannered Danny Ozark – and some say he kicked and screamed the Phillies to their first World's Championship.

The Phils would win another flag in 1983 under onetime general manager and longtime farm director Paul "The Pope" Owens and their last one of the 20th Century in 1993 under Jim Fregosi. (The next World's

Championship, their second, didn't come until 2008 under Charlie Manuel.)

ANDY COHEN

Thirty-nine different men wore the mantle of "Phillies manager" in the 20th Century. One of them, Andy Cohen, wore it but for just two games (he split the contests) between Eddie Sawyer, who quit after an opening day loss in 1960 saying "I'm 49, I'd like to live to be 50" and the irrepressible Gene Mauch. (The picture of Cohen is from his 1933 Goudey Baseball card when he was playing for the New York Giants.)

Two men who most Phils fans expected to, one day, manage the team never did. One was Andy Seminick (the man behind the plate for most of the Whiz Kid's 1950 pennant run) and Rich Ashburn. Both admitted they considered it. Seminick managed in the minors, had two stints as a coach with the big club. Ashburn, at one time, considered coming down from the broadcast booth to take the job – and then had second thoughts. Ashburn's logic was "manager's get fired" and he had a job he loved as a broadcaster. He did return to uniform from time-to-time in the spring (as Mike Schmidt does, and Robin Roberts did) and in old-timers games, but once he retired after the '62 season he was done.

Ted Taylor

In 1976, long after he retired (but was still working locally as a sales rep for the Plymouth Golf Ball Company) we hired Eddie sawyer to be celebrity autograph guest (along with Del Ennis) at the 2nd annual Philadelphia Baseball Card & Sports Memorabilia Show at Spring Garden College – where I was athletic director. We promoted the show aggressively and my partner, Bob Schmierer, and I created a postcard sized promotion piece with Sawyer's picture on the front and info on the back about the show. We also reproduced a copy of the T-206 Honus Wagner card, also with show info on the back. Both cards were distributed all over the Delaware Valley (twice, with the Phils permission at Veteran's Stadium).

The Glenside Kid Remembers...

On the day of the show Mr. Sawyer shows up at the college and tells one of our staff members (Patricia Dieterly) to "tell Mr. Taylor I've arrived". Pat had no idea who he was and she asked him. Sawyer replied "I'm the guy on the card". Still having no clue was to whom he was, but seeing a T-206 repro on the table, she picks up the microphone and announces "Honus Wagner is here to sign autographs". Needless to say, lots of people were excited in anticipation of meeting the long-dead Pirate Hall of Famer.

20th Century Phillies by the Numbers

The Philadelphia Athletics played in the same city for 54 of the same years. They had one manager for 50 of them (Connie Mack) and two others (Jimmie Dykes and Eddie Joost). The A's won nine AL pennants and five World's Championships. Is it any wonder that longtime Phils President Bill Giles once said to me, "The wrong team left town".

The 20th Century Phillies Managers

The 1915 NL Champion Phillies, Pat Moran, manager

Name	Years	Won – Lost
Bill Shetsline	1898-1902	367-303
Chief Zimmer	1903	49-86
Hugh Duffy	1904-06	206-251
Bill Murray	1907-09	240-214
Red Dooin	1910-14	392-370
Pat Moran	1915-18	323-257
Jack Coombs	1919	18-44
Gavvy Cravath	1919-20	91-137

20th Century Phillies by the Numbers

Manager	Years	Record
Bill Donovan	1921	31-71
Kaiser Wilhelm	1921-22	83-137
Art Fletcher	1923-26	231-378
Stuffy McInnis	1927	51-103
Burt Shotton #26, 27	1928-33	370-549
Jimmy Wilson #12	1934-38	280-477
Hans Lobert #25, 1, 2	1938, 1942	42-111
Doc Prothro #1	1939-41	138-320
Bucky Harris #24	1943	40-53
Fred Fitz Simmons #33, 14	1943-45	102-179

Phils manager Ben Chapman poses with Jackie Robinson in 1947 (in a UPI photo) to alleviate some of the racial tension associated with Robinson's first visit to Shibe Park. Prior to Brooklyn's visit Phillies GM Herb Pennock called Dodger GM Branch Rickey and begged him not to bring Robinson to town, the city was "just not ready for that sort of thing" he said. But Robinson and the

Ted Taylor

Dodgers came and over 40,000 people attended the Sunday doubleheader (which the Phils swept) to witness history. Chapman had a reputation for being an Anti-Semite, so it was no surprise that he wasn't going to be kind to baseball's first African American player. Pennock died in January of the next year and Chapman's days as Phils skipper were numbered.

Ben Chapman #34, 7	1945-48	197-277
Dusty Cooke #32	1948	6-6
Eddie Sawyer #7, 24	1948-52, 58-60	390-424
Steve O'Neill #24	1952-54	182-140
Terry Moore #8	1954	35-42
Mayo Smith #24	1955-58	264-281
Andy Cohen #39	1960	1-1
Gene Mauch #32, 4	1960-68	645-684
George Myatt #1, 47	1968, 1969	21-35
Bob Skinner #1	1968-69	92-123
Frank Lucchesi #1	1970-72	166-233
Paul Owens #8, 5	1972, 83-84	161-158
Danny Ozark #3	1973-79	594-510
Dallas Green #46	1979-81	169-130
Pat Corrales #8, 5	1982-83	132-115
John Felske #7	1985-87	190-194
Lee Elia #4	1987-88	111-142

20th Century Phillies by the Numbers

John Vukovich #7	1988	5-4
Nick Leyva #16	1989-91	148-189
Jim Fregosi #11	1991-96	431-463
Terry Francona #7	1997-2001	285-363

The Coaches –

Never underestimate the value of a good coach. Some managers simply appoint their cronies from their playing days but the more confident ones usually select men that can teach and, in some cases, actually succeed them in their job.

The Phillies, on the list that follows, have had both kinds. The long-term ones are usually the teachers and, frequently, they stayed on even after the club changed managers.

It isn't surprising that the best coaches are often men who were the foot soldiers during their careers. The utility infielders, back-up catchers, mop-up relievers. Those men usually became keen observers of what's happening and had the time to consider what the manager did right, what he'd do wrong and, more importantly, what they'd do in such a situation.

Eddie Sawyer, winner of the 1950 pennant, inherited the heart of his coaching staff from Ben Chapman –

Ted Taylor

Benny Bengough, Cy Perkins, Dusty Cooke - and they were still there when he left. Coach Maje McDonnell had joined the Phillies after World War II and was elevated to coach status in 1948 (and then stayed with the club for the rest of his life in various posts). Onetime A's star hurler, George Earnshaw, joined Sawyer in 1949 and lasted only one more campaign (he is oddly missing from most Whiz Kids team photos).

Ironically, even though the other coaches had seniority, the 1948 Phils tapped Allen "Dusty" Cooke, (left) a big league outfielder for eight seasons, 1930-38 (Yankees, Red Sox, Reds) as manager between Chapman and Sawyer – and he won six of 13 games (one was a tie)! Bengough had a ten-year-career as a backup catcher with the Yankees (1923-30) and the Browns (1931-32). Perkins career was mostly spent with the Philadelphia A's (1915-30) and one year stints with the Yankees (1931) and Tigers (1932). He accompanied Mickey Cochrane to the Tigers as a player and also served as a coach with the Bengals.

20th Century Phillies by the Numbers

Coaches – Name & Years Served

Ruben Amaro Sr. #12
1980-81

Benny Bengough #11
1946-58

Carroll Berringer #1, 5
1973-78

Larry Bowa #2
1988-96

Dave Bristol #4, 2
1982-85, 1988

Dick Carter #21
1959-60

Dave Cash #30
1996

Galen Cisco #42, 43
1997-2000

Andy Cohen #31
1960

Earle Combs #31
1954

Wid Conroy
1922

Dusty Cooke #32
1948-52

Chuck Cottier #3
1997-2000

Gavvy Cravath
1923

Benny Culp #25
1946-47

Jim Davenport #2
1986-87

Brandy Davis #2
1972

Billy DeMars #46, 3, 2
1969-81

George Earnshaw #38
1949-50

Doc Edwards #5
1970-72

Lee Elia #3, 2, 4
1980-81, 85-87

John Felske #7
1984

Tom Ferrick #51
1959

Ramon Henderson #59
1998-2010

Don Hoak #3
1967

Newt Hunter #27
1928-31, 33

Deron Johnson #2
1982-84

Syl Johnson #3
1939-41

Bubber Jonnard #10
1935

Bill Killifer #2
1942

Ted Taylor

Chuck Klein #3, 8, 26
1942-45

Darold Knowles #3
1989-90

Hal Lanier #22
1990-91

Bob Lemon #2
1961

Hans Lobert #50, 25, 2
1934-41

Peanuts Lowrey #21, 3
1960-66

Eddie Mayo #32
1952-54

Maje McDonnell #40
1948-57

Cal McLish #2
1965-66

Hal McRae # 56
1997-2000

Denis Menke #4, 14
1989-96

Ben Meyer
1925-26

Brad Mills #9
1997-2000

Wally Moses #32
1955-58

Dan Murphy
1927

George Myatt #1, 47, 2
1964-72

Bob Oldis #27
1964-66

Jack Onslow #27
1931-32

Claude Osteen #3
1982-88

Cy Perkins #31
1946-54

Johnny Podres #46
1991-96

Bill Posedel #31
1958

Pat Ragan
1924

Johnny Riddle #39
1959

Joe Rigoli #59
1996-97

Ray Ripplemeyer #4
1970-78

Mel Roberts #26
1992-95

Mike Ryan #5, 9
1980-95

Andy Seminick #21, 2, 48
1957-58, 1967-69

Merv Shea #9, 25
1944-45

Larry Shepard #5
1967

Ken Silvestri #31
1959-60

20th Century Phillies by the Numbers

Dick Spalding #51
1934-36

Herm Starrette #4
1979-81

Joe Sugden
1926-27

Jesse Tannehill
1920

Tony Taylor #12
1977-79, 88-89

Bob Tiefenauer #5
1979

Del Unser #25
1985-88

Al Vincent #1
1961-63

John Vuckovich #18, 3
1988-2004

Earl Whitehill #23
1943

Al Widmar #3, 2, 49
1962-64, 68-69

Kaiser Wilhelm
1921

Bobby Wine #1, 7
1972-83

Jim Wright #58
1996

Whit Wyatt #31
1955-57

Ted Taylor

The Glenside Kid Remembers...

My Uncle, Ernie Lay, promised me that we'd go to a World Series game if the Phillies won the pennant. I was psyched. So the Phillies win the pennant and Unc goes on a ticket quest – and comes up dry. This man was the biggest Phillies fan in the world and he couldn't score two tickets. So he has to tell his 10-year-old nephew that we're not going. His wife, my Aunt Florence worked for Western Union and the day before the series began she got assigned to the press box at Shibe Park. She didn't even like baseball. The game is played, my uncle and I are listening on the radio, my aunt is watching it from the press box. How fair was that?

Chapter 5
Phillies in the Post Season

The Phillies spent the 100 years of the 20th Century winning just one World's Championship (1980) and five National League pennants (1915, 1950, 1980, 1983, 1993).

The Phillies got close to a league pennant in 1976, losing the NL Championship to the Reds, who swept them in three games. In 1977 they lost in the league championships to the Dodgers three games-to-one. In 1978 they, again, lost to the Dodgers by the same count. In 1980, setting the stage for their World Series win they beat Houston three games-to-two in, what some say, was the most exciting league playoff series ever. In 1981 because a player's strike disrupted the season, the Phils and Montreal Expos ended up in a split-season playoff – and the Expos took both games.

The World Series – 1915

The Phillies had finished fifth in 1914 and no one expected Pat Moran's club to dominate the NL the following season, but they did. Moran's team started the year 8-0 and Grover Cleveland Alexander's 31 wins (pictured left) paced the staff followed by Erskine

Ted Taylor

Meyer's 21 wins and 14 more from Al Demaree. Gavvy Cravath won the homerun title with 24 of them; Dave Bancroft was a rookie and played short like he invented the position. First baseman Fred Luderus batted .315 and Cravath stroked the ball at a .285 clip. The Phils were 90-62 and finished seven games ahead of second place Boston. Ironically, their AL rivals, the always dominant Athletics (winners of the AL crown in 1914) crashed to earth losing 109 games against just 43 wins.

Their rivals in the World Series were the Boston Red Sox. The AL winners had won 101 games (against 50 losses). Boston was deep in pitching and had a 20-year-old kid lefty, Babe Ruth, who had notched an 18-6 won-lost record. Rube Foster won 20 for Bill Carrigan's club and Ernie Shore notched 19. Tris Speaker was their leading hitter (.325) and Ruth's four homers (as a pitcher, remember) were the most on the team (he also batted .315).

The Phillies won game one at home with Alexander besting Shore, 3-1. The Phils managed just five hits, the Sox had eight. Attendance was 19,343.

Foster beat Meyer in game two, 2-1. The Sox had ten hits, the Phillies just three. This time 20,306 Philadelphians paid their way in to expanded seating capacity.

Veteran Dutch Leonard (14-7 on the regular season) bested Alexander in game 3, 2-1, Boston scoring in the bottom of the ninth. The Sox had six hits, the Phils just three. It was Alexander's second complete game. 42,300 Bostonians showed up.

Game four went to the Sox 2-1 as Shore, pitching his second complete game, bested George Chalmers. The Sox had eight hits, the Phils 7. 41,096 were there in Beantown.

Up to this point, every hurler for both clubs had pitched a complete game and three of the four games had ended 2-1, the other 3-1.

In game five, back in Philadelphia, the Phils jumped out to a 2-0 lead then saw the Sox tie the game in the third. The Phils scored two more in the fourth and were up 4-2. Moran had replaced starter Meyer in the third with Eppa Rixey – and he pitched the rest of the way giving up two runs in the eighth and one in the ninth and the Sox had won the championship! Babe Ruth never pitched, despite is 18 regular season wins, and was 0-for-1 as a pinch hitter. 20,306 paid their way in again and this was because the Phils had added extra seating. Some say the extra seats cost them game five when three Red Sox homeruns fell in to the seats – which had reduced the dimensions of the park. In those days, if something could go wrong it usually did.

Winner's share-per-player was $3,780, the Phillies players each got $2,520.

Ted Taylor

1915 Phillies Roster

Manager – Pat Moran 90-62
Pitchers – Alexander, Mayer, Demaree, Rixey, Chalmers, McQuillan, Oeschger, Baumgartner, Tincup.
Catchers – Killefer, Burns, Adams
Infielders – Luderus, Nehoff, Bancroft, Byrne, Stock, Dugey
Outfielders – Cravath, Paskert, Whitted, Becker, Weiser

The World Series – 1950

DICK SISLER

It had been 35 years between pennants and the Phillies almost let this one get away too. It all came down to one game – Oct. 1, 1950 - at Ebbetts Field where 35,073 Dodger faithful were rocking and rolling in anticipation of a second straight NL title. Actually a win for Burt Shotton's team would have left both clubs tied for the NL lead with a one-game playoff looming. If not for a heroic tenth inning three-run-homerun by Dick Sisler, a yeoman-like performance from Robin Roberts on the mound (his third start in five days) and Rich Ashburn's on-target throw nailing Cal Abrams at the plate the city might have waited another 30 years.

20th Century Phillies by the Numbers

Called "The Whiz Kids" because it was, indeed, a youthful nucleus of players (with a sprinkling of seasoned vets in the wings). Catcher Andy Semnick was called "Grandpa Whiz" and he was just 29. But they were mostly kids – Curt Simmons (17-8) was just 21; Roberts, Granny Hamner and Ashburn were all 23; Willie Jones, Mike Goliat and hurler Bob Miller were 24; Del Ennis was 25 and Sisler was 29.

The Phillies were badly wounded warriors going to the World Series against Casey Stengel's mighty Yankees. Phils ace lefty Simmons was gone – called up by the National Guard on September 10, Bubba Church stopped a line drive with his face on September 15 and Bob Miller's arm was aching.

For game one Manager Eddie Sawyer knew that he couldn't go with Robin Roberts and so, for the first time all season, he gave the start to 33-year-old reliever Jim Konstanty. The professorial-looking hurler had a 16-7 record in an incredible 74 appearances (almost every-other-game) and would go on to be named the NL's MVP.

The Yankees started 21-game-winner Vic Raschi in game one at Shibe Park and for eight innings the clubs battled tooth and nail – the Yanks holding a one-run-lead. Russ Meyer came on and pitched the ninth frame. The Yankees won 1-0 on five hits, the Phillies

Ted Taylor

managed just two – and both came in one inning, the fifth.

In game two Roberts got the start (he had gone 20-11 in the regular season); Casey Stengel countered with 16-game-winner Allie Reynolds. The Yankees won again, 2-1, this time in extra innings as Joe DiMaggio launched a 400-foot plus rocket in to the upper deck in left. Both starters pitched complete games. The Yanks had 10 hits, the Phillies seven – and left runners in scoring position in five innings.

Game three, the first game at Yankee Stadium, ended in the Yankee's favor, 3-2. Veteran Ken Heintzelman started as Sawyer was running out of options and for 7 $2/3^{rd}$ innings the veteran lefthander was in charge – and then his control deserted him. Konstanty came on in the eighth to finish the frame and Russ Meyer pitched the ninth. Eddie Lopat started for New York; Tom Ferrick pitched a scoreless ninth. Going back to 1915 this marked the Phillies seventh consecutive one-run-loss in World Series play.

Bob Miller started game four, a do or die affair, for the Phils and he never got out of the first inning. He got just one out and Konstanty came in (his third appearance of the series, just like the regular season). He pitched until the seventh, Roberts came on in the eighth – but the party was over. Whitey Ford started for the New Yorkers and Reynolds closed it out in the ninth. The Yankees won 5-2, sweeping the Phils in four games.

20th Century Phillies by the Numbers

The winning Yankees each got $5,737, the losing Phils each got $4,081.34. When they arrived at 30th Street Station after the loss of game four a just a handful of fans were there to greet them.

But given the youth of the ball club the majority of the Phillies fans were not dissuaded by the 4-0 sweep believing that this was just the beginning of a long run by the locals. It wasn't.

1950 Phillies Roster

Manager – Eddie Sawyer 91-63
Pitchers – Roberts, Simmons, Konstanty, Miller, Meyer, Church, Johnson, Heintzelman, Donnelly, Candini, Borowy, Brittin, Stuffel, Ridzik, Thompson.
Catchers – Seminick, Lopata, Silvestri
Infielders – Waitkus, Goliat, Hamner, Jones, Bloodworth, Caballero
Outfielders – Ennis, Ashburn, Sisler, Whitman, Nicholson, Mayo, Blatnik, Hollmig

The Glenside Kid Remembers...

It's the late sixties and I'm running (with partner Bob Schmierer) the annual Philadelphia Baseball Card & Sports Memorabilia Show at the George Washington Motor Lodge in Willow Grove PA.

Our featured guest is **Dick Sisler**. *He agreed to come and sign autographs and we paid his expenses and a stipend. When Dick arrived at the convention center (we had him picked up at the airport) I met him at our motel room. Sisler looked at me and said, "I think you've wasted your money, nobody will even* remember me." He was being honest and quite humble.

I walked him across the driveway and in the packed hall (10,000+ collectors) and a loud round of applause began. Sisler was surprised. No one else was. Sisler was our "Bobby Thomson" and his dramatic homerun in 1950 sunk the Dodgers in the last game, just as Thomson's would do a year later.

My Mother Helen, 71-at-the-time, eyed up Dick and said, "You were handsome in 1950, you are still handsome today." He blushed.

The World Series – 1980

1980 Phillies

It had been 30 years since the last National League pennant and the city of Philadelphia was ready. And, as in 1950, it almost didn't happen. In fact the whole ball of wax was decided in a nail-biting game five of the

20th Century Phillies by the Numbers

National League playoffs against those pesky Houston Astros.

On October 1, 1980 the Phils, losers of three National League playoffs (1976-77-78), hosted the Astros and, with Steve Carlton on the mound, and two innings of sterling relief from Tug McGraw the Phils won 3-1. Bob Forsch pitched a complete game for the Astros – and lost.

Houston topped the Phils 7-4 in game 2. Dick Ruthven started, but Ron Reed was the loser in relief giving up four runs in one and $1/3^{rd}$ of an inning.

Game three was in Houston and the Phils lost 1-0 in the eleventh inning, Tug McGraw was the losing pitcher. Dick Ruthven had started for the Phils against Joe Niekro.

Carlton started the die-or-die fourth game against Verne Ruhle and was off his game. In fact Lefty lasted just 5 $1/3^{rd}$ innings and left the game trailing 2-0. The Phils took a 3-2 lead in the eighth, but the Astros tied it up in the bottom of the ninth. In the tenth when with Pete Rose on first, Greg Luzinski pinch hit for Bake McBride and scorched a double to left. Rose (left) never broke stride and leveled Houston catcher Bruce Bochy with a forearm to the face before crossing the plate. Manny Trillo singled the Bull home with an insurance run. McGraw shut down the Astros in the bottom of the tenth and a fifth game was on tap.

Game five was played in Houston and they trotted out ace Nolan Ryan, the Phils countered with Marty Bystrom – and for seven innings it seemed to be working for them. The Texans owned a 5-2 lead with Ryan hurling bullets going in to the eighth. But then the roof fell in and the Phils roughed up Ryan, Joe Sambito and Forsch in that frame scoring five runs and taking a 7-5 lead. But the Astros weren't dead yet, putting two runs over the plate in the bottom of the inning (McGraw gave up the two runs). Dick Ruthven came in for the Phils and would pitch two scoreless innings as Dallas Green's club won in the tenth as Del Unser scored on a Garry Maddox double.

The Phillies were back in the World Series for the first time in thirty years and their foes would be the Kansas City Royals.

Game one was at Veteran's Stadium and Green trotted out rookie Bob Walk (his pitching staff was worn out from the Astor series). The Royals countered with ace Dennis Leonard and the Royals hopped out to a 4-0 lead – this before the Phillies used Leonard for batting practice, chasing him after 3 2/3rd innings, playing six runs on six hits. The Phils tacked on single runs in the next two years and that was good because in the eighth inning the KC club added two runs. McGraw came in, again, and shut them down over the last two frames and the Phils had a 7-6 first game win.

20th Century Phillies by the Numbers

The Phils went two games up in the second contest notching a 6-4 win – another come-from-behind affair as the Phillies scored four in the eighth to overcome a 4-2 hole. Steve Carlton went eight for the win; Ron Reed came in for the save. Larry Guar went six for the Royals and Dan Quisenberry pitched two.

Game three was in Kansas City and the Royals pleased the home folks with a 4-3 tenth inning win. Dan Quisenberry, their top reliever, got the win, McGraw got the loss. Phils starter Dick Ruthven went nine, allowing three runs on nine hits.

Game four was also in KC and the Royals knotted the series at two wins each as they notched a 5-3 win. Larry Christensen started for the Phils, gave up four runs and five hits in one-third of an inning and it was pretty much over. Dickie Noles, Kevin Saucier and Warren Brusstar pitched the rest of the way allowing just one more run on five hits. Dennis Leonard got the win, Quisenberry the save.

The Phillies too game five 4-3 by scoring two runs in the bottom of the ninth. Marty Bystrom started and gave up three runs and ten hits over five-plus frames. Tug McGraw, who pitched the last three fames (allowing no runs, one hit – but loading the bases in the ninth) got the victory. Dan Quisenberry got the loss.

The Phils were up three games-to-two and to-a-man as they boarded the flight home they agreed that they'd end the series in game six – and they did.

Ted Taylor

It was Tuesday, October 21, with 65,838 fans (your author included) in the stands. Steve Carlton was masterful for seven innings allowing just three hits, struck over seven. They had a 4-0 lead and, frankly, the fans were feeling the win coming. But Carlton started to tire and allowed the first two runners in the eighth to reach base. Green made the sign to the pen and in trotted, who else? Tug McGraw. Tugger loaded the bases and gave up a Royal's run.

The climactic ninth is the stuff of legend. McGraw (left) struck out Amos Otis for the first out, but then loaded the bases on a walk to Willie Mays Aitkens and singles by John Wathan and Jose Cardenal. Frank White was the next batter, but before he could step in, Skipper Green went to the mound – and most of us thought Tug was gone. Green, though, had a message for Tug, he said "Let's not make this son-of-a-bitch as overly exciting as you are trying now" and turned and walked back to the dugout.

White lifted a pitch pop fly foul in front of the first base dugout (directly in front of where I was sitting) and both Bob Boone and Pete Rose converged on the ball. Boone waived Rose off and then dropped the ball, but somehow Rose caught the rebound. Two out.

Willie Wilson was next up. The game, the series, a century of futility, all on the line. McGraw worked a 1-2

20th Century Phillies by the Numbers

count on Wilson and then blew a fastball by Wilson for strike three. It was 11.29 PM and a century of no championships ended. McGraw looked at third base and waited for Mike Schmidt to meet him on the mound as the celebration erupted. Years later Schmidt would recount how he and Tug, who drove in together that day, they talked about how the catcher is always in the picture of a championship last pitch. Schmidt said he'd like to be in that picture too, so Tug waited for him.

A picture of McGraw in the ensuring parade holding aloft a copy of the *Philadelphia Daily News* with the simple headline "We Win!"

It would be 28 years before the Phillies would win their second World's Championship.

1980 Phillies Roster

Dallas Green, manager 91-71

Pitchers – Carlton, Ruthven, Walk, Reed, Saucier, Bystrom, Christenson, McGraw, Lerch, Espinosa, Brusstar, Lyle, Munninghoff, Davis, LeGrow, Larson

Catchers – Boone, Moreland, McCormack, Virgil

Infielders – Rose, Trillo, Bowa, Schmidt, Unser, Aviles, Aguayo, Loviglio, McCarver, J. Vukovich

Outfielders – McBride, Maddox, Luzinski, Gross, L. Smith, G. Vukovich, Dernier, Isales

The Glenside Kid Remembers...

I was with my friend Ken Bukantis and when the sixth game ended the entire field was surrounded by mounted police and some pretty fierce looking dogs. Ken said, "How nice, a pet show". The real reason, of course, was to discourage the fans from dismantling the field and it worked. We stood in our seats and simply cheered for, what seemed like, an hour. Nobody wanted to leave. It was time for the ages and, to this day, remains my most exciting sports moment. There was no point in trying to drive out of there because everything was grid-locked. When we finally left the park somebody handed me a beer, I have no idea who it was – or where it came from. It was one of those times. We got back to Glenside around 5.30 AM.

The World Series – 1983

The year was, to be kind, strange. Pat Corrales, a loyal team soldier, had been named manager in 1982 replacing Dallas Green. Under the ex-catcher the Phillies finished in second place, three games back of the Cardinals with a solid 89-73 record. Hopes for 1983 were high, yet with the Phils in first place under Corrales (43-42) he got fired and was replaced by GM Paul Owens – his second trip to the dugout. The Pope guided them to a 47-30 finish; six games ahead of the second place Pirates.

The road to the '83 World Series included a best-of-five league championship against the Los Angeles

Dodgers. Unlike 1980, however, this wasn't quite so dramatic. The Phillies won three of the first four and were, again, World Series bound.

It was an I-95 World Series as the Phillies were matched up with the Baltimore Orioles. This club featured a mini reunion of "The Big Red Machine" – Pete Rose, Joe Morgan (left) and Tony Perez. The press labeled the, mostly, veteran team "The Wheeze Kids". A kid catcher named Darren Daulton came up at the end of the season and saw action in two games (batting .333). He watched the World Series from the bullpen where he served as a warm-up catcher.

As World Series go this one isn't terribly memorable, and I was there for three of the games in Philly. The Phillies took game one in Baltimore 2-1. John Denny got the win, Al Holland, a fire-balling reliever, got the save. Scott McGregor took the loss. Joe Morgan got two of the Phillies five hits.

The O's evened things in game two winning 4-1. Charlie Hudson started for the Phillies and never got out of the fifth inning. Mark Boddicker hurled a complete game to get the win for the AL club. The Phillies managed just three hits.

Ted Taylor

The mood was up-beat when Manager Paul Owens' team returned to Philadelphia. Everyone figured a split in Baltimore removed the home team advantage. Little did they know.

The Orioles won game three, 3-2. Mike Flanagan got the win, Steve Carlton, who pitched six and $2/3^{rd}$ innings took the loss. The Phillies bats remained silent mustering just two hits.

Baltimore took game four, 5-4. Both clubs managed ten hits. Bo Diaz and Rose had two each. Storm Davis won the game with five innings of work, John Denny was the loser.

Things looked bad for the Phillies heading in to game five. They'd have to win all three to regain the title they had won in 1980 – but it wasn't to be. Scott McGregor pitched a five-hit shutout and the Phillies went meekly in to the night.

The Phillies offense had taken a vacation. As a team they batted .195 (31 hits, 159 at bats). Joe Morgan had two of the team's four homers – Garry Maddox and Gary Mathews had the other two.

It would be ten years before they'd return to the World Series.

20th Century Phillies by the Numbers

1983 Phillies Roster

Pat Corrales (43-42), Paul Owens (47-30), managers

Pitchers – Denny, Carlton, Reed, Holland, Hernandez, Hudson, Bystrom, K. Gross, Monge, McGraw, Altamirano, Christensen, Andersen, Comer, Ghelfi, Ruthven, Carman, Farmer

Catchers – Diaz, Virgil, Daulton

Infielders – Rose, Morgan, DeJesus, Schmidt, Perez, Milbourne, Garcia, Matuszek, Samuel, Jeltz, B. Robinson, Corcoran, Aguayo, D. Roberts

Outfielders – Hayes, Maddox, Mathews, G. Gross, Dernier, Lefebvre, Lezcano, Stone, Sanchez

The Glenside Kid Remembers...

I was in the press box for this World Series covering it for "Sports Collectors Digest" a weekly hobby publication based in Iola, WI. I was, at one time the magazine's editor, but at this time I was a featured columnist and reporter. My wife, Cindy, was a South Philly native so for the Phillies three home games (#3, 4, 5) I camped out at my in-laws home (Vince and Gilda DeMarco) and had my sister-in-law drive me to the park and then pick me up when the game was over. My mother-in-law, Gilda, took very good care of me. I took my brother-in-law, a Vietnam Vet, David DeMarco, to game four and my son Brett to game five. After the first game the attendant in charge of the press box told me I could bring someone along to the next two. After game three my son Brett, then 14, met Reggie Jackson (a fellow Cheltenham High graduate) and Howard Cosell. It took some of the sting out the Phillies losing the series.

Ted Taylor

The World Series – 1993

The 1993 Phillies were a prime example of what happens when a lot of diverse personalities mesh and become a cohesive unit. It was team that shouldn't have won the pennant but did so in a cake walk. Jim Fregosi was the manager (some said he was the ringmaster) of the club. The names Kruk, Daulton, Incaviglia, Schilling, Hollins, Eisenreich, Williams will resonate in the annals of baseball history whenever Phillies fans talk about those "special teams".

The Phillies, who had cruised to the NL East division title with a 97-65 record and then got to the World Series by winning the National League Championship Series with the Atlanta Braves. The Phillies stunned the 104-win Braves, who were bidding for their third consecutive World Series appearance, and won the NLCS 4–2.

The World Series opened in Toronto where the defending AL champions sent their ace Juan Guzman against the best the Phillies had to offer Curt Schilling (left). The result was less than a pitcher's duel, however, as both teams scored early and often.

With Toronto behind 4–3 in the fifth inning, Devon White hit a solo home run to tie the game. The next inning, John Olerud hit a solo home run of his own to put Toronto on top. Toronto added three insurance runs in the bottom of the seventh and held on to win 8–5. Al Leiter pitched 2 $\frac{2}{3}$ innings—in relief of an erratic Juan Guzman, who walked four in just five innings—for his first World Series win. John Kruk (famous for once telling a fan who chided him about his weight, "I'm not an athlete lady, I'm a baseball player") had three hits for Philadelphia.

In Game two also in Toronto, Dave "Smoke" Stewart was on the mound for Toronto and the always underrated Terry Mulholland started for Philadelphia. The Phils jumped out to an early lead: in the third inning, Jim Eisenreich followed John Kruk and Dave Hollins RBI singles with a three-run home run to deep right-center. Toronto got on the scoreboard in the fourth inning courtesy of a Joe Carter two-run home run to left, but the Jays were unable to mount a significant offensive push later in the game. Philadelphia held on to win 6–4. Terry Mulholland pitched 5 $\frac{2}{3}$ innings, allowing three earned runs, for the win.

The Phillies came home to Veteran's Stadium with a split. They felt good about that. For Toronto, Pat Hentgen faced off against Philadelphia starter Danny Jackson in Game 3. Hentgen pitched a strong six innings, allowing just a single run, and the Toronto offense took care of the rest. In Jackson's last postseason start against the Blue Jays, he had recorded a shutout (in the 1985 American League Championship Series) but he was not nearly as effective in this game as he was rocked for three runs in the first. Toronto prevailed, 10–3.

Toronto manager Cito Gaston was faced with a difficult decision prior to game time. As the Series switched to the National League ballpark, Gaston was forced to sit one player from his regular line-up as the designated hitter (DH) would not be allowed to play. As regular DH Paul Molitor had been a hot hand in the line-up, Gaston elected to sit first baseman John Olerud and position Molitor at first base. The decision was controversial as Olerud had led the American League in batting over the season with a .363 average; moreover, Molitor was the less sure-handed fielder. Molitor, however, put these concerns to rest, going 3-for-4, hitting a home run in the third inning and driving in three runs, while playing adequately at first base.

Game four was crucial to the Phillies and it was a heartbreaker (and I was there). Toronto sent Todd Stottlemyre to the mound while Philadelphia countered with Tommy Greene. It had been a rainy day in Philadelphia, which water-logged the aging turf at Veteran's Stadium, making for particularly slippery conditions. There was some talk about postponing the game – but MLB prevailed, tickets were sold, TV time was paid for.

Early in the game, Stottlemyre, trying to go first to third on a Roberto Alomar single in the second inning, did a

belly flop diving into third base, where he was called out. Todd's awkward dive resulted in an abrasion on his chin and appeared to shake him up in the next inning, during which he surrendered a two-run home run to Lenny Dykstra (left). Stottlemyre was pulled after the second inning, having already given up six runs. Greene fared little better for the Phillies, being pulled after giving up seven runs in three innings.

Philadelphia took a commanding 12–7 lead in the fifth inning, courtesy of two-run home runs from Dykstra and Darren Daulton, and a run-scoring double from Milt Thompson. The fans, my son Chris and I included, were very happy at that point.

We all sat there in shock as Toronto fought back from a 14–9 deficit in the eighth inning, scoring six runs on hits from Paul Molitor, Tony Fernández, Rickey Henderson, and Devon White. Duane Ward earned the save, retiring the last four Phillies batters. Three new World Series records were set, including the longest game (4:14), most total runs scored in a single game (29), and most runs scored by a losing team (14).

Two death threats directed towards Mitch Williams were phoned into Veterans Stadium as soon as it became evident that he was going to be the losing pitcher of Game 4. Williams wasn't aware of the death threats until after Game 5. (In later years he would become a popular local TV figure and then move on to a national prominence with ESPN and, later, MLB Network.)

So now it came down to game five. The Phillies needed to win this one and the next two if they were going to take the crown. The offenses were due for an off-day, and it came in Game 5 courtesy of a Curt Schilling and Juan Guzman pitching duel. Schilling shut down the previously unstoppable Toronto offense, limiting the team to just five hits and no runs. It was only the

Ted Taylor

second time all season that Toronto had been shut out. Guzman pitched well in a losing effort, allowing only two runs and five hits in seven innings of work.

The two runs scored as a result of scrappy play from the Philadelphia offense, so typical all season long. This team simply didn't like to lose. In the first inning, Lenny Dykstra walked, stole second, moved to third on a Pat Borders throwing error, and scored on a John Kruk ground out. In the second inning, Darren Daulton opened with a double, took third on a ground out, and scored on a Kevin Stocker single.

Back to Toronto for game six. The Jays needed one win, the Phillies needed two. The sixth game in the Series was a rematch between Game 2 starters Terry Mulholland and Dave Stewart, who would have similar results. Toronto scored in the bottom of the first with a run-scoring Paul Molitor triple, Joe Carter sacrifice fly, and Roberto Alomar RBI single. Paul Molitor added a solo home run in the fifth inning while the Toronto fans were chanting "MVP" for Paul, bringing the score to 5–1 for Toronto. Ultimately, Molitor became the first player in World Series history to have at least two home runs, two doubles, and two triples.

In the seventh inning, Philadelphia fought back with five runs to take a 6–5 lead. Lenny Dykstra hit a three-run home run, Dave Hollins had an RBI single and Pete Incaviglia hit a sacrifice fly. The inning brought an end to Stewart's night, leaving the game with six innings pitched and four runs given up.

20th Century Phillies by the Numbers

Closer Mitch Williams (left) came on to pitch the bottom of the ninth with his team clinging to a 6–5 lead (the TV cameras showed Phils ace Curt Schilling hiding his head under a towel – he just couldn't look). After beginning the inning by walking Rickey Henderson, Williams tried to counter Henderson's speed by using a slide-step style of pitching delivery. Prior to that game Williams never used the slide-step delivery in his career, and this may have cut back on his velocity. The walk to Henderson was followed by a Devon White fly out and a single by Paul Molitor that moved Henderson to second.

Joe Carter came up next and, with the count 2–2, he hit a three-run home run to win the game and the World Series crown. Just before the fifth and final pitch to Joe Carter, CBS Sports announcer Tim McCarver (a former Phil) commented that Carter (relatively unproductive in the Series up to that point) looked awkward and uncomfortable at the plate. The same pitch allowed Blue Jays radio announcer Tom Cheek the opportunity to utter his famous "Touch 'em all, Joe" quote, when Joe Carter clinched the series. Carter joined Pirates Hall of Famer Bill Mazeroski as one of the only two players to win a World Series with a home run in the bottom of the ninth inning of the deciding game.

Ted Taylor

The Blue Jays became the second expansion team to win two World Series championships, following the New York Mets in 1986. With the Montreal Canadiens winning the 1993 Stanley Cup Finals five months earlier, it marked the only time Canada celebrated two world championships in the same calendar year..ever.

Manager Jim Fregosi in an interview with Inquirer sportswriter Bob Brookover called his '93 team "the most unique group of individuals I ever managed. They were the last team I think that you could call 'baseball rats'. They enjoyed each other and they cared about each other."

The Phillies wouldn't return to the post season until 2008 – when they won their second World's Championship.

1993 Phillies Roster

Manager – Jim Fregosi, 97-65

Pitchers – Tommy Greene, Schilling, Rivera, Mulholland, Jackson, West, Mason, DeLeon, Thigpen, Andersen, Mitch Williams, Ayrault, Pall, Davis, Mike Williams, Mauser, Tyler Green, Brink, Fletcher, Foster

Catchers – Daulton, Pratt, Lindsey

Infielders – Kruk, Morandini, Stocker, Hollins, Duncan, R. Jordan, Batiste, Bell, Millette, Manto

Outfielders – Eisenreich, Dykstra, M. Thompson, Incavigia, W. Chamberlain, Amaro Jr., Longmire

20th Century Phillies by the Numbers

The Glenside Kid has an opinion...
It's popular to name "all time" teams. Everybody does it. To end the speculation I have picked two such teams – dividing the 20th Century in half and then picking two clubs from 1950-75, another from 1976-2000. Agree, disagree, it's my book.

1950-75 – 1b-Eddie Waitkus, 2b-Tony Taylor, SS-Granny Hamner, 3b-Dick Allen; Outfielders – Rich Ashburn, Del Ennis, Johnny Callison; c-Andy Seminick. Starting pitchers – Robin Roberts, Curt Simmons, Jim Bunning, Chris Short, Art Mahaffey. Reliever – Jim Konstanty. Manager – Gene Mauch.

1976-00 – 1b-Pete Rose, 2b-Dave Cash, SS-Larry Bowa, 3b-Mike Schmidt. Outfielders –John Kruk, Garry Maddox, Greg Luzinski, c-Darren Daulton. Starting pitchers – Steve Carlton, Curt Schilling, Terry Mulholland, Dick Ruthven, John Denny. Reliever – Tug McGraw. Manager-Dallas Green.

I wasn't around for very much of the first half of the century but there were some great players – Grover Cleveland Alexander, Chuck Klein, Cy Williams to name just a few.

Chapter 6
Player Profiles (A-J)

Close to 2,000 players wore Phillies uniforms in the 20th Century. In Chapter 11 you'll find a complete listing, by numbers, of every manager, coach and player. The 450 random player profiles that follow over the next three chapters are based on the Glenside Kid's impressions of selected players that made an impact in Phillies spangles.

Richie Ashburn, of (#1, 1948-59) – The highly skilled outfielder actually began in pro ball as a catcher. But by the time he got to the high minors he was an outfielder and stayed that way. Later he became one of the Phillies broadcast team, partnered with his pal Harry Kalas – "Harry the K". His famous "Hard to believe Harry" quote following an unusual play is the stuff of many stories. (There has always been a nagging question about a photo taken of Ashburn in Spring Training – 1948 – that clearly shows him wearing #8 or 9, yet he never wore it in any game that we can tell. His 1950 Bowman card is a version of that photo.)

Ted Taylor

George "Sparky" Anderson, 2b (#2, 1959; #45, 1959) – Acquired from the Dodgers, his one year as a player in the big leagues was with the Phillies. His .218 batting mark in 152 contests suggested his baseball future was as a manager. He earned Hall of Fame credentials as a highly successful manager with the Reds and Tigers. His '59 Topps card, as a Phillie, was really an airbrushed picture of him in his Dodgers uniform.

Morrie Arnovich, of (#3, 1936-38; #24, 1939-40) – A five-year starter with the Phils (pictured left), the media played up that he was Jewish (there were not many players of that faith). Mo batted .288 for the Phils over 442 games. His lifetime batting average of .287 was one point less than his Phillies tenure. He was sold to the New York Giants in 1941, went in to the service for four years, came out and played one game with the Giants and retired.

Harry "The Horse" Anderson, 1b-of (#9, 1957-60) – Played most of his career with the Phillies, batting .264 in 438 games. Finished up with the Reds, 1960-61. Had as many homeruns (60) as Babe Ruth, difference was it took him five years. A graduate of West Chester State College, Harry stayed with the Phils until they dealt him to Cincinnati in a deal that brought Tony Gonzalez to the Phils.

20th Century Phillies by the Numbers

Ruben Amaro Sr., coach/if (#12, coach, 1980-81; #20, ss, 1960-65) – Father of current Phils GM Ruben Jr. Was an excellent shortstop, batted .241 in 668 games. Came up with the Cardinals in 1958, also played with the Yankees (1966-68) and Los Angeles Angels (1969)

Dick Allen, 3b-1b (#15, 1964-69, 1975-76; #32, 1964) – One of the most prodigious sluggers to come out of the Phillies farm system. His off-beat personality was usually at the root of his problems. A fist-fight with veteran third baseman Frank Thomas in 1964 may have cost the Phillies the pennant. He lost a battle with a car headlight in front of his Mt. Airy home – no one ever could fully explain that one. He was traded a few times – Cardinals, Dodgers, White Sox – and then came home, more mellow, to finish out his career. Two-time homerun king with the White Sox. Lifetime batting average of .292 included .351 homeruns. His stats, under normal circumstances, should say "Hall of Famer". Scouted and signed by Johnny Ogden, one of baseball's super scouts.

Baseball historian John Shiffert adds, "To summarize Allen's contributions on the field in the briefest of fashions, using the best and most comprehensive measure of hitting, he still is the 19th best hitter in major league history, tied with Willie Mays and Frank Thomas for that honor, and just ahead of Hank Aaron, Joe DiMaggio, Mel Ott, Frank Robinson, Honus Wagner, Nap Lajoie and a bunch of other immortals. This is using the metric Adjusted OPS. That is, On base Plus Slugging, adjusted for the era and the parks wherein the individual played, widely considered to be the best single means of judging offensive contributions."

Allen is pictured above with the author at a 2006 Baseball Card show in a fire house near Hammonton (Central) New Jersey.

Ruben Amaro Jr., of (#37, 1966; #33, 1992-93, 96-98) – Half of the only father & son team to ever play for the Phillies – his Grandfather, Santos Amaro, was one of Latin America's greatest players. In the majors between 1991-98, he was drafted by the Angels. Also played with Cleveland. Career 485 games, .235 lifetime batting mark. With Phils 421 games, .239. Ruben, not so much a great player, but his Stanford education served him well as he served in numerous Phillies front office jobs before succeeding his mentor, Pat Gillick, as Phillies GM. The jury remains out on what kind of a GM he has become.

Larry Andersen, p (#47, 1983-86, 93-94) – A 17-year-career that started in 1975 and ended in 1994 with the Phillies saw Larry go 40-39 lifetime in 699 games, mostly as a reliever. With the Phils he was 11-14 over six years and 241 games. Andersen was the only player to be a member of both the 1983 and 1993 NL Championship teams. Darren Daulton was on the '83 roster for two games, was not in the World Series (he was a bullpen catcher). Daulton was on the 1993 squad, of course.

Andersen, after toiling as a pitching coach for the Phillies minor league clubs for several seasons moved in to the broadcast booth and became a very popular analyst on the club's radio network.

Bobby Abreu, of (#53, 1998-99) – Abreu was the team's right fielder well in to the 2000's and was a steady hitter. Nine seasons with the Phils resulted in a .303 average (1,353 games). Broke in with Houston in 1996. After Phillies played for the Yankees, Angels and Dodgers – lifetime .292 batting mark, 2,347 games. Biggest complaint was that he often played as if he really wasn't interested. At age 40 – and out of baseball for a year – Abreu signed a 2014 minor league contract with the Phillies, attempting a comeback but didn't stick with the club. He saw big league action in 2014 as a member of the Mets and then retired at the end of the season.

Carroll Berringer, coach (#1, 1973-77; #5, 1978) – Known as an excellent pitching coach, he never pitched in the majors. Spent 13 years (plus two out for military service) in the Dodgers organization. Came on board with fellow Dodger Danny Ozark when he was named skipper. Was 145-82 as a minor leaguer.

Dick "Rowdy Richard" Bartell, if (#2, 1932-33; #20, 1934) – In his time with the Phils he batted .295 in 587 games. Career began in 1927 with the Pirates, ended in 1946 with the Giants – that's 18 years, 2,016 games and a lifetime .284 bating average.

Ted Taylor

Dave Bristol, coach (#2, 1988; #4, 1982-85) – Everybody (including the Philly media and Bristol himself) expected him to, one day, be the Phils manager. It never happened. He was a big league pilot for 11 years with the Reds, Brewers, Braves and Giants.

Larry Bowa, ch/ss (#2, coach, 1989-96; #10, ss, 1970-81) – Bowa would later become Phillies manager (in the 2000's), after leaving them in the 90's to become manager of the Padres. The shortstop of the World Championship team and a catalyst for the fine teams of the 1970's. He and Ryne Sandberg were traded to the Cubs for, of all people, Ivan DeJesus – in a swindle engineered by Dallas Green who had left Philadelphia to become the Cubs' GM. Bowa's patented intensity usually ends up costing him whatever job he has at the moment. His baseball acumen is second to none. Played 16 years, .260 batting mark. Returned to Phillies colors in 2014 as Sanberg's bench coach.

Ed Bouchee, 1b (#5, 1957-60, #39, 1956) – After a marvelous 1957 rookie season (.293, 17 homers) Ed ran afoul of the law in the off-season and missed half of the '58 campaign while in counseling. He returned the next season (cured, they said), but was never quite the same player again. He was traded to the Cubs in 1960, finished with the 1962 Mets. Seven years, .265, 61 homers.

20th Century Phillies by the Numbers

Walter "Boom Boom" Beck, p (#7, 1942; #10, 1942; #11, 1942; #15, 1943) – Started out with the St. Louis Browns in 1924, with the Dodgers in 1933-34. Came to the Phillies in 1939, also with the Tigers and Reds and finished with the Pirates in 1945.The nickname comes from sound of line drives – that started out as Beck pitches - booming off the wall in the outfield. Even changing his number three times in 1942 didn't fool the opposition. Career was 12 years, he won 38, lost 69. Lost 20 for the Dodgers in 1933 (12 wins). On the same Phillies teams with him was "Losing Pitcher" Mulcahy (he lost 20 twice). It gives you an idea of what Phillies fans of that era had to deal with.

Buddy Blattner, if (#7, 1949) – Just missed the 1950 NL flag, batted .247 in 64 games for the '49 version. Broke in with the Cardinals in 1942, with the Giants 1946-48, finished with the Phils. Career five seasons, 272 games, .247 lifetime. Went on to become a popular baseball broadcaster after his playing days were over.

Bob Boone, c-1b-3b (#8, 1973-81, #40, 1972) – Son of infielder Ray Boone, Bob was the quarterback of the World's Champions as well as the other solid 1970's Phillies teams. In 1,125 games for the Phils he batted .259 and was part of the fluke pop foul out in Game Six of the '80 World Series when he muffed the catch but Pete Rose caught the rebound.

"Bouncing" Benny Bengough, coach (#11, 1946-59) – This former big league catcher came to the Phillies as a coach with Ben Chapman in 1946 and remained

Ted Taylor

through five more managers before retiring. Played with the Yankees 1923-30 and St. Louis Browns (1931-32). In 455 career contests has a .255 lifetime batting average. Graduate of Niagara University in his hometown of Buffalo NY.

Jim Bunning, p (#14, 1964-67; 1970-71) – Hall of Famer and three-time 19-game-winner for the Phillies. Pitched a perfect game on Father's Day 1964 against the miserable New York Mets at Shea. Earlier, as a member of the Detroit Tigers, he pitched his first "no no". Later he became a Republican Congressman and U. S. Senator. I met him at a Philly card show in the early 80's, decided I didn't like him very much.

Johnny Blatnick, of (#16, 1948-50) – Is sometimes listed as a 1950 "Whiz Kid" but saw very little action that season (4 games) and wasn't around for the World Series. Best year was 1948 when he played in 121 games for the Phils and batted .260, including six homers. Nice 1949 Bowman baseball card of him (above) that I got as a boy. Batted .258 in 131 games over three seasons with the Phils. Also saw action with the St. Louis Cardinals where he was swapped late in 1950.

20th Century Phillies by the Numbers

.**Bobby Bragan, c-if (#20, 1940-42)** – Broke in with the Phils and had a productive big league career, also was a big league manager with the Pirates (1956-57), Indians (1958), Milwaukee Braves (1963-65) and Atlanta Braves (1966). In Philly, however, he batted just .233 in 395 games. Also played for the Brooklyn Dodgers. Career, seven years, .240 lifetime average in 597 contests.

Forrest "Smoky" Burgess, c (#21, 1952-55) – Traded to the Phillies to replace Andy Seminick, the little round catcher quickly became a fan favorite. Later in his career (as he got even rounder) the one thing he could do was hit and he became baseball's premier pinch-hitter. Someone once said that Burgess could be awakened out of a sound sleep in the middle of the night and he'd still hit a line drive.

Kenny Brett, p (#31, 1973) – The wrong Brett brother. A fair pitcher, fair hitter, but did neither well enough to enjoy the same kind of career as George. He was 13-9 in 31 games for the Phils. I still think they should have made an outfielder out of him. His career spanned 14 seasons and he was 83-85 playing with the Red Sox, Brewers, Pirates, Yankees, White Sox, Angels, Twins and Dodgers. He probably gets a lot of old-timer game invitations. Won 13 games-in-a-season three times.

Ted Taylor

Bo Belinsky, p (#33, 1965-66) – Flamboyant, cocky, media savvy, a left-hander, would all describe Bo. He was married to a screen sex queen, Mamie Van Doren, at one point. Best year of his eight year big league career was his first (1962), 10-11 with the LA Angels. On May 5 of that year he no-hit the Orioles 2-0. For the Phils he was 4-11 in 39 games. After two years with the Phils he also pitched for Houston, Pittsburgh and Cincinnati – not with much success. Career shows a 28-51 record in 146 games. The ladies liked him a lot.

Mack Burk, c (#34, 1956, 58) – Another Phillies Bonus baby that didn't work out. Was in sixteen games (lots of pinch-running) and got to the plate twice, had one hit. That was that, a lifetime .500 batter.

Paul Byrd, p (#34, 1998-99) – Had a long big league career – Mets, Braves (twice), Angels, Indians and finished with the Red Sox. While with the Phillies he was named to the NL All-Star team. Lifetime he was 190-96. Noted as a very "nice guy".

Marty Bystrom, p (#39, 1980; #50, 1980-84) – Some say his 5-0 record down the stretch in 1980 is why the Phils won the pennant, then the World Series. But that was pretty much his "glory". Over 69 games for the Phils he was 24-22 with a 4.23 ERA. Some will remember that when the player's went on strike and the major league clubs were hiring replacements, Marty returned to the Phillies. Has done some TV pre and post game work for the Phils in recent years.

20th Century Phillies by the Numbers

Steve Bedrosian, p (#40, 1986-89) – They called him "Bed Rock" and the man could pitch. He was 21-18 with a 3.04 ERA in 218 games – with 103 saves as a Phillie.

Warren Brusstar, p (#40, 1973-75) – A sportswriter, the late Bill Conlin I think, said he had "Gun Fighter eyes". 18-11 in 179 games as a reliever, he notched six saves.

Ricky Bottalico, p (#52, 1994-97) – After his playing days were over he returned to Philadelphia as a popular radio/TV Phillies host on Comcast. A reliable reliever over his seven Phils campaigns, he saved 78 games went 15-25. Career 12 years, 33-42, 116 saves.

Tony Barron, of (#53, 1997) – Picked up from the Expos. Tony played in 57 games, batted .286, hit four homers – then hit the road.

Hank Borowy, p (#20, 1949-50) – He was 12-12 in 31 games over two seasons. ERA was 4.24.

The Glenside Kid Remembers...

At the height of the hobby (early-to-mid 90's) Hank Borowy got the idea that, as a member of the '50 Phillies, he was something special and began demanding ridiculous prices for his autograph at baseball card shows and through the mail. Lots of us did without his signature, though I did finally get one

Ted Taylor

from him at a show at the Armory in Northeast Philadelphia.

Jose Cardenal, of (#1, 1978-79) – Broke in with San Francisco in 1963, also played with the Angels, Indians, Cardinals (of course), Brewers, Cubs, Mets and Royals. His two Phillies years were not that noteworthy, though he got in to the NLCS in 1978. He was a member of the Royals when the Phillies won the World's Championship in 1980 (he was 2-for-10). Batted .241 as a Phil in 116 games.

Ben Culp, c/coach (#2, 1944; #20, 1944; #23, 1944; #25, 1942, 46-47; #29, 1943; #31, 1944) – Seemed like he was always around, but really only logged playing time in three seasons – and then it was only 15 games. Batting average was .192.

Ralph "Putsy" Caballero, if (#2, 1948; #3, 1950-52; #9, 1949; #20, 1944; #27, 1947; #28, 1945) – New Orleans born and bred, he was the consummate utility infielder, popular with the fans, but could never seem to crack the starting lineup. Signed first Phillies contract when he was 16. Was with the club for eight seasons, got in to 322 games, batted .238. Only once did he get in to over 100 games (1948, 113, splitting time between third and second.)

Jim Command, 3b (#5, 1954; #18, 1955) – Lots of promise, disappointing results. Jim appeared in just 14 games, hit .174. Perpetual prospect, batted .328 with 94 RBI's for Terre Haute in 1951.

20th Century Phillies by the Numbers

Pat Corrales, c/coach/mgr (#5, 1983; #8, 1982; #10, 1965; #18, 1983) – This poor guy was fired as Phils manager with the team in first place (left). Paul Owens came down from the front office replacing him all the way to the World's Series. As a player, he saw action in just 65 games, batting .223. Had a long career as a big league coach after he left the Phils.

Billy Crouch, p (#6, 1941) – Won 2, lost 3 in 20 games, one save a 4.42 ERA.

Johnny Callison, of (#6, 1960-69) – A very good Phillies player for almost a decade, but never quite the player that the Chicago White Sox expected when they first signed him. Callison also played with the Cubs and the Yankees and then retired back to the Philadelphia area, settling in Glenside – where he remained until his death. Callison did not have it easy after he retired and spent several years working as a bartender. He wrote an interesting book about his life and, briefly, played semi-pro baseball for the Jenkintown Steel Quakers. (I saw him play a game and the pitchers didn't have a chance.) Batted .271 lifetime, 1,432 games, 185 homers. His walk-off homerun won the 1964 All-Star game for the National League. Lived in Glenside PA until his death.

Ted Taylor

A Glensider enjoys his moment in time...
Johnny Callison was an adopted "Glensider" and he lived on Oakdale Avenue in that small Philadelphia suburb until he passed away. He was a fine ball player and accomplished a lot in his long career but his signature "moment in time" came on July 7, 1964 at the All-Star game at Shea Stadium in New York City. In front of 50,850 fans Johnny delivered a two-out ninth inning three-run homerun to give the NL a 7-4 victory, Callison was a last minute addition to the team and one that the senior circuit would never regret. Giants hurler Juan Marichal got the win.

Tony Curry, of (#7. 1960-61) – A pure hitter and a 14-carat liability with a glove. He was a designated hitter in an era before there was such a thing. One night "The Glenside kid" was at a game in Shibe Park, the batter lofted a soft pop fly to shallow left field. Shortstop Joe Koppe yelled "I got it", but he never did. Curry came flying in from left field and mowed Koppe down. The ball dropped for a double. Koppe was carried off the field on a stretcher. His defensive failings meant he got in to only 110 games over two seasons and batted .253.

Clarence "Choo Choo" Coleman, c (#12, 1961) – Not a very good catcher, but a terrific nickname. Ended up as a member of the incredibly bad 1962 Mets. His Phils career produced a .128 batting average in 34 games. Ouch.

20th Century Phillies by the Numbers

"Fidgety" Phil Collins, p (#16, 1933; #18, 1932; #40, 1934-35) – Phil was a pretty good pitcher on some pretty bad clubs. Phils record was 72-79 in 265 games with an ERA of 4.67.

Doug Clemens, of (#17, 1966-68; #18, 1968) – Decent pinch-hitter (26-for-116 as a Phil). Overall in 177 games batted .223. Broke in with the Cardinals.

Milo Candini, p (#18, 1950-51) – After baseball Milo opened a liquor store on the west coast. He used to tell people that he was the pitcher that won the NL pennant for the Phillies in 1950. His logic? He was 1-0 as a pitcher, the Phillies won the pennant by one game. Career with the Phils 2-0 in 33 games. Broke in to the big leagues with Washington in 1943, was with them until 1948. Drafted off the roster of the PCL Oakland Oaks after then '49 season. First career in pro ball he was 21-7 with El Paso (that was 1937).

Emory "Bubba" Church, p (#23, 1950-52) – Stopped a screaming line drive with his face and was never the same again. He was 23-17 for the Phils in 71 games before they dealt him to Cincinnati. Best Phils (and career) year was 1951 when he went 15-11. The Reds swapped him to the Cubs in 1953 and that was pretty much it, he was in two games for Chicago in 1955.

Ted Taylor

Dolph Camilli, 1b (#24, 1934-36; #27, 1937) – Phils long-ball hitter, stroked 92 homers for the Quakers, batted .295 in 540 games.

Gene Conley, p (#29, 1959-60) – In addition to being a pretty decent big league hurler, Conley also played pro basketball with the Boston Celtics. 20-21 with the Phils in 54 games with a 3.35 ERA.

Dave Cash, 2b (#30, 1974-76, 96 as a coach) – The Phils mid-70's slogan "Yes we can" originated with Dave. In 484 games he batted .296. Good guy, very popular with the Phillie Phaithful.

Wes Chamberlain, of (#31, 1990-91; #44, 1992-94) – Popular player, always seemed more formidable than he really was. With Phils for five seasons, 315 games, .260 with 38 homers. Lifetime 6 years, 385 games, .255, 43 homers.

Dusty Cooke, coach/manager (#32, 1948-52) – When the Phillies fired Ben Chapman as manager, Dusty took over as interim skipper until Eddie Sawyer was able to get there. He went 6-6-1, not bad.

Steve Carlton, p (#32, 1972-86) – Other pitchers have been called "Lefty" only he and Lefty Grove really deserve that nickname. Both great hurlers toed the slab for Philadelphia ball clubs. I was at the park the night he needed three strikeouts for 3,000. Certificates were printed and everyone in attendance got one. Carlton faced three Expos in the first inning and struck out each one. Tim Wallach, a pretty good hitter, was the 3,000th and he didn't have a chance. Over breakfast in York, PA before a card show/signing event that I ran

20th Century Phillies by the Numbers

with partner Jeff Stevens, I mentioned to Carlton that I was there that night. He said, "Yes it was a distraction and I wanted to get it over as soon as possible." He did, three strikeouts on ten pitches. Carlton never threw a no-hitter, but I saw him come close. One game against the Atlanta Braves he was mowing them down and in the eighth inning the Braves sent up reserve catcher (and former Phillie) Bill Naharodny as a pinch-hitter. Naharodny lined a single up the middle. It was the only Braves hit. I asked Carlton what he thought, he said, "Naharodny? You had to be kidding." Career saw 241 wins, 161 losses, 3.09 ERA.

Ben Chapman, manager (#34, 1945; #7, 1946-48) – Savaged in the Jackie Robinson movie "42" as a race-baiting bigot, clearly the film's chief bad guy. People who know say that in real life he was pretty much as described, but not nearly as bad as portrayed in the film. Phils were 196-276-2 under his leadership.

Norm Charlton, p (#37, 1994-95) – They called him "The Sheriff" and at one time he was a pretty fair reliever. That time, however, didn't include the two years he was cashing Phillies paychecks. He spent all of '94 on the DL and then the next year went 2-5 with zero saves in 25 games and was sent back to Seattle from whence he came. In fact he had three stints with the Mariners. Lifetime 13 years, 51-54, 97 saves.

Larry Christensen, p (#38, 1973-84) – A fan favorite, Larry was 83-71 in 243 games and a 3.79 ERA. Active in the Philadelphia community I worked with him at a Variety Club charity golf event with him shortly after he retired. Nice guy.

Pat Combs, p (#38, 1989-91; #21, 1992) – Won 17, lost 17 in 56 games for the Phils over four seasons. He was 10-10 in 1990 and that's as close as he ever came to all the predictions made of his coming greatness.

Andy Cohen, coach/manager (#39, 1960) – One season as a coach, managed Phils for two games between Eddie Sawyer and Gene Mauch. He was 1-1. Big league career with the Giants (1926-29) batted .281 in 262 games. Mainly played second base.

Don Carman, p (#39, 1983-84; #42, 1984-90) – Spent eight of his ten big league years with the Phillies (53-52 lifetime). Won 13 games in 1987, lost 15 in 1989 to gain the dubious distinction of most NL losses that year.

Joe Cowley, p (#39, 1987) – Won 33 games in the three seasons prior to coming to the Phillies – Atlanta, Yankees, White Sox. He went 0-4 for the locals in the five games he played (four were starts) and was finished.

John "Wes" Covington, of (#43, 1962-65) – Boy was he fun to watch. Came to the Phillies from the Braves. The man could hit and over 11 lifetime seasons he batted .279 with 131 homers. Best year (of his four with the Phils) was 1963 when he batted .303 with 17 homers in 119 games.

Don Cardwell, p (#46, 1957-60) – 14 years in the majors, broke in with the Phillies in 1957. Best year for them was '59 when he went 9-10. Saw action with the Cubs, Pirates, Mets and Braves during his career. Total of 410 games, lifetime 102-138 record with a 3.92 ERA.

20th Century Phillies by the Numbers

George "Kiddo" Davis, of (#1, 1932; #31, 1934) – Did well in two tours with the Phillies (.309 in 137 games in '32; .293 in 100 games in '34), but seemed destined to move from team-to-team. Started with the Yankees, was also with the Giants, Cardinals and Reds. Career spanned eight years, batted .282.

Alvin "Blackie" Dark, if (#1, 1960) – All American football player at LSU, All-Star baseball player. He had a 14 year career – and in 55 games, batted .242 with the Phils in part of a season. Played in 1,828 games, lifetime .289 hitter, 126 homers. Batted over .300 four times. Played with Braves (broke in with Boston, returned later with Milwaukee), Giants, Cardinals, Cubs. Managed for 13 years, took Giants and A's to World Series and won (in 1974) with Oakland.

Billy DeMars, coach (#2, 1973-81; #3, 1970-72; #46, 1969) – Longtime Phillies hitting coach, DeMars broke in as an infielder with the Philadelphia A's (1948) and then was swapped to the St. Louis Browns (1950-51, pictured on is '50 Bowman card). He was, for the longest time, the last living alum of both those long-gone clubs still wearing a uniform. His whole playing career was three seasons, 80 games and a .237 batting average.

Ted Taylor

Babe Dahlgren, 1b (#3, 1943) – One season with the Phils, batted .287 in 136 games with just five homers. Career spanned 1935-46, 1139 games, .261 average, 82 homers. Claim to fame is that he replaced Lou Gehrig at first base, ending the Iron Man's career. The name "Babe" fits the Yankee model. His given name, Ellsworth, not so much.

Virgil "Spud" Davis, c (#4, 1939; #8, 1933; #6, 1932; #28, 1938) – Played two games for the Cardinals in 1928 and then was swapped to the Phils. Spent eight of his 16 big league seasons with the Phils. Best year was 1933 when he batted .349 – and that got him traded back to the Cardinals the following year. Batted over .300 nine times. Also played for the Reds and the Pirates. Lifetime 1,458 games and a .305 batting average. Interim manager of the Pirates in 1946 (3-1). Not a Hall of Famer, some think he should be.

Lenny "Nails" Dykstra, of (#4, 1989-98) – Broke in with the Mets in 1985, spent five seasons with them and was traded to the Phils where he became the catalyst for the '93 pennant and hugely popular with the fans. Best year was 1990 when he batted .325 with league-leading OBP (.418) and hits (192). Phils career included 734 games, .289 batting average, 51 homers. Lifetime 1,278 games, .285 batting mark, 81 homeruns.

Bo Diaz c (#6, 1982-85) Very popular player during his four year Phillie stint. In 333 games Bo batted .256 with 36 homers. His career, with the Red Sox, Reds and Indians created a 13 year career, 993 games, .255 average. He retired in 1989 (age 36) and the following November (11/23/90) he fell off the roof of his home in

Venezuela and was killed. Some stories said he was fixing his TV antenna at the time.

Vince DiMaggio, of (#7, 1945; #34, 1946) – Three DiMaggio brothers played in the big leagues. There was Hall of Famer Joe, Dom (who should be in there too) and Vince, the one who the Phillies ended up with. It always happened that way. Broke in with the Braves in 1937 (a year after Joe came up with the Yankees, three before Dom made the Red Sox), then to the Reds, Pirates, Phillies and, finally, the Giants. In 1,110 games, he batted .249 with 125 homers. He was the oldest DiMaggio brother. Played in 127 games for the '45 Phils (batting .257) – hitting four grand slam homers - and after six games with them in '46 he was dealt to the New York Giants where he finished his career.

Darren "Dutch" Daulton, c (#10, 1985-97; #29, 1983) – Rated with Bob Boone, Andy Seminick and Mike Leiberthal among the best Phillies catchers ever. Not so sure that Jimmie Wilson shouldn't be on that list too. One of the most popular Phils players in recent history (the ladies sure liked him). Played 14 years in the majors – all but 52 games with the Phillies. He was, to many, the glue that held the '93 NL pennant winners together. As a Phil appeared in 1109 games, batted .245 and stroked 134 homers. Knee problems limited his playing time as he aged and his best batting mark (.300) came as a part-timer in 1994 (69 games). Swapped to Miami in mid-1997 he was with the Marlins team that won the World Series (he got his ring). He retired at the end of 1997.

Clay Dalrymple, c (#11, 1960-68) – Not a bad catcher either. Batted .234 in 1,006 games. Played three years with the Baltimore Orioles after leaving Philly. Like Callison, Dalrymple was a Glenside PA resident at one time.

Ivan DeJesus, ss (#11, 1983-84, #18, 1982) – He came to the Phillies in that dreadful deal that sent Larry Bowa and Ryne Sandberg to the Cubs. It didn't matter how good he was – and he wasn't really that bad – Phillies fans felt robbed (and they were). Batting .249 in 463 games didn't allow anyone to feel good about the deal. Ironically Sandberg returned to the Phils, first as a minor league manager, then a coach with the big club and, finally, as skipper in mid-2013. Who did he name as bench coach for 2014? Larry Bowa.

Ryne Duren, p (#18, 1963-64; #30, 1965) – He could throw the ball through a brick wall (at least so it seemed) and he wore glasses so thick people assumed he was half blind and maybe he was. The result was that hitters were terrified to bat against him. In 41 games he went 6-2 and logged two saves. He had a tidy 3.39 ERA, mostly because no one dared dig in on him.

Murry Dickson, p (#20, 1954-56) – His best years were with the Cardinals, then the Pirates. With the Phils he went 22-34 in 79 games. His ERA wasn't bad – 3.71 – but the Phils of his time were. He also got one save along the way.

20th Century Phillies by the Numbers

Karl Drews, p (#22, 1951-54) – Solid hurler for the Phils. Appeared in 93 games, won 25, lost 25. Had an ERA of 3.74 and three saves. He was mostly a starter, with 30 relief appearances also on his Phils resume.

Bobby Dernier, of (#22, 1982, 88-89; #24, 1982-83; #29, 1983; #30, 1980-81) – Highly touted player, two stints with the Phils (best years in between with the Cubs). In 439 games batted .241.

Don Demeter, 1b-3b-of (#24, 1961-63) – Batted .276 in 413 games. Long ball threat, popped 71 homers for the Phils. Broke in when the Dodgers were still in Brooklyn (3 games, 1956) ended up with the Indians in 1967. Had a .265 lifetime mark over 11 seasons and 1109 games.

Sylvester "Blix" Donnelly, p (#30, 1946-50) – Broke in to majors with the Cardinals in 1944 and went 1-0 in the World Series (vs. the Browns). Dealt to the Phillies in 1946 he stayed with them through the Whiz Kid campaign (he was 2-4, did not pitch in the series). Finished up with the Boston Braves in 1951. In eight seasons, Blix won 27, lost 36 – mostly as a reliever, though he did notch 27 complete games over the years. Magic was his hobby and some opposing hitters swore that's what his curve ball was – magic.

John Denny, p (#40, 1983-85) – Solid starter for the Phils. Notched a 37-29 record over 95 games. His ERA was a stellar 2.80..

Ted Taylor

Curt "Coonskin" Davis, p (#42, 1934-36) – Pretty good pitcher on some pretty bad teams. Went 37-35 in 105 games with a 3.42 ERA.

Mark Davis, p (#43, 1980-81; #48, 1993) – Can you say disappointing? Davis was the Phils first round draft pick in 1979 and went on to a 15 year career in the majors. Why? I have no idea. He never won more than nine games in any season, with the Phils over three he was 2-6. Spent five seasons each with the Padres and the Giants (he won 25 for them, lost 45). Lifetime he was 51-84 with a 4.17 ERA in 624 games. I guess the only explanation was that he was left-handed and good lefties are hard to find. (See Davis, Mark).

Jose DeLeon, p (#48, 1992; #50, 1992-93) – Has the dubious distinction of twice leading the league in losses (19). He was 2-19 with the '85 Pirates, 7-19 with the 1990 Cardinals. He also was a 16 game winner for the Cards the year before. With the Phils he got in to 27 games, going 3-1. Lifetime 13 years, 86-119 in 415 games.

Lee Elia, coach/manager (#2, 1985; #3, 1980-81; #4, 1986-88) – Born in Philadelphia, but never played with the Phillies. Spent one season with the White Sox (1966, 80-games, .205) and one with the Cubs (1968, 15 games, .176). Worked in the Phillies farm system as manager and coach – was with the World's Champions. Named Cubs skipper in 1982 and 83 and was fired 123 games in to the '83 season for a melt-down he had with the media. Back to the Phils as a coach in '85, named manager in 1987 (replacing John Felske and going 51-50) and then piloted the team in 1988. Career as a skipper, 238-300.

Jim Eisenreich, of (#8, 1993-96) – Overcame Tourettes Syndrome to craft a 15 year big league career. A key member of the Phils early 90's successes ('93 NL flag), Eisenreich batted .324 for them over 499 games (24 homers). In 1996 he appeared in 113 games and batted .361. Career 1,422 games, .290 batting average. Played six seasons with the Kansas City Royals. Finished with the LA Dodgers.

Del Ennis, of (#14, 1946-56) - A native son, Del came back from serving in World War II and immediately began being productive. Without his big year in 1950, the Phillies don't win the pennant. Broke in to the majors with the Phils in 1946, batted .313, hit 17 homers, drove in 70. Drove in over 100 runs seven times (in his 14 year career), hit 20-or-more homeruns ten times, 30-or-more twice. Was NL RBI leader in 1950 (126) on the way to the pennant. Career batting mark .284, 288 homeruns, 1,284 RBI's. Look like Hall of Fame numbers to me.

The Glenside Kid Remembers...
One of the worst days of my life came when I discovered that Del had been traded to St. Louis for Eldon "Rip" Repulski over the winter of '56. My first thought was that somebody had lost their mind. Del will always be the only Phillies player worthy of number 14. When partner Bob Schmierer and I were putting together our second "Philly Show" (Baseball Card & Sports Memorabilia Show) we needed a guest and drove to Del's Huntingdon Valley PA bowling alley. Del

Ted Taylor

was less than excited about the idea, but his wife (Liz) said "Do it Del, give the boys a hand". We paid him with a $25 gift certificate to Strawbridge's (a Jenkintown department store where my Mom worked).

"Jumbo" Jim Elliott, p (#17, 1933; #21, 1932; #43, 1934) – Steady hurler for some not-so-hot teams. In 129 games he went 36-35 with a 4.53 ERA.

Bobby Estallela, c (#27, 1996-99) – He was the son of longtime Philadelphia A's outfielder, Bob Estallela Sr. Broke in with the Phils in '96, got in to 76 games over four years batting .218 with 14 homers. Career spanned nine years, several teams, 310 games, .216 average with 48 homers.

Nino Espinosa, p (#35, 1979-81) – A member of the '80 World Champs. Went 19-22 in his short Phillies career. Appeared in 59 games.

George Earnshaw, coach (#38, 1949-50) – One of two men to have been a member of pennant winning A's (1929-31) and Phillies (1950) teams (the other was Cy Perkins, a backup A's catcher in 1929-30). Pitched for the A's 1928-33 and was traded to the White Sox for '34 (as part of Connie Mack's depression era fund raising). Dealt to Brooklyn by the Chisox in mid-1935 he finished up with the Cardinals in 1936. For his career he was 127-93. He won 20-games-or-more three straight years with the A's (24 in 1929, 22 in 1930 and 21 in 1931). His World

Series record was 4-3 in eight starts all for the A's. Nickname was "Moose", he stood 6'4, weighed 210.

Fred Fitz Simmons, mgr (#14, 1944-45) – Nickname was "Fat Freddie" (he was 5'11, 205) – and he was robust. In a 19 year career as a pitcher he was 217-146 with the Giants and the Dodgers – he was also once a 20-game-winner (1928). Not so much a success as a skipper, his Phils teams were 105-181-2. Later he returned to the majors as a pitching coach with the Dodgers, Braves and Giants.

Jimmie Foxx, 1b-p (#4, 1945) – The "Right-handed Babe Ruth", Jimmie Foxx's career was in the rear view mirror when he joined the Phils just as World War II was winding down. But, oh what a player he was during his 20-year-career, especially with Connie Mack's Athletics and the Boston Red Sox. In 89 games for the '45 Phils Foxx batted .268 and hit the last seven homers of his career. Foxx also pitched in nine games that year, went 1-0 with a 1.52 ERA. The career shows 2,317 games, a lifetime .325 batting average and 534 homeruns. Nicknamed "Double X" and "The Beast". As an A's historian it bothers me that on Foxx's Hall of Fame plaque his hat reflects a Boston "B". Foxx spent 12 years with the A's, a little over six with the Red Sox.

Ted Taylor

Gene "Augie" Freese, 3b (#4, 1959) – With the Phils just one season, got in to 132 games and batted .268. Started with the Pirates in 1955, ended up with Houston in 1966. Along the 12 seasons he played in 1,115 games, batted .254. His brother George played in the majors for parts of three seasons.

Mickey Finn, 2b (#7, 1933) – Sounds like a drink, real name Cornelius (Neal). Was in 51 games, batted .237. Four years in the bigs got him in to 321 games and a .262 lifetime batting mark.

John Felske, manager (#7, 1984-87) – Almost three years as skipper. His clubs went 190-194. A catcher, he played parts of three seasons (Cubs, Brewers), saw action in 54 games and batted .135.

Terry "Tito" Francona, manager (#7, 1997-02) – Francona's career as a manager began in the White Sox farm system where he had the unenviable job of being Michael Jordan's first baseball skipper. Jordan was a great NBA player, not so much as a pro baseball player – in fact he was pretty bad. Francona had to play second fiddle to the media attention generated by a guy who really couldn't play the game very well. Later, as Red Sox skipper, he'd break "The Babe Ruth Jinx" and win it all. After a sort-of player mutiny in Boston, Francona got fired, spent a year as a broadcaster and then became skipper of the Cleveland Indians.

20th Century Phillies by the Numbers

Bob Finley, c (#9, 1944; #15, 1943; #31, 1944) – Sally League All-Star catcher in 1943 with Knoxville, came to the Phils in July of that year and batted .259 in 28 games. His first big league hit was a homerun against the Cardinals. Hit .251 in 122 career games. Pictured left on a TCMA Play Ball 1944 card.

Bernie Frieberg, if-of (#11, 1932) – With the Phils 1925-32 played in 795 games and batted .274. He was the consummate utility man – really played everywhere but pitcher.

Jim Fregosi, mgr (#11, 1991-96) – Phils skipper for six years – won the '93 pennant, lost to the Blue Jays in the series. Record 431-463. Spent 18 years as a big league player (1,902 games, .265, 151 homers), none as a Phillie. As a big league skipper for 15 years also piloted Angels, White Sox and Blue Jays (1028-1094).

Woody Fryman, p (#14, 1968; #22, 1968-70; #35, 1970-72) – Reliable hurler, worked 157 games in his Phils career, went 46-52 with 3.75 ERA.

Howie Fox, p (#18, 1952) – Earned his chops with the Cincinnati Reds, came to the Phils and went 2-7 in 13 games, 5.08 ERA. Died young and as a result collectors seek his, oft-forged, autograph on early 50's cards.

Ted Taylor

Julio Franco, if (#15, 1982) – Seems like he was in baseball forever, but only one of those years was with the Phils – 16 games, batted .276. Actually was with eight different teams over 23 years (1982-2007), appearing in 2,527 games, batting .298 with 173 homeruns. Typical of the Phils, despite much bally-hoo about him the minors he got just a scant look here and then was shipped off for 22 very good big league years elsewhere. He as playing for the San Antonio Cats in an independent league at age 55 in 2014.

Roger Freed, of (#20, 1970-71) – Hit the first homer at the Vet but never set the town ablaze. In 191 games he averaged .222. Mike Schmidt had more success with this number.

Dick "Turk" Farrell, p (#32, 1967-69; #39, 1967; #44, 1956; #43, 1957-61) – Studley Phils relief hurler. Had 65 saves in 359 games and a 3.26 ERA. Won 47-lost 47. Part of the media-created "Dalton Gang".

Chico Fernandez, 2b-ss (#45, 1957; #16, 1958; #17, 1958-59) – Chico came to the Phillies from the Dodgers and was seen as a long term solution to the revolving door at shortstop since the departure of Granny Hamner. Chico was not the answer. Played 342 games for the Phils, batted .242. Good fielder, though.

Marvin Freeman, p (#48, 1986-90) – Some called him "Marvelous Marv" (mostly because of his name, I guess) but he wasn't all that marvelous. Got in to 31 games, went 4-5. Also called "Starvin' Marvin. Perhaps because he was thin.

20th Century Phillies by the Numbers

Tom Ferrick, coach (#51, 1959) – Someone once asked Ferrick if he ever had a sore arm. He replied, "Just once, but it lasted from 1941 to 1952". In other words in the days that he played pitchers did not report sore arms because, with just 16 teams, if you were lame you may have been finished, too. Broke in with the Philadelphia A's in 1941, ended with the Washington Senators in 1952 – also saw action with the Browns and the Yankees. Lifetime 40-40 in 323 games.

Bill Glynn, 1b (#3, 1949) – Played in just eight games, batted .200. Later would spend three years with the Indians. Career was 310 games, .249 batting average. As a kid I got a Bill Glynn '54 Topps baseball card of him and somebody told me "he lived in the area" (they said Melrose Park). I tried to find out exactly where. His card said he lived in Franklin, NJ – wherever that was.

Al "Lefty" Gerheauser, p (#6, 1943; #11, 1943-44; #24, 1944) – Mostly a starter, Lefty saw service in 68 games going 18-35 with a 4.05 ERA.

Mike Goliat, 2b (#9, 1949-51) – Second baseman for the Whiz Kids. Short big league tenure. One year he had it, the next he didn't. Go figure. Played 241 games for the Phils over three years, batted .227. Ended big league career with the St. Louis Browns, but played several more good years in the Pacific Coast League.

Ted Taylor

Jim Greengrass, of (#10, 1955, #23, 1956) – My friend Carolyn Scott and I were at Shibe Park on the day in 1955 that the trade was announced. Greengrass was coming from the Reds and old pal Andy Seminick was coming back too. I remember the buzz as if it were yesterday. In 180 games he batted just .245.

Greg Gross, of (#21, 1983-88; #23, 1979-82) – Played in 1,547 games – a lot of them as a pinch-hitter, something at which he excelled. Batted .279. Actually pitched in one game, too. No record, though. Long career as a Phils batting coach extending in to the 21st Century.

Ruben Gomez, p (#22, 1959-60, 67; #32, 1967; #40, 1959) – Probably left all his good pitching behind with the San Francisco Giants. As a Phil he got in to 49 games, won 3, lost 11. His ERA was 5.63.

Tony Gonzalez, of (#22, 1960-61; #25, 1962-68; #12, 1962) – Popular, good hitting outfielder, came over in a deal with Cincinnati. Got in to 1,118 games as a Phil, batted .295. Nine years as a very popular player in Philly. He over .300 three times (hit .339 in 1967) but was never a long-ball threat.

Oscar Gamble, of (#23, 1970-72) – There's a memorable baseball card of Gamble with an Afro hairstyle that looks like one of those hats the Queen's Guards wear in England. The guy doing the airbrushing for Topps should have been fired. Batted .241 in 254 games, hair not withstanding.

20th Century Phillies by the Numbers

Dick Groat, ss (#24, 1966-67) – A very good shortstop, Groat was also an All-America college basketball player. Broke in with the Pirates in 1952 and stayed with them until traded to the Cardinals in 1963. On the Bucs World Championshp team in 1960 he led the NL in hitting with a .325 average. To the Phils in 1966 where he hit .254 for the Phils in 165 games over two seasons. Finished with the Giants in 1967. Lifetime 14 seasons, 1929 games, batted .286.

Dallas Green, p/mgr (#26, 1960-64, 67; #47, 1967; #46, 1979-81) – Green was a 20-game-winner in the big leagues, but it took him eight years to get that total (he lost 22). Besides pitching for the Phillies he saw action with the Senators (1965) and the Mets (1966). He came back to the Phils in 1967, though for only eight games. He then settled in to a series of administrative posts. They brought "Big D" down from the front office to light a fire under the Phillies in late 1979 and light it he did (they were 19-11 for the rest of that season). Big and gruff (6'5, 210) and clearly the boss, he motivated the club to its' first World's Championship in 1980 (91-71). Left Phils after '81 season for a front office job with the Cubs, later (1989) managed the Yankees (56-65, partial season).

Ted Taylor

Gene Garber, p (#26, 1974-78) – Had 51 saves in 250 games, all in relief. Won 33, lost 22. Had a nifty 2.68 ERA. Solid career with the Phils and was eventually traded to the Braves so the club could re-acquire Dick Ruthven. With Atlanta he was a key figure as the Braves won the 1982 NL West flag. Another claim to fame came when, in 1978, he struck out Pete Rose to end his 44-game hitting streak.

Tyler Green, p (#28, 1993, 1995-99) – A Phils first round draft pick out of Wichita State University in 1991 (10th overall). Green was with the Phils for four years (he sat out 1994 with an injury) and fashioned an 18-25 record. Spent seven years in the minors going 32-47.

Johnny Gray, p (#38, 1958) – Broke in with the Philadelphia A's, came to the Phils in '58, saw action in 15 games, but had no decisions. ERA was 4.15.

Kevin Gross, p (#46, 1983-88; #48, 1983) – Went 60-66 in 203 games for the Phils. Had a decent 3.87 ERA. After leaving the Phillies he pitched a no-hitter as a member of the Los Angeles Dodgers.

Tommy Green, p (#49, 1990-96) – Tommy came to the Phillies in '90 (from Atlanta) and had two solid seasons (1991 when he went 13-7, and 1993 when he had the best record on the staff, 16-4, as they won the NL flag). Overall, though, Green was on the DL more than he played. His Phils career shows 36-22.

Granny Hamner, ss-p (#1, 1948; #2, 1949-59; #6, 1945; #17, 1948; #37, 1946; #35, 1947; #21, 1944; #33, 1948) – Granny wore more numbers than any other Phillies player. Most of us who recall the Whiz

Kids remember him as #2, their ace shortstop. But it took a while for Granny to catch on, breaking in with the club in 1944 and it seemed like every time he was with the club he got another number. Played 17 years in the majors, 1,531 games, batted .262. All playing time was with the Phils except for 27 games with the Indians in 1959 and three with the '62 Kansas City A's – where he was trying to make it as a pitcher. The A's took a chance after Hamner, as a fulltime pitcher at the age of 35, had pitched for Binghamton of the Eastern League and gone 10-4 in 22 games. The Phils toyed with the idea of using his strong arm from the mound and he saw mound action in four games for them. He lost a decision in 1956, another in 1962. His brother Garvin played in 32 games for the Phils in 1945, batting .189.

Rollie Hemsley, c (#2, 1946; #32, 1947; #47, 1946) – Ironically Rollie ended his big league career as a coach (for manager Eddie Joost) with the 1954 Philadelphia A's, the last year the team played in Philadelphia. Batted .225 in 51 games for the Phils as a player.

Don Hurst, 1b (#4, 1932; #15, 1933) – Career with the Phils began in 1928 and it was a productive one. In 854 games he compiled a .303 batting average. (See more about Don in the players-by-season chapter.)

Solly Hemus, if (#4, 1956-58) – Solly Joe came over from the Cardinals and became a fan favorite over the three seasons he was here. Batted .269 in 352 contests, mostly as a utility infielder. Later he'd manage the Cardinals for three seasons.

Ted Taylor

Larry Hisle, of (#4, 1969; #22, 1970-71; #24, 1968) – One of those highly heralded, loaded with potential, but gets low results, players that the Phillies always seem to find. He got in to 314 games, batted .236.

Al "Boots" Hollingsworth, p (#7, 1939; #17, 1938-39) – Why they called him "Boots" is beyond me. They should have called him losing pitcher, except that belonged to Hugh Mulcahy. In 39 games, 31 as a starter, he won 6, lost 25. The man would go on to become a pretty decent pitching coach. Go figure.

Juan Francisco "Pancho" Hererra, 1b-2b-3b (#7, 1961; #18, 1958, 60-61) – Picture Ryan Howard playing second base and that's what it looked like when they tried to make a second sacker out of the hulking (6'3, 220) Mr. Hererra. It didn't work. The big guy batted .271 in 300 games. He managed 31 homeruns. He would play 16 seasons in the minors at various levels (mostly AAA) and craft a .291 lifetime batting mark with 239 homers. He retired from baseball in 1974 at age 40.

Garvin "Wes" Hamner, 2b (#8, 1945) – For one season Garvin and brother Granny formed the Phillies keystone combination. In 32 games, batted .198. He was three years old than his brother.

Charlie Hayes, 3b (#8, 1989-91; #13, 1995) – After being the Phils regular third sacker 1989-91, he returned to the team in '95 and picked up where he left off. Hayes batted .275 in 141 games in '95. In his earlier stint he hit .248 in 378 contests.

Von Hayes, of-1b (#9, 1983-91; #26, 1983) – The "5-for-1" tag that came with him in the trade from Cleveland hung around his neck like a rock. The fans (encouraged by a negative news media) never liked him very much but he batted .272 in 1,208 games and that's not too shabby.

Don Hoak, 3b, coach (#12, 1963-64, #3, 1967) – You had to like Don, he was a rough neck, dirty uniform player, but his best days were behind him when he wore Phillies colors. In two visits he batted .228 in 121 contests. He was once married to pop singer Jill Corey.

Kirby Higbe, p (#14, 1939-40) – His reputation as a nasty player lives on. With the Phils he was 24-33 in 75 games – his best days were still to come. He broke in with the Cubs in 1937, dealt to the Phils in '39. After winning 14 games for Philly in 1940 he was traded to the Dodgers where he went 22-9 in 1941 and was one of their best hurlers until losing two seasons in the military. Came back from the Army, had a falling out with Dodger brass over Jackie Robinson and they dealt him to the woeful Pirates. He ended his career going 0-3 with the Giants in 1951. Lifetime he was 118-101.

Ted Taylor

Tommy Hutton, 1b (#14, 1972-77) – A fan favorite, Tommy batted .253 in 651 games for the Phils. A very good fielder. Broke in with the Dodgers in 1966, dealt to the Phils in 1972 and with them until the end of the '77 season. Dealt to Toronto for 1978 and then to Montreal where he finished his career in 1981. Lifetime, 12 seasons 952 games, .248 batting mark.

Dave Hollins, 3b (#15, 1990-94) – Tough guy third baseman who spent all or parts of seven seasons in Philly. Best year was '92 when he batted .270 with 27 homers in 156 games. He hit .273 for the '93 NL pennant winners with 18 homers. Career 12 years batted .260 with 112 homers. Traded to the Red Sox in mid-95 he became a baseball nomad playing for the Twins, Seattle, Angels, Toronto and Cleveland. Returned to Phils in '02 for 14 games.

Stan Hollmig, of (#17, 1949-51) – This powerful Texan was a three-year member of the "Whiz Kids". Stan could never crack the starting lineup and got in to 94 games over three years, batted .253.

Terry Harmon, if (#17, 1970-77; #34, 1967) – Capable utility infielder and popular with Phils fans, Harmon got in to 547 and batted .233.

Richie Hebner, if (#18, 1977-78; #19, 1969) – Had the unusual off-season job as a grave digger. With the Phils "Digger" batted .284 in 255 contests. Started with Pittsburgh in 1968 and with them until traded to the Phillies for 1977. With the Mets in 1979, then to the Tigers, back to the Pirates and finished with the Cubs in 1985. Career spanned 18 seasons, batted .276 in 1908 games.

20th Century Phillies by the Numbers

Al Holland, p (#19, 1983-85) – Al, a reliever, really threw heat. I recall being in the press box at the 1983 World Series (there were so many people with press credentials that the press box ringed the stadium). My seat was above the Phil's bullpen and I remember listening to Al warming up. I could hear the ball going in to the catcher's mitt. Al had one great season and 1983 was it. In is Phils career he earned 55 saves in 139 games, ERA of 2.85.

Ray Hamrick, 2b-ss (#20, 1943-46, #37, 1946) – First joined Phils in 1943 after batting .310 for Nashville in 106 games. Got in to 118 games and batted .204 for his tenure at Shibe Park.

Andy Hansen, p (#20, 1951-53) – A onetime New York Giants hurler (came up to them in 1944 from Jersey City), Andy was drafted by the Phils in the 1950 fall rule 5 lottery as a reliever, got in to 97 games, won eight, lost nine had a 3.34 ERA and seven saves.

Harvey "The Kitten" Haddix, p (#20, 1956-57) – Haddix broke in with the Cardinals just as the career of pitcher Harry "The Cat" Brecheen was ending. Some deep thinker decided that Haddix was the next Brecheen, so he became the kitten. With the Phils he was 22-21 in 58 games. A decent batter, he occasionally saw duty as a pinch hitter.

Don Hassenmayer, if (#21, 1945; #40, 1946) – Lived in Warrington PA and became active in the early days of the Philadelphia A's historical society. You could always count on Don for autograph events. Saw action in just 11 games and batted .100 (3-for-30).

Ted Taylor

John Hernnstein, 1b-of (#21, 1962; #22, 1960-61, #44, 1963) – A big guy, former grid star, Johnny got in to 213 career games and batted just .222.

Jim Hearn, p (#22, 1957-59) – Once one of the Sal Maglie-Jim Hearn 1951 knockout punch of the New York Giants. A poem of the day, attributed to an NL player (identity long forgotten) said "The luck of the Irish, we've money to burn, we don't have to face either Maglie or Hearn". Jim went 10-6 with the Phils with three saves over three years.

Bucky Harris, mgr (#24, 1943) – Hall of Fame skipper, once known as "The Boy Wonder" Harris managed in the big leagues for 29 years – Washington (3 times), Detroit (twice), Red Sox, Phillies, Yankees. His clubs won three World's Series titles. As a skipper he was 2157-2218-31. Only lasted part of a season in Philly, quitting after a tiff with the owner – his club was 38-52-2 at the time.

Frederick "Newt" Hunter, coach (#26, 1933; #27, 1933) – Newt never cracked the lineup, he was a coach. Played one big league season, 1911, with the Pirates and batted .254. He managed five seasons in the minors and finished first every year. As a player he spent 17 seasons in the minors.

20th Century Phillies by the Numbers

Ken Heintzelman, p (#27, 1947-53) – A solid member of Eddie Sawyer's Whiz Kids pitching staff. Kenny won 40, lost 55 with a 3.83 ERA in 165 games. Broke in with Pittsburgh in 1937, came to the Phils in 1947. In 13 seasons he was 77-98 in 319 games with a 3.93 ERA.

Dick Hall, p (#27, 1967-68; #35, 1967) – Swarthmore College grad, Hall went 14-9 for the Phils – all in relief, but one. That one start was a complete game. Appeared in 80 games with a 3.14 ERA.

Jim "Shanty" Hegan, c (#39, 1958-59) – Came to the Phils pretty much at the end of his career. Was an outstanding catcher with the great Cleveland Indians teams of the late 40's and early 50's (with the Tribe from 1941-47). Sportswriter's dubbed him "The Quarterback of the Tribe". He was in 50 games for the Phils, 25 each in 1958 and 59. Batted .232. Also played with Detroit, San Francisco and the Cubs. Saw action in 1,666 games (lost three years to World War II) and batted .228.

Joe Hoerner, p (#43, 1970-72, 75) – Phils reliever went 13-12, fashioned a 2.28 ERA in 133 games. He notched 21 saves. Saw action with Houston (came up in 1963), then the Cardinals, Phils (twice), Braves, Kansas City A's, Texas and Cincinnati. In 14 years was 39-34 in 493 games with a 2.99 ERA.

Ted Taylor

Charlie Hudson, p (#43, 1983; #49, 1983-86) – Charlie never lived up to his promise. He went 32-42 with a 4.02 ERA in 127 games, mostly as a starter. Also pitched for the Yankees and Tigers. Career spanned seven years, went 50-60 with a 4.14 ERA in 208 contests. Best year (11-7) with the 1987 Yankees.

Guillermo "Willie" Hernandez, p (#43, 1983; #48, 1983) – Was 8-4 for the Phils in 1983 with the Phils. Came up with the Cubs in 1977, dealt to the Phils in 1983 and then off to Detroit the next year where he stayed until he retired in 1989. Went 70-63 in 744 games over 13 years.

Ken Howell, p (#43, 1989-92) – Came over from the Dodgers (he was there 1984-88) and then to the Phils where he won 20, lost 19 over two seasons. Career shows a 38-48 record over seven seasons.

Pete"Inky" Incaviglia, of (#9, 1996; #22, 1993-94) – One of the key ingredients in the unlikely Phillies NL pennant win in 1963. "Inky" they called him and he was big and loud and quite a presence. Drafted number one by the Montréal Expos in 1985 and then was traded to Texas. Came to the Phils in 1993, appeared in 116 games, batted .274 and belted 24 homers. He was a traveler and played in the bigs, also, for the Astros, Tigers and Orioles. Lifetime, 12 seasons, .246 and 206, mostly long, homeruns.

Willie Jones, 3b (#6, 1949-59; #12, 1947; #37, 1948) – "Puddin' Head" Jones was one of the NL's top third sackers in the 1950's. Nickname came from a song "Wooden Head, Puddin' Head Jones". Signed by the Phils for a $16,000 bonus – after having spurned a

$9,000 offer from Connie Mack's A's. Began his 15 year big league journey with the Phils in 1947 and was with them until 1959. Best year was '50 when he helped spark the Whiz Kids to the pennant – batting .267 with 25 homers and 88 RBI's. Career (after the Phils with the Indians, then the Reds) totaled 1,691 games, .258 batting average and 190 homeruns. A slick fielder, Jones always played to win.

Vernal "Nippy" Jones, 1b (#9, 1952) – Gained fame in the 1957 World Series while playing for Milwaukee. He claimed he was hit by a pitch, the ump said he wasn't. Jones asked him to check the ball and, like magic, black shine from his shoe was, indeed, on the ball. "Take your base, Jones", the ump said. Played six of his eight years with the Cardinals, really only 8 games with the Phils (batting .167 with just five hits, one a homer) and the Braves. Lifetime 412 games, .267 batting average.

Silas "Si" Johnson, p (#8, 1942; #10, 1943; #16, 1942; #46, 1934; #34, 1940-41) – Pitching for some really bad clubs, Si went 26-48 in 137 games. He crafted a 4.02 ERA along the way.

Ted Taylor

Deron Johnson, 1b-coach (#11, 1969-73; #2, 1982-84) – Came over from the Braves to become one of the Phillies most popular players of that time period. He banged out 34 homers for the '71 Phils, batting .265 with 95 RBI's. Had a run of four homeruns in four straight at-bats in 1971 against the Expos. He homered in his last at-bat the night before and then banged three more in his next three trips to the plate the following day. Lifetime in the bigs, including stops with Oakland and the Red Sox showed 1,765 games, a lifetime .244 mark and 245 round trippers.

Stan Jok, 3b (#12, 1954) – Signed originally by the Philadelphia A's. Stan got in to three games as a pinch-hitter for the Phils and is still looking for his first hit. Played nine games for the White Sox in 1954 and 55 and actually hit a homerun for them. He played 14 seasons in the minors, 1,731 games, had a career .278 batting mark and 192 homeruns.

Davey Johnson, 2b (#15, 1977-78) – Slugging second baseman who would go on to a successful career as a big league manager – and was still doing it in to his 70's (last stop, Washington Nationals in 2013). Hit the majors with Baltimore in 1965 and was a fixture with the O's until swapped to Atlanta in 1973. From there it was the Phils in 1977-78 and then, finally, to the Cubs. In 1435 games he batted .261 with 136 homeruns.

20th Century Phillies by the Numbers

Steve Jeltz, ss (#15, 1983-84; #30, 1984-89) – A switch-hitter he once hit homeruns from each side of the plate in the same inning. He didn't him them – or anything else – very often. His career homerun title was just five. He left the Phils after the 1989 season and ended with the Royals for his last season. Over eight seasons, Jeltz batted .210 in 727 games.

Ken Johnson, p (#16, 1950; #39, 1951) – A Whiz Kid, he was 4-1 in 1950 after coming over from the Cardinals (broke in with them in 1947). Career six years, 12-14. Ended with Detroit in 1952.

Jay Johnstone, of (#21, 1974-78) – They called him "Crazy Jay" for good reason. When he hit his 100th career homerun he ran the bases backwards – but in the right order. He had a 20-year big league career, saw action in 1748 games, batted .267. With the Phils he batted .295, .329, .318 and .284 and then got dealt to the Yankees.

Stan Javier, of (#22, 1992) – Typical of the Phillies, they got the wrong Javier. Julian, Stan's father, had a solid career with the St. Louis Cardinals. Stan, not so much. In 74 games, batted .261. Broke in with the Yankees in 1984, also played for the A's and the Dodgers. Career 8 years, 758 games, .246.

Alex Johnson, of (#26, 1964-65; #60, 1964) – First two years with the Phils (1964-65) then played with the Cardinals, Reds, Angels (with whom he won the AL batting crown in 1970, batting .329), Indians, Rangers, Yankees and the Tigers. Nobody kept Alex long. Thirteen seasons, 1322 games, lifetime .288.

Ted Taylor

Grant Jackson, p (#29, 1965-70) – Spent 18 years in the majors (six of them with the Phils, won 14, lost 18 for them in 1969). Saw action also with the Orioles, Yankees, Pirates, Expos and Royals. Career 86-75 won-lost mark.

Ferguson Jenkins, p (#30, 1966; #46, 1965) – One the Phillies let get away. Fergie was traded to the Cubs in early 1966 and that's where he began earning his Hall of Fame credentials. He also played basketball for the Harlem Globetrotters. With the Phils he was 2-1 in 1965-66, with the rest of baseball he was 282-225 over 19 years. He was a 20-game-winner seven times.

Jeff (Jesse) James, p (#30, 1968-69) – He was 6-6 over two years. Got in to 35 games and never appeared in the majors again.

Niles Jordan, p (#41, 1951) – The Phils really thought they had something in Jordan. In 1951 he went 2-3 in five games as a starter. In 1952 he was swapped to the Reds went 0-1 in three games and that was that.

Larry Jackson, p (#46, 1966-69) – Jackson was in the big leagues for 14 years, three of them as a Phils starter. He went 15-13, 13-15, 13-17 and retired. Broke in with the Cardinals in 1955. Career 194-183 record.

Chapter 7
Player Profiles (K-Z)

Chuck Klein, of, coach (#1, 1938; #3, 1932-33, 42, #8, 1943; #26, 1939, 44-45; #29, 1940-41; #36, 1936-37; #44, 1946) – When the Phillies decided to begin retiring player numbers it was obvious that one of those players should be Klein. The problem was, however, that he wore so many different numbers with the club that there really never was one he was identified with. Two of his numbers (#1 and #36) were retired for others. So they solved the problem by not retiring his number, but acknowledging that he was a "retired" number player. Whatever that meant. With the Phils, Cubs and Pirates Chuck appeared in 1,753 games between 1928 and 1944. He batted .320 with an even 300 homers and 1,201 RBI's.

Bill Killefer, coach (#2, 1942) – A longtime big league manager (Cubs, 1921-25 and St. Louis Browns, 1930-33), Bill spent just one year on the Phils coaching lines. He was a member of the Phillies, 1911-1917 including being on the NL pennant winning 1915 Phils. A catcher, Bill broke in with the Browns in 1909 and finished up as a player with the Cubs in 1921. Lifetime

Ted Taylor

13 years, 1,035 games and a lifetime .238 batting average. Brother "Red" Killefer spent seven journeyman years in the majors.

Ted "Killer" Kazanski, ss-2b (#7, 1953-58) – One of the large crop of bonus baby's that the Phillies booked in the early 50's. Given $100,000 a few days after graduating from high school, Kazanski started in the minors in 1951 and by mid-season 1953 while playing for the AAA Baltimore Orioles (and batting .290) he was hailed as the best shortstop in the minors. He joined the Phils for 95 games that season, but was overmatched by big league pitching and batted a mere .217. Sent back to the minors in 1955 (Syracuse AAA) he found that pitching to his liking and was batted .307 getting him another shot in 1956. He was the starting second baseman for the Phils that year but, again, found big league pitching a mystery, batting just .211. As a utility man in 1957 (62 games) he batted .265, but in 1958 fell to .228 and was gone from the big leagues.

John Kennedy, ss (#8, 1957) – John was the first African-American player to make the Phillies varsity roster based on a .330 batting average in 1957 spring training. Sadly, Kennedy didn't last very long, appearing in just five games, going 0-for-2. Prior to the Phils he had played in the Negro Leagues for the Birmingham Black Barons and the Kansas City Monarchs.

20th Century Phillies by the Numbers

Darold Knowles, p/coach (#3, 1989-90, #32, 1966; #33, 1990) – Appeared in 69 games, going 6-5 with a 3.05 ERA. 16 years as a big league left-handed relief ace. Broke in with the Orioles in 1965, also played for the Senators, A's, Cubs, Rangers, Expos and Cardinals. In 765 games, won 66, lost 74 but saved 143.

John Kruk, 1b-of (#11, 1989; #19, 1990; #28, 1990; #29, 1991-94) – Famous for his quote in reply to a lady who said he seemed fat for an athlete, "Lady, I'm not an athlete, I'm a baseball player". I worked with him on a photo shoot when he and Darren Daulton served as spokespersons for our Fleer baseball card line. He's just as good a guy in person as he appears on network TV. Odd stats. He played in 1200 games over ten seasons, batted an even .300 for his career and had exactly 100 homeruns. Actually batted .300 or better eight times. Had 592 career RBI's. Came up with the Padres in 1968, to the Phils in 1989 and finished with the White Sox in 1995.

Joe Koppe, ss (#15, 1959-61) – I was attending a game at Connie Mack Stadium and a high pop up went in to shallow left field – Koppe's ball all the way – when out of nowhere came left-fielder Tony Curry who ran in to Koppe at full speed and, of course, the ball and Koppe fell to the ground. Koppe left the field on a stretcher. Curry couldn't catch a cold, let alone a fly ball.

Ted Taylor

Hal Kelleher, p (#24, 1938; #42, 1937; #43, 1936-37) – A native Philadelphian, Hal was a right-hander starter who won his first two games (2-0) in 1935. In 1936, however, things turned south for him and he went 0-5 in 14 games. Last season was 1938, lifetime he was 4-9 with a 5.95 ERA.

Jerry (Kooz) Koosman, p (#24, 1984-85)- An ace with the Mets, not so with the Phils. His career was winding down but he still had something left in the tank. He won 14 games (lost 15) in 1984, went 6-4 in 1985. His 19 big league years saw a 222-209 record (mostly with the Mets). He was 3-0 in World Series competition with the Mets.

Casimir "Jim" Konstanty, p (#26, 1948; #35 1949-54) – When the Phillies took over the Toronto Maple Leaf franchise (AAA) in 1947 Konstanty was on the roster. He had failed earlier big league chances (Reds and Braves) and even Connie Mack's A's (owners of the Toronto club when Konstanty joined the team) passed on the big hurler – and Lord knows, Mack could always use pitching. But instead of helping the A's as they made a run at the 1948 pennant, he was pitching for the Phillies that year. 1950 was his defining career-year. He was both an All-Star and NL MVP. He appeared in 74 games for the Phils (all in relief) winning 16, losing 7, saving 22. He started game one of the World's Series because Eddie Sawyer didn't have anyone rested enough to do it – and though he lost he did fine. With the Phils from 1948-54 and then dealt to the Yankees where he spent three years, going 8-3 for the Bombers. Career 11 seasons, 66-48, 433 games, 72 saves.

20th Century Phillies by the Numbers

Thornton Kipper, p (#34, 1953-55) – A tall (6'3) right-hander, Kipper went 3-3 in 20 games for the '53 Phils and then was up-and-down the next two campaigns. Career he was 3-4 in 55 contests.

Jim "Kitty" Kaat, p (#30, 1976-79) – A very good left-handed pitcher who, later in life, took up golf and could play from either side. Soon Kaat was holding contests. The right-handed Kaat versus the lefty. He'd hire two caddies, have two sets of clubs and set off for 18 holes. Lefty usually won – because he was a winner. He actually spent 25 seasons in the majors (1959-83) and finished with 283 wins against 237 losses. With the Phils he went 27-30. Bulk of his career was with the Twins and his best season was 1966 when he won 25 games (against 13 losses).

Mike Krukow, p (#39, 1982) – He was 13-11 in his one year with the Phils, lifetime 124-117 in 14 seasons (divided between the Cubs and the Giants). Was a 20-game-winner for the '86 Giants.

Johnny Kilppstein, p (#45, 1963-64) – Spent 18 years in the majors (1950-67) but only one full season with the Phils (5-6 in '63, 2-1 in '64). He was 101-118 in his career, some of which can be attributed to the fact he never played on very good teams.

John Bernard "Hans" Lobert, manager & coach (#1, 1942; #2, 1939-42; #25, 1938; #50, 1934-37) – Nicknamed "Hans" because people noted a strong resemblance to Hall of Famer Honus "Hans" Wagner. Had a 14 year playing career as an infielder, got in to 1317 games, batted .274. Started with Pittsburgh in 1903, then to the Cubs, the Reds and played for the

Ted Taylor

Phils 1911-14. Finished with the New York Giants in 1917.

Frank Lucchesi, manager (#1, 1970-72) – Career Phillies minor league skipper who finally got his chance to manage (not well, sadly) the big club. Also managed the Cubs and Texas Rangers – not much success at either place. Never cracked a big league boxscore.

Harry "Peanuts" Lowery, of/ch (#3, 1955, 1961-66; #21, 1960) – Came to the Phils in 1955, played in 54 games, batted .189. Came back in 1960 as a coach under Eddie Sawyer, stayed with Gene Mauch. Broke in with Cubs in 1942 also played with the Reds and Cardinals. In 13 years, 1401 games, he hit .273.

Danny Litwhiler, of (#4, 1940-41, 43; #7, 1942; #11, 1942; #28, 1940; #31, 1942) – Broke in with the Phils, batted .345 in 36 games in 1940 – then hit .305, .271 and .259 before being swapped to the Cardinals. Played also with the Braves and the Reds. Eleven years, 1057 games, batted .281.

Jack "Lucky" Lohrke, if (#7, 1952-53) – Came by his nickname honestly surviving a bus crash in the minors where several players lost their lives. Broke in with the New York Giants (1947-51) and then dealt to the Phils where he hit .207 in 1952 and .154 in 1953. Luck never accompanied him to the batter's box.

20th Century Phillies by the Numbers

Joe Lonnett, c (#7, 1959; #8, 1958; #35, 1956-57) – Four years with the Phils, 143 games, .166 batting average, He hit six homers.

Bobby Locke, p (#14, 1962; #34, 1963-64) – Two seasons with the Phils, no wins, no losses in 17 games. Career nine years, 165 games, 16-15.

Nick Leyva, manager (#16, 1989-91) – Another Phillies lifer. He waited his turn and got a chance at the brass ring. The ring turned out to be tin.

Johnny Lindell, p-of (#18, 1953-54) – After a long career with the Yankees as an outfielder, Lindell went to the minors and re-invented himself as a knuckle ball tossing pitcher. It got him back to the show and also got his personal catcher Mike Sandlock another trip to the bigs. With the Phils he was 1-1 in 1958 (they got him from the Pirates late in the season, he was 5-16 at the time). He also pitched in 1942 for the Yankees, went 2-1 that time. As a hitter for the Phils he batted .389 in 11 games in 1953, .200 in seven games in 1954 (and then released). Career as a batter (with the Yankees, 12 years, .273 batting average.)

Phil Linz, if (#18, 1966-67) – Phil might be baseball's most famous harmonica player. Started out as a Yankee in 1962, swapped to the Phils in 1966 (batted .200), started next year with Philly but was dealt to the Mets where he finished his career. Seven years, 519 games, .235.

Ted Taylor

Greg "The Bull" Luzinski, of (#19, 1971-80; #42, 1970-71) – "the Bull" and Mike Schmidt came up at approximately the same time and most baseball people expected Luzinski to be the big star. It didn't work out that way, though Luzinski did have a solid career and posed a long-ball threat at each at-bat. Batted .276 over 15 seasons, had a .276 lifetime mark with 307 homers. Batted .300, .304 and .309 1975-77 with 39 homers in 1977. Funny but nobody ever says he has "Hall of Fame" stats – but he's darn close. When the new stadium (Citizen's Bank Park) opened in 2004 Luzinski was back in town – as host of a eatery on Ashburn Alley (in deep right field) called "Bull's Bar-Be-Cue". Greg holds court at most home games signing autographs.

Emil "Dutch" Leonard, p (#20, 1947-48) – Two of his 20 year big league career were spent with the Phils. He went 17-12 in 1947, 11-18 in 1948, Broke in with Brooklyn in 1933, also played with Washington Senators and the Cubs. In 640 games he went 190-182. Won 20 games in 1939 for Washington.

Mike Leiberthal, c (#24, 1994-06) – Phils first round pick (3rd overall) in 1990 draft out of Westlake CA High School. Made the bigs at age 22 in June 1994 and stayed until finishing up with the Dodgers in 2007. Mike's best year was 1999 when he batted .300 for the Phils in 145 games, stuck 31 homers and drove in 96 runs. Career 1212 games, .274 batting average.

Joe Lis, of (#25, 1971-72; #46, 1970-71) – Cobbled together eight big league seasons (Phils, Twins, Indians and Seattle). Saw action in 356 games, batted .233 with 32 homers.

20th Century Phillies by the Numbers

Stan "Stosh" Lopata, c-1b (#29, 1949-58; #41, 1948) – The big catcher adopted the "crouch" batting stance of his idol Stan Musial and, all of a sudden, he became a power hitter. Hit 32 homers in 1956, his best year, batting .267. Ended career with the Milwaukee Braves in 1960. I was at the park one night when he crushed a ball to dead center field – and it was going up, up, up when it hit the Ballentine Beer sign. Stan lived in Abington after he retired and I got to meet him several times (usually at the local super market). His hobby was painting historic baseballs – when a player achieved a landmark Stan would decorate the ball for him. Lifetime 13 years, .254, 116 homers.

Art Lopatka, p (#32, 1946) – Played a year before Stan Lopata joined the team or a "Lopatka-Lopata" battery might have happened. It wouldn't have lasted, Art was 0-1 in four games.

Jim Lonborg, p (#41, 1973-79) – 15 year career, won 17 games in 1974, 18 in 1976. Broke in with the Red Sox in 1965, Phils got him from the Brewers in 1972. In 15 years he was 157-137. Today he is a dentist.

Lynn Lovenguth, p (#43, 1955) – One year with the Phils (0-1, 14 games, 1955) and one with the Cardinals (0-1, 2 games, 1956).

Angelo LiPetri, p (#45, 1956; #46, 1956; #50, 1958) – Two seasons, no record, ten games.

Randy Lerch, p (#47, 1975-81, 86) – Began with the Phils in 1975, ended with them in 1986. Along the way he also played for Milwaukee, Montreal and San

Ted Taylor

Francisco. He was 36-42 in Phils colors, overall 60-64 over 11 seasons.

"Irish" Danny Murtaugh, 2b (#1, 1943; #16, 1941; #27, 1942) – Irish Danny played with some of the worst teams in Phillies history but he, himself, was a decent player. Broke in with them in 1941 as a good field, little hit second sacker. Swapped to the Braves in 1947 and then to the Pirates in 1951. Nine years, 767 games .254 average. Went on to win a World Series as manager of the Pittsburgh Pirates.

Joe Morgan, 3b (#1, 1960) – Not the Hall of Fame second baseman, but Joe did become a big league manager with the Red Sox. With the Phils in 1960 he got in to 26 games and batted .133. Seven seasons saw him "get a look" from some team or another – including Milwaukee, Kansas City, Cleveland and the Cardinals – in addition to the Phils. Remarkably he got in to 88 games over those eight years and batted .193.

Elisha "Bitsy" Mott, if (#1, 1945) – Great baseball name, he stood 5'8 (not that bitsy). He got in to 90 games before the soldiers returned home. Hit .221 and that was that.

Hersh Martin, of (#2, 1943; #25, 1939-40; #30, 1937) – A Phils regular, Martin batted .286 in 405 games for some pretty poor teams. Ended up with the Yankees. In six seasons and 605 games, batted .285.

Merrill "Pinky" May, 3b (#2, 1943; #26, 1942; #19, 1939-41) – 665 games with the Phils resulted in a .275 batting mark. Best year was 1940 when he batted .293.

Had no pop in his bat at all and in five years stroked just four homeruns.

Ford "Moon" Mullin, if-c (#2, 1944; #17, 1944) – Came to the Phils from the PCL, he was a University of Oregon grad. Played that one season while the regulars were at war, got in to 118 games, batted .267, mostly played second, but caught one game.

Bobby Malkmus, if (#2, 1960; #19, 1961-62) – One of a parade of utility infielders that trooped through town in those days. Broke in with the Braves, also played for the Senators. Had a six year career, 268 games, .215 batting mark.

Bobby Morgan, 2b (#3, 1957; #4, 1954-56) – Came over from the Dodgers in 1954 with much fanfare, he was a middle-infielder. Swapped to the Cardinals at the end of 1956 and then they traded him back (but not for long). He hadn't gotten any better and the Phils dealt him to the Cubs where his career ended in 1958. Broke in with Brooklyn in 1950. In eight years he was in 671 games, batted .233.

Dale Murphy, of (#3, 1991-92) – Let me get this out of the way, Murphy belongs in the Hall of Fame. Period, no question. Not as a Phillie of course, but for all his years with the Atlanta Braves. Saw action in 153 games in 1991 (hit .252 with 18 homers) and had limited service in 1992 (18 games) and was finished. In 17 years he hit .266 in 2154 games with 398 homers. If there was a Hall for great human beings he'd be in the charter class.

Ted Taylor

Art Mahan, 1b (#4, 1940) – Short big league career, long career as Baseball coach and Athletic Director at Villanova University. Played in 146 games in 1940, batted .244 and that was all there was.

Gene "The Little General" Mauch – (#4, 1961-68; #32, 1960) – Never much of a player, Mauch came on like gangbusters as a manager with the Phillies – following the mellow Eddie Sawyer. Mauch was anything but laid back, he was a dynamo and urged a really bad club to work hard – not with a lot of success at the beginning, but by 1964 he almost pulled off a miracle. Broke in as a player with Brooklyn in 1944, also with the Pirates, Cubs, Braves, Cardinals and Red Sox. Career was 9 years, 304 games, .239. A classic pose, his 1951 Bowman card (shown here) was turned in to a Yankee player and used on the cover of one of their early 50's yearbooks.

Eddie Miller, if (#5, 1948-49) – Just missed being a Whiz Kid. A utility infielder for them, Miller was in 215 games, batted .232. Broke in with the Reds in 1936, to the Boston Braves in 1939, back to Cincinnati in 1943, to the Phils in 1948 and finished with the Cardinals in 1950. Career 14 years, .238 in 1512 games.

20th Century Phillies by the Numbers

Don Money, 3b (#5, 1968-69; #16, 1970-72) – Vineland NJ's answer to the Phils third base problems was in place for 524 games, batted .241. He was dealt to Milwaukee where he became a fixture for eleven seasons. He had a 16 year career, saw action in 1720 games, batted .261.

Keith Moreland, c (#6, 1980-81; #12, 1974-80; #34, 1978-79) – Broke in with the Phils in 1978 (1 game) and was pretty much a back up catcher. Then the Cubs snatched him away and he caught fire. Keith hit over .300 for them twice as their regular backstop. His 12 year career ended in 1989 with the Orioles. (**Glenside Kid note**: I saw him play for the Phillies AA Reading farm club a year or so before he came up, he looked like the real deal to me.)

Harry "Hal" Marnie, if (#7, 1942; #9, 1941; #15, 1942; #18, 1940; #24, 1941) – Wore lots of numbers, couldn't hit in any of them. Saw action in 96 games and batted .221.

Hugh "Losing Pitcher" Mulcahy, p (#9, 1939-40; #15, 1938-42; #17, 1945; #40, 1935; #37, 1942; #48, 1946) – If that nickname wasn't bad enough, he was also the first big league player drafted in to the Army in World War II. Even giving him five different numbers didn't help – the opposing batters still recognized him. He doesn't get all the blame, the teams he played with were awful. He played all but one season of his nine in the majors with the Phils – finished with a two-game stint with the Pirates in 1947. Lost 18 games in 1937, 20 in 1938, 16 in 1939 and a league leading 22 in 1940 – he came by the nickname honestly. In 220 games he went 45-89 with a 4.49 ERA.

Ted Taylor

Jerry Martin, of (#11, 1974-75; #25, 1975-78) – Good defensive outfielder that Danny Ozark didn't use late in a Playoff game (to replace Luzinski who dropped a crucial fly ball). Batted .254 in 444 contests.

Len Matuszek, 1b (#12, 1982-84; #24, 1982; #26, 1981) – Got in to 167 games, batted .237 and disappointed everyone who had heralded him as the first baseman of the future. He wasn't.

Mickey Morandini, 2b (#12, 1990-97) – I played in the Richie Ashburn Golf Classic with Mickey one year. He was a good guy, but even a worse golfer than me. Came back to the organization in the 2000's as a minor league manager and coach. First came up with the Phils in 1990 and by 1992 he was the regular second sacker. Traded to the Cubs for 1998 and then back to the Phils in 2000. Finished that season and his career with Toronto. Eleven years, 1298 games, .268 batting average.

Rube Melton, p (#17, 1941-42) – Played with arguably the worst teams in Phillies history, went 10-25 over two years. Mostly a starter, he did record four saves (which with those clubs was a miracle).

Pete Mackanin, if (#17, 1979; #24, 1978-79) – Only got in to 18 games, batted .176 as a Phil. Broke in with Texas in 1973, also played with the Expos and the Twins. In 548 games he batted .226. Pete keeps turning up in Philadelphia, though, and his latest incarnation is as third base coach for Ryne Sandberg's Phils.

Don McCormack, c (#17, 1980-81) – Highly touted prospect but never reached potential. Saw action in just five games. Had five at-bats, got two hits. That makes his career batting average with the club .400.

Jackie Mayo, of (#18, 1948; #15, 1949-53) – They kept waiting for Jackie "to happen". He never did. Best thing that did happen to him was being a reserve fly chaser on the Whiz Kids. Career with the Phils 139 games, .213 batting mark.

Arnold "Bake" McBride, of (#21, 1977-81) – They called him "Shake and Bake" and he was a key player on the 1980 World's Championship club. For the World's Champs McBride batted .309 in 137 games. Came to the Phils in 1977 from the Cardinals, finished up with Cleveland. In 11 seasons and 1071 games he batted .299.

Stu Miller, p (#25, 1956) – His pitches were so slow they called him "Stutterball Stu". He was small and the wind at San Francisco's Candlestick Park once blew him off the mound. With the Phils, mostly as a starter, he went 5-8 in 24 games.

Guillermo "Willie" Montanez, 1b (#25, 1982; #27, 1971-75; #33, 1970) – He was "Willie the Phillie" and hugely popular in town. Came as a result of the Curt Flood deal (he was the compensation from the Cardinals).Batted .266 in 651 games for the Phils. Actually broke in with the Angels (8 games) in 1966 (four years later, as Cardinals property he came to the

Ted Taylor

Phils). His journeyman career also took him to San Francisco, Atlanta, Mets, San Diego, Texas, Montreal, Pittsburgh and then back to the Phillies to finish it out in 1982. Career spanned 14 years, 1632 games and a .275 batting average.

Barney Mussill, p (#27, 1944; #29, 1944) – A big lefty who really mowed 'em down as a pitcher in the Army (1942-43) – he was a sergeant. Had gone 15-7 with Trenton in 1941. He was 19-2 for Fort Warren (Army) in 1943. He was 0-1 in 16 games for the '44 Phils.

Garry Maddox, of (#29, 1975; #31, 1975-86) – He was such a great centerfielder that they called him "The Secretary of Defense". Broke in with the Giants in 1972, traded to the Phils in 1975 and remained with them until 1986. Batted .412 in World Series competition for the Phils (1980, 83). Playoff average .333, LCS stats 19 games, five years, .286. Big league career 15 years, 1749 games, .285.

Eddie Mayo, coach (#32, 1952-54) – Phillies fans expected him to be elevated to manager in 1955, instead they hired another Mayo, Mayo Smith. Spent 9 years in the big leagues (1943 with the Philadelphia A's). In 834 games, he batted .252.

20th Century Phillies by the Numbers

Bob Miller, p (#41, 1949; #19, 1950-58) – Spent his entire big league career with the Phillies. Record was 42-42 in 261 games (only 68 of them as a starter). Most wins were 11 in 1950 (against 6 losses). He got a start for the Whiz Kids in the 1950 World Series and lost the game. Career ERA was 3.96, a native of Detroit.

Jack Meyer, p (#42, 1955-61) – Logged seven big league seasons, all with the Phillies had a 24-34 record in 202 games. Died at age 34 in 1967.

Gary "Sarge" Matthews, of (#43, 1981-83) – Broke in with the Giants in 1972, dealt to Atlanta in 1977 and then to the Phillies in 1981. Following the Phils he played with the Cubs and Mariners. Career 16 seasons, .281 batting mark, 234 homers. After his playing days Sarge became the Cubs hitting coach and then ended up in the TV booth for the Phillies. He and Chris Wheeler got unceremoniously dumped after the 2013 season. Both stayed on with the club in other roles.

Mike Maddux, p (#44, 1986-89) – Another "wrong brother" example. He's the older brother of the great Greg Maddux. With the Phillies for four seasons, also played for the Dodgers and Padres. Over seven seasons he was 19-18 in 189 games and fashioned a 3.74 ERA. Did go on to become a very good big league pitching coach.

Frank "Tug" McGraw, p (#45, 1975-84) – One of the most beloved of the Phillies, the "Tugger" was the man who fanned Willie Wilson for the last out in Game 6 of the 1980 World Series, giving the Phils their first-ever World's championship. Tug is also credited with starting the idea of teams wearing green for St. Patrick's Day games in Spring Training. Tim McGraw, the popular country singer, is Tug's son and often wear's Tug's '80 championship ring at concerts.

Calvin "Buster" McLish, p/coach (#2, 1965-66; #26, 1962-64) – Pitched three seasons for the Phils at the end of a 15-year-career. He went 24-17 for the locals. Career he was 92-92. Cal was a 19-game-winner for Cleveland in 1959. Born in Oklahoma, his full name was Calvin Coolidge Julius Caesar Tuskahoma McLish. No wonder he went by Cal – or Buster.

Tim McCarver, c (#6, 1970-72; #11, 1975-80) – Now in the Hall of Fame as a broadcaster, Tug was Steve Carlton's personal catcher on the Phils during Lefty's best years. Also had a solid career as a starting catcher with the Cardinals. In 628 Phils games (two tours) he batted .272 in 268 contests.

Roger McDowell, p (#13, 1989-91) – Became pitching coach of the Atlanta Braves when his playing days ended. As a Phil, 12-17 (all in relief) in 154 games, He had 44 saves and a 2.90 ERA.

20th Century Phillies by the Numbers

Frank "Buck" McCormick, 1b (#26, 1946-47) – Just spent '46 and part of '47 seasons with the Phils, 150 games, .279 batting average and 12 homers. Broke in with the Reds in 1934, ended with the Boston Braves in 1948. Career (13 seasons) shows 1,534 games, .299 lifetime batting average and 128 homers. He led the NL in RBI's (128) with the '39 Reds, three times lead the league in hits and twice topped at-bats.

Maje McDonnell, coach (#40, 1949-57) – Never threw a pitch in the big leagues but was a key player in the Phillies organization for decades. The Phils designated him as a "Goodwill Ambassador" after he took off his uniform and he served in that role the rest of his life. A star college pitcher at Villanova, he joined the Phils as a batting practice pitcher after World War II. He was elevated to coach by Eddie Sawyer in 1949. Never made a big league box score but often pitched (early on in his Phillies career) in exhibition games.

Ron Northey, of (#4, 1944, 46-47: #14, 1943; #26, 1957; #30, 1942; #33, 1942) – Ron was a big guy and by the time he returned to the Phillies as a pinch-hitter in 1957 he had the nickname "Round Ron" was as wide as he was tall – but the man could flat out hit. Signed originally by the Philadelphia A's. I saw him get a pinch single in 1957 and it took forever for him to get to first (he turned a sure double in to a single). With Phils for 600 games, in three tours, lifetime .269. Played for the Cardinals. Reds, Cubs and White Sox. Career 12 years, .276 with 108 homeruns.

Ted Taylor

Skeeter Newsome, if (#6, 1947; #29, 1946) – It's a shame that the Phillies couldn't give him #2. He was one of three 's players nicknamed "Skeeter" who got that number (the others were Webb and Kell) and that resulted in the sub-title of my A's book "The Philadelphia A's by the Numbers; Let's Give Skeeter #2". In 207 games with the Phils he hit .231.

Bill Nahorodny, c (#9, 1976) – His lone claim to fame was as a member of the Atlanta Braves when later in his career, he broke up a Steve Carlton no-hitter in the eighth inning with a single up the middle. I was at that game and groaned along with the rest of the crowd. One day over breakfast in York, PA I asked Carlton if he remembered that hit, he smiled and said, "What do you think?" Only played three games with the Phils, batted .200.

Bill "Swish" Nicholson, of (#12, 1949-53) – Broke in with the A's, finished with the Phillies (part of a trivia question). A long-ball hitter he won a homerun crown as a member of the Cubs. Diabetes cut his career short. As a Phil he got in to 317 games, batted .238. Graduate of Washington College in Chestertown MD where he resided most of his life.

Constantine "Gus" Niarhos, c (#25, 1954-55) – Signed by the Yankees in 1941 out of Auburn University, Went in to the service for three years, came back and hit .321 in 1947 for the AAA Kansas City Blues. Advanced to the Yankees in 1948, batted .268 in 1948, .279 in 1949. Swapped to the White Sox in 1950, Gus batted .324 in 42 games. With the Phils he was almost invisible appearing in only ten games, batting .143.

20th Century Phillies by the Numbers

Dickie Noles, p (#34, 1990; #48, 1978-81; #60, 1990) – A front office fixture with the Phils in the 2000's, Dickie got in to 76 games, won 6, lost 10, had six saves.

Lou "The Mad Russian" Novikoff, off (#39, 1946) – I have no idea what he was mad about. Maybe it was because he only got one season with the Phils. He batted .304 in 17 games and that was that.

Danny Ozark, manager (#3, 1973-79) – "Half this game is ninety percent mental," is the line that this Phillies manager will always be known for. Danny was pretty much under-rated and he positioned the Phillies for the 1980 title – but it took Dallas Green's kicking some butts (he replaced Ozark late in 1979) to get the team over the finish line. Came out of the Los Angeles Dodgers farm system where he had been a highly successful skipper. After the Phils he managed the Giants for part of the 1984 season. When he retired Danny spent a lot of time playing in and often winning celebrity golf tournaments – I played in a "Baseball for Kids" tourney with him in 1997 in Clearwater. (Real name, Daniel Leonard Orzechowski.)

Bob Oldis, c-coach (#5, 1964-66; #10, 1962-63; #34, 1964) – Played for the Phils for two of his seven big league years (also played for the Senators and Pirates). Got in to 135 games total, batted .237.

Ted Taylor

Johnny Oates, c (#6, 1975-76) – Had an 11 year career (two with the Phils). Broke in with the Orioles in 1976, then Atlanta. After his Phils stint he saw action with the Dodgers and Yankees. Career 593 games, .250 batting mark.

Jim Owens, p (#18, 1955; #39, 1956; #49, 1959-62) – Spent seven of his 12 big league seasons with the Phillies. Broke in with them in 1955 but didn't win his first big league game until 1958. In '59 he went 12-12, his best career year. Dealt to the Reds in 1963, with the Astros for the last four. In 286 games he was 42-68 with a 4.31 ERA.

Steve O'Neill, manager (#24, 1952-54) – A successful manager elsewhere, Stout Steve didn't have much luck with a Phillies team still trying to replicate 1950. He was a big league manager for 14 years – Cleveland, Detroit and the Red Sox (1879-1040).

Eddie Pellegrini, if (#13, 1951) – Another one of a string of utility infielders that came and went on a regular basis. Got in to 86 games, batted .234. His journeyman career included stops with the Red Sox, Browns, Phils, Reds and Pirates. Eight years, 563 games, .226.

Claude Passeau, p (#13, 1938-39; #48, 1936-37) – Workhorse pitcher, mostly a starter. Phils career spanned 151 games, won 38, lost 55. Overall he pitched for the Pirates and Cubs as well as the Phils over 13 seasons. Lifetime 162-150 in 444 games with a 3.32 ERA.

20th Century Phillies by the Numbers

Lance Parrish, c (#13, 1987-88) – First the Phillies couldn't wait to lure him away from the Tigers as a free agent. Once they got him they couldn't wait to get rid of him. He didn't stink up the place, but he wasn't the catalyst they expected. Over two seasons in 253 games he batted .230.

Wally Post, of (#14, 1958-60) – Came over from the Reds in 1958, appeared in 276 games during his stay, batted .269. Was a power-hitter for Cincinnati from 1949-to-1957. Stroked 40 homers for them in 1955. After the Phils he played for the Reds, again, Minnesota and Cleveland. Over 15 seasons he batted .266 in 1204 games with 210 circuit smashes.

Stan Palys, of (#15, 1954-55; #23, 1953) – Lots of promise, not a lot of chances. Got in to just 19 games, hit .276.

Les Powers, 1b (#16, 1939) – Phillies got him from the Giants after the '38 season (he was in three games for them, recorded no stats – but hit .293 for them in AAA Jersey City) and then, in 1939, he appeared in 19 Phillies games, batted .346 and was never back in the big leagues. Go figure.

John Podgajny, p (#17, 1941, 43; #20, 1942; #22, 1940) – 20-33 in 94 games playing for some of the worst Phils teams ever. ERA of 3.91. Also played for the Pirates and Indians. He was 0-4 for everyone not the Phils.

Adolfo Phillips, of (#23, 1965-66; #54, 1964) – Broke in with the Phils played two-plus seasons with them and was swapped to the Cubs in the Ferguson Jenkins deal, later to the Expos. In eight years and 649 games he batted .247.

Tony Perez, 1b (#24, 1983; #37, 1983) – Key ingredient of the Big Red Machine who came to the Phils toward the end of his career and went 1-for-1 for them in the '83 World Series as one of the "Wheeze Kids". In one season as a Phillie, he appeared in 91 games, batted .241 with six homers. Began and ended his career with the Reds (1964-86) – also played with the Red Sox and Montreal. In 2777 games he batted .279 with 379 homers.

Lowell Palmer, p (#26, 1969-70; #40, 1970-71) – Always lots of promise, not much in the way of results, though. He was 3-10 in 67 Phils games. ERA was 5.39. After the Phillies he pitched for Cleveland, St. Louis and San Diego – he was a combined 2-8 with them.

Robert Person, p (#31, 1999-2002) – Person hit two homeruns in one game versus the Montreal Expos and I was there (it was 2001). It was an incredible performance. Broke in with the Mets (1995-96), then the Blue Jays (1997-99) who traded him to the Phils where he remained until 2002. Finished with Boston in 2003. Lifetime nine years, 51-43, 4.64 ERA. Best year was 15-7 with '01 Phils.

Kent Peterson, p (#33, 1952-53) – Just 18 games for the Phils, 0-1 with a 5.29 ERA (he had two saves). Came over from Cincinnati where he was a workhorse on the mound. Sadly all that work didn't yield much (other than he was an innings eater). In 1947 he was 6-13, 1948 he was 2-13. He was 0-3 in 1950. You get the idea. Did I mention that he was a lefty.

Duane Pillette, p (#33, 1956) – Toward the end of his career. In 20 games he had no decisions and a 6.56 ERA. Come up through the Yankees farm system, dealt by them to the Browns in early 1950, he went 3-5 with them in 24 games. Broke in with the Newark Bears in 1946 where he went 11-10.

Hugh Poland, c (#34, 1947) – Four games, 0-for-8.

Robert Pena, ss (#34, 1968) – Batted .260 in 138 games for 1968 club. Broke in with Cubs in 1965 with them two years, then to Phils. Padres in 1969, Oakland A's and Brewers in 1970, finished with Milwaukee in 1971. Six years, 587 games, .245.

Johnny Podres, coach (#46, 1991-96) – An excellent pitching coach for the Phils following a brilliant pitching career mostly with the Dodgers. In 15 years he was 148-116 and 4-1 in four World Series with Brooklyn and LA.

Ted Taylor

Vic Power, 1b (#62, 1964) – Vic's career was pretty much over when the Phils acquired him – for a player to be named later - from the Angels in the 1964 pennant stretch drive. He didn't contribute much and at the end of season the Phils sent him back to Los Angeles as the "player to be named later". Originally signed by the Yankees and traded to the Philadelphia A's in 1954 when, in Power's own words, "The Yankees realized I was going to turn white". He was a fine player for a lot of years and in retirement I met him at A's Society event and he was still the fancy dresser and smooth talker he always was. He only got in to 18 games with the Phils batting just .208. His career, though, spanned 12 years, 1627 games and a .284 average. The A's first year in Kansas City was his best. He batted .319 in 147 games with 19 homers and 91 RBI's.

Tom "Money Bags" Qualters, p (#33, 1953-54, 1957-58) – Another bonus baby mistake that the Phillies made (Mack Burk, Teddy Kazanski, Ed Keegan). He never earned a decision in the big leagues – not a win, not a loss. He even pitched for the White Sox after the Phils and still no wins or losses.

20th Century Phillies by the Numbers

Paul Quantrill, p (#49, 1994-95) – Claimed being a distant relative of the Civil War marauders "Quantrill's Raiders". If that is in my background I'd have probably kept it a secret. Broke in with the Red Sox in 1992, came to the Phils for two seasons (1994-95) where he got in to 51 games and went 13-14. Always a reliever, Paul managed one complete game in the 841 games he appeared in. Also with Blue Jays, Dodgers, Yankees, Padres and Marlins. 68-78 overall.

"Irish" Mike Ryan, c/coach (#5, 1980-89; #9, 1968-73, 93-95; #25, 1983-84, 92) – A longtime fixture with the Phils both as a player and a coach. In 392 he earned a .190 lifetime batting average. Imagine.

John Russell, c (#6, 1986-88; #29, 1984-85; #37, 1984) – Ended up managing the Pittsburgh Pirates at one point. In 259 games for the locals he batted .232.

Ken Raffensberger, p (#7, 1944; #15, 1943, 45; #16, 1946-47) – Went on to a solid career with the Reds after the Phils. With the Quakers he was in 92 games, won 23, lost 45 with a respectable 3.42 ERA. Two-thirds of his Phils appearances were as a starter. Brief look with the Cardinals in 1939, two seasons with the Cubs prior to the Phils. Broke in to baseball in 1937 with Cambridge of the Eastern Shore League.

Connie Ryan, 2b (#8, 1952-53) – Batted .257 in 244 games over two seasons. Began in baseball in 1940, made the majors with the Giants in 1942. Traded to the Braves in 1943 and to the Reds in 1944. Had one season out for the service.

Ted Taylor

Eldon "Rip" Repulski, of (#14, 1957; #15, 1958) – The acquisition half of one of the most unpopular trades in Phillies history. Del Ennis was sent to the Cardinals in exchange for Repulski. To make matters wore, they gave him Del's number in 1957 but had enough sense to change it the following season. In 1957 he batted .260 in 134 games with 20 homers. His career spanned 9 seasons, 928 games and he had a .269 lifetime average.

Pete Rose, 1b (#14, 1979-83) – Quite simply, the Phillies do not win the 1980 World's Series without "Charlie Hustle". When he played for the Reds we all hated him because he always found a way to win (ask catchers Bruce Bochy and Ray Fosse how hard he played). Rose was a great baseball player, not so much as a human being and that has kept him out of the Hall of Fame. His penchant for (a.) gambling, (b.) not always telling the truth and (c.) women were his undoing. Still, if I had to choose one player in his prime to build a team round, it's Pete Rose. In 24 years, Pete batted .303 with the all-time record of 4256 hits. He played in 3562 games. The man even hit 160 homeruns.

Carvel "Bama" Rowell, if (#15, 1948) – Only one of his seven years was with the Phils (77 games, .240). With Boston Braves 1939-47. In six seasons he batted .275 in 574 games.

20th Century Phillies by the Numbers

Octavio "Cookie" Rojas, 2b (#16, 1963-69) – Broke in with the Reds in 1962, dealt to the Phils in 1963 and stayed with them until 1969. Later played with the Cardinals and the KC Royals (for eight years). Sixteen seasons produced a .263 batting mark in 1822 games. Batted .303 in '65 for the Phils, his best mark.

Ed Roebuck, p (#17, 1964-65; #26, 1966; #54, 1964) – His last two seasons (of 11) were with the Phils and he went a combined 5-5 in 50 games. Began with the Brooklyn Dodgers in 1955, also played with the Washington Senators. Career 52-31 in 460 games.

Lynwood "Schoolboy" Rowe, p (#19, 1946-49; #22, 1943) – Not only was he a great pitcher (especially with Detroit, best year 24-8 in 1934) but he could flat out hit, too. In 15 years (six with the Phils) he went 158-101. Spent 1942 with Brooklyn and Detroit. As a hitter he batted .263 with 18 career homers – hit over .300 three times, was in 83 games as pitcher/hitter for the '43 Phils and batted an even .300 with four homers. At one point sportswriters assumed he'd be a lock for the Hall of Fame but it never happened. One day pitching he yelled to his wife from the mound "How am I doing Edna?" From then on Mrs. Rowe was famous, too.

Steve Ridzik, p (#20, 1950; #27, 1966; #37, 1952-53, 55; #42, 1966) – Appeared in one game for the Whiz Kids (but that gets him in the club). Career spanned 12 seasons (the first five, last one with the Phils). Also with the Reds, NY Giants, Indians and Senators, In two games in 1966 for the Phils, same record as 1950, 0-0.

Ted Taylor

Saul Rogovin, p (#26, 1956-57) – Saul's pitches had three speeds – slow, slower and how the heck did it get to home plate? Eight years he was 48-48 appearing with Detroit (broke in with them in 1949), White Sox and the Orioles besides the Phils. He was 7-6 for the Quakers in 1956.

Mel Roberts, coach (#26, 1992-95) – Career Phils player/coach. Outstanding scholastic football player in the Philadelphia area.

Mike Rogodzinski, of (#28, 1973-75; #29, 1973) – A baseball card show promoter (perhaps "shameless" belongs in the description) once advertised that the biggest name on the Phillies was going to be a guest at his show (he didn't name the player). He justified the claim to the legions who complained by pointing out that there were eleven letters in his last name, a bigger name than anyone else on the roster. Truth is, at times, stranger than fiction. In just 99 games over three years he batted .219.

Shane Rawley, p (#28, 1986-88; #48, 1984-86) – Solid big league hurler for 12 seasons. With the Phils (1984-88) he was 59-48. Career 469 games, 111-118.

Humberto Robinson, p (#34, 1959-60) – With the Phils he was 2-8, with the rest (Milwaukee and Cleveland) he was 4-5. Broke in with the Braves in 1955 and went 3-1.

20th Century Phillies by the Numbers

Robin Roberts, p (#36, 1948-61) – One of the Phillies all-time greats. A Hall of Famer and a wonderful gentleman. His 19-year-career produced 286 wins (245 losses) – he wanted 300 so bad he even agreed to a Phils minor league contract (at Reading) to work his way back. He struggled in the minors (he was 40 by then) and gave in to Father Time. He won twenty-plus six times and 19 another. Played, also, with Baltimore, Houston and the Cubs.

Dick "Rufus" Ruthven, p (#40, 1973-75; #44, 1978-83) – Traded to Atlanta then encountered some marital problems there – and got traded back. Broke in with the Phils in '73 and was dealt to the Braves in 1876, and back again in 1978. The Phils swapped him, again, in 1983 to the Cubs with whom he finished his career in 1986. In 14 years he won 123, lost 127. Best year 17-10 for the 1980 World Champions.

Ron Reed, p (#42, 1975-83) – One of those great athletes, good enough for two big league sports. Reed also played in the NBA. 19 years in the majors and on the '80 Champions. Broke in with Atlanta in 1960, finished up with the White Sox in 1984. In 751 games he logged a 146-140 record.

Bruce Ruffin, p (#47, 1986-71) – Seven years in the majors, mostly with the Phils (Milwaukee in 1972). In 223 contests he went 43-64.

Bob Skinner, manager (#1, 1969; #19, 1968) – Dick Allen caused his demise. He simply couldn't deal with the meteoric third baseman. As a player he saw action in 1381 games, batted .277 and stroked 103 homers. Played with the Pirates, Reds and Cardinals.

Ted Taylor

Andy Seminick, c/coach (#2, 1967-68; #15, 1943-44; #21, 1948-51, 1955-58; #24, 1944-48; #48, 1969) – Andy was "Grandpa Whiz" on the 1950 Phillies. Even though he was just 29 he was the elder statesman on the over-achieving "Whiz Kids". A longtime Philly favorite, there was always the assumption (never fulfilled) that he'd, one day, become the Phillies skipper. Broke in with them in 1943, swapped to the Reds in 1952 and back in 1955. Total of 15 years, 1304 games, .243 average with 164 homers. Managed in the Phils farm system for years, even coached on the big league club. Just never the manager.

Roy Sievers, 1b (#5, 1962-64) – AL rookie of the year in 1949 with the St. Louis Browns batting .306 in 140 games. Dealt to Washington in 1954, White Sox in 1960 and to the Phils in 1962. Then in 1964 they sent him back to Washington. Career 17 years, 1887 games, 318 homers. He batted .301 for Washington in 1957 and .295 three times during his career.

Gus Suhr, 1b (#6, 1939-40) – Came to Philly at the end of his career, but did hit .303 in 1939 (.318 with the Phils after they acquired him from the Pirates). Broke in with the Buccos in 1930, ended with the Phils in 1940 (hitting .160 in ten games). Career 11 seasons, 1435 games, .279 with 84 homers.

20th Century Phillies by the Numbers

Dick Sisler, 1b-of (#6, 1948; #8, 1949-51) – Son of Hall of Famer George Sisler and bother of former big league pitcher Dave Sisler, Dick will forever be remembered as the man who hit the homerun that put the Phillies in the 1950 World's Series. Broke in with the Cardinals in 1946, dealt to the Phils in 1948. Swapped to the Reds (a team he'd later manage) and the back to St. Louis. Batted .296 for the Whiz Kids with seven homers (including the big one at Ebbetts Field). Career just eight seasons, 799 games, .276, 55 homers.

Eddie Sawyer, manager (#7, 1948; #24, 1949-52, 58-60) – Pilot of the Whiz Kids, Eddie was the right man at the right time to take the young Phils to their first pennant in 35 years. Never played in the big leagues, but spent several years in the Yankee farm system. He was once a college professor (biology and physiology) and never got a shot at a big league playing job due to an injury he sustained while playing in the Yankees farm system. Phils GM Herb Pennock hired him to manage their Utica NY farm club and after guiding them to two pennants was primed to succeed Ben Chapman as Phils skipper, which he did.

Ted Savage, of (#7, 1962; #14, 1962) – Highly touted outfielder came up in '62 after a fantastic year at the Phils AAA Buffalo farm club where he batted .325 with 24 homers in 149 games. The Philly sportswriters had him as a lock to the Hall of Fame. With the Phils he appeared in 127 games, batted .266 and was dealt to the Pirates – and there his nomadic career began also playing with the Cardinals, Cubs, Dodgers, Reds, Braves and Royals – over the next seven years.

Ted Taylor

Career, 9 years, 642 games, .233 lifetime batting average and 34 homers.

Dick "Dr. Strange Glove" Stuart, 1b (#7, 1965) – To be honest, the man could flat out hit, he could not field. He was a perfect "designated hitter" at a time when no such position existed. Broke in with the Pirates and spent five years there. Dealt to Boston where, in 1963, he was the AL RBI leader (118), hit 42 homeruns and struck out 144 times! To the Phils for one season (1965, batted .234 with 28 homeruns in 149 games). Played, too, for the Mets, Dodgers and Angels. Lifetime, ten years, 1112 games, 228 homeruns, .264 batting average. He also had the nicknames of Boston Strangler and Stonefingers.

Juan "Sammy" Samuel, 2b (#8, 1984-89; #9, 1983; #16, 1983) – After his playing days, Juan spent time with the Orioles as a coach (an interim manager) and then assumed coaching duties with the Phils under both Charlie Manuel and Ryne Sandberg. Broke in with the Phillies (1983-89) then to the Mets, Dodgers, Royals (twice), Tigers and Blue Jays. Twice NL leader in triples – four time leader in most times struck out in a season. In 16 years and 1720 games, he hit 161 homers and batted .259.

Danny "Shotgun" Schell, of (#10, 1954-55) – A perpetual prospect, Schell batted .307 for Schenectady in 1951 with 16 homers and 85 RBI's. Total of 94 Phils games, batted .281 lifetime, hit seven homeruns (92 games in '54, two in '55).

Jeff Stone, of (#14, 1986-87; #23, 1983; #26, 1984-86) – Another one of those "get ready for Cooperstown"

20th Century Phillies by the Numbers

prospects that didn't happen. With the Phils 1983-88, then the Orioles, Rangers and Red Sox. In 1984 he batted .362 for the club in 51 games and boy were we all excited. The next season in 88 games, he batted almost 100 points less. That was even good as things turned out. Career over 8 years (1983-90) includes 372 games, .277 batting average, 11 homeruns.

Eddie Sanicki, of (#15, 1951; #33, 1949) – Eddie homered in his first Phillies at-bat in 1949 and his career went down hill from there. Injuries kept him off the Whiz Kids, back with the club in '51 for a cup of coffee – probably decaf. Appeared in 20 games in those two seasons, batted .294 and had five homeruns. He was a guest at one of the early Philadelphia Baseball Card & Sports Memorabilia Show and lamented "how close" he got to being on the Whiz Kids.

Rick Schu, 3b (#15, 1985-87; #27, 1991; #53, 1984) – With the Phils 1984-87, then back again in 1991. Also played for the Orioles, Tigers, Angels (and in 1996) one game for the Expos. Nine years, 580 games, .246 with 41 homers/

Clyde "Lefty" Smoll, p (#16, 1940) – Once the property of the Detroit Tigers he was among the players liberated by Judge Landis over some of their signing "irregularities". Smoll went 12-9 for Atlanta (fanning 102 in 186 innings) in 1939 and the Phils acquired him.

Ted Taylor

Charley Schanz, p (#16, 1944-45; #18, 1946-47; #22, 1944) – A 6'4 hurler, Charlie came to the Phils from San Diego of the PCL after winning 17 games (against 18 losses) in 1943 appearing in 44 games and 276 innings.

Bobby Gene Smith, of (#16, 1960-61) – Broke in with the Cardinals (1957-59), spent next two seasons with the Phils where, in 177 games he batted .271 with six homers. Off to the Mets, Cubs, back to the Cardinals, then to the Angels. Career seven years, 476 games, 13 homers and a .243 batting mark.

Roy Smalley Jr., ss (#17, 1955-58) – A very good field, not so much a hitter, shortstop. Broke in with the Cubs in 1948, to Milwaukee Braves for 1954, then the Phillies 1955-58 (186 games, .204, 8 homers). His son Roy III was also a big league shortstop in a career spanning 13 years. Dad's lifetime 11 years, 872 games, 61 homers, .227.

Chris Short, p (#18, 1959; #41, 1960-73) – Outstanding Phils lefty before Carlton arrived on the scene. His wins still stack up well against other longtime Phils hurlers (132-127 over 14 seasons). Chris broke in with the club in 1959 and pitched all but one of his 14 big league seasons with them (he finished with the Brewers in 1973, going 3-5). Chris won 20 games (against 10 losses) in 1966 and was 19-13 in 1968.

20th Century Phillies by the Numbers

Benito Santiago, c (#18, 1996) – The man hardly ever walked (unless it was intentional), though in his one year with the Phils he took a free base 49 times – no other season was he ever close to that. He would swing at anything even close to the plate – and he was quite a dangerous hitter. Spent 20 years in the majors, got in to 1978 games, batted .263 with 217 homeruns. His teams-played-for list would make AAA envious. Padres (1986-92), Marlins (1993-94), Reds (1995, 2000), Blue Jays 1997-98), Cubs (1999), Giants (2001-03) and then to the Pirates and Royals. With the Phils in 1996, 136 games, .264, 11 homeruns.

Kevin Stocker, ss (#19, 1993-97) – Spent five seasons trying to become a fixture at shortstop (they hadn't had one, really, since Larry Bowa). With the club he was in 545 games and batted .262. Dealt to Tampa Bay in November, 1997, for Bobby Abreu. A great deal for the Phils, for Tampa Bay not so much. Career (also including a stop in Anaheim at the end) 846 games, .254 batting mark.

Mike Schmidt, 3b (#20, 1973-89; #22, 1972) – One of the greatest (if not the greatest) third sackers ever to play the game. (See Hall of Fame listing.) The stats show 18 years, 2404 games, .267 batting mark and 548 homeruns. Returned to the Phils as a part-time TV sportscaster in 2014 and was quite good. Also managed on the minors for the Phils at one time.

Ted Taylor

Edward "Mayo" Smith, manager (#24, 1955-57) – Onetime Philadelphia A's outfielder (73 games, .212 batting average in 1945), found managerial success after leaving the Phils with Detroit. Guided Tigers to the 1968 AL pennant and then won the World's Series. Also one season as interim skipper in Cincinnati. In nine years 662-612 record.

Ryne Sandberg, 2b (#24, 1981) – Dallas Green, then Cubs GM, snookered the Phils in the Larry Bowa deal and got them to "throw in" Ryno. All he did was become a Hall of Famer. Back now as Phils skipper. Got in to 13 games with the 1981 Phils (.167) and then off to the Cubs (1982-1997, he sat out 1995). In 2164 games, batted .285 with 282 homers. Three time runs leader in the NL and, in 1990, the Homerun King with 40.

Ken Silvestri, c/coach (#25, 1949-51; #31, 1959-60) – backed up Andy Seminick and Stan Lopata with the Whiz Kids. Came back later as a coach. Broke in with the White Sox in 1939 and played three seasons for them. Lost four years to military service and came back with the Yankees (1946-47). Played for the Yanks Newark AAA Bears in 1948 (129 games, .218, 12 homers) and the Phils picked him up in the Rule 5 draft. The word was, at the time, that he was the best catcher in the minors. Spent three years (1949-51) as backup catcher and got in a total of 19 games and batted .212.

20th Century Phillies by the Numbers

Burt "Barney" Shotton, manager (#26, 1932-33; #27, 1933) – The Phils fired him as manager in 1933 and then got him fired from the same post with the Brooklyn Dodgers in 1950 (he was the Dodgers skipper when the Phils beat the Bums in the final game of the season to win the pennant). It's likely that the Phils were not his favorite organization. Spent 14 seasons in the big leagues (1909-1923). Strictly an outfielder he played for the Browns, Senators and Cardinals, appeared in 1388 games, batted .270.

Lonnie "Skates" Smith, of (#27, 1978-81) – It's likely that the Phils gave up on the exciting Mr. Smith too early. For the '80 World's Champs he hit 339 in 100 games (highest in his career) and came the following year in 62 games and batted .324. It seemed the Phils just didn't know where to play him. Dealt to the Cardinals in 1982 he also played for the Royals, Braves, Pirates and the Orioles. Batted .315 for Atlanta in 1989 and .305 for them in 1990. Career spanned 17 years, 1613 games and the fleet fly chaser swiped 370 bases in his career.

LeGrant Scott, of (#28, 1939) – Played with the Phillies in 1939, batted .280 in 76 games and then was released to Indianapolis. They gave him another chance in 1940 but he didn't make the club. Known as a solid defensive outfielder.

Curt Simmons, p (#28, 1948-60; #32, 1947) – Outstanding lefty and many feel his call to the Army right before the '50 World Series may have cost them a chance at becoming World's Champs. In that pennant-winning campaign Curt went 17-8 in 31 games with a 3.40 ERA. Simmons lost part of a toe to a lawnmower after he returned from the service. Signed for $60,000 bonus by the Phils – GM Herb Pennock saw him as "a second Rube Waddell". Released by the Phils in 1960 (115-110 with them over 13 campaigns) he hooked on with St. Louis and was a member of the '64 Cards championship team, going 18-9. (Tell me the pitching poor '64 Phils couldn't have used him.) He spent seven years with the Cards (69-58) and he played in '64 World Series, for St. Louis not the Phils. Also pitched for the Cubs and Angels at the end of his career. Career 20 years, 193-183 and a 3.54 ERA.

Paul Stuffel, p (#34, 1953; #39, 1950; #41, 1952) – Great things were expected from Stuffel who, in 1951 at Schenectady went 15-10 striking out 183. In the five years prior he whiffed over 1,000 minor leaguers.

Bobby Shantz, p (#35, 1964; #53, 1964) – Bobby was the American League MVP in 1952 while pitching for the Philadelphia Athletics (24-7). A broken wrist in late '52 (Senators hurler Walt Masterson did the deed) pretty much ended Bobby's career as a starter. He enjoyed success with the Yankees (1957-60) and the little lefty's last stop was with the ill-fated '64 Phillies, making him another answer to the trivia question "Name a player who began and ended his career in the same city but with a different team". With the Phils in just 14 games in '64 he went 1-1. For his 16-year career Bobby was 119-99 in 537 games with an ERA of 3.38. His brother

20th Century Phillies by the Numbers

Wilmer (Billy) played briefly with the A's and he and Bobby formed a brother battery combo for a time.

Nick Strincevich, p (#36, 1948) – Nick was walking out of the Phillies clubhouse, newly released, when Robin Roberts, fresh from the minor leagues, walked in. Strincevich tossed him his jersey #36 and said, "Hey kid I hope you have more luck with this number than I did." History reports that he did.

Curt Schilling, p (#38, 1992-99) – An excellent pitcher with a prickly personality that got him traded often despite his talents, his career spanned 20 years, 1988-2007. A key member of the '93 NL pennant winners (he went 16-7). Broke in with the Orioles, dealt to Houston from whom the Phils acquired him in 1992 in a deal for Jason Grimsley. At that point his entire career record was 4-11 and nobody got all that excited. But in Philly he found a home – and confidence – and over the next nine seasons he went 101-78. Was with pennant winners in Arizona (won 22 games in '01) and the Red Sox (won 21 in '04). Very active in fund raising for the ALS charity (named his son Gehrig).

Jack Sanford, p (#39, 1957-58; #48, 1956) – Came up with the Phils in 1956 and, in 1957, won 19, against 8 losses. He also was the NL strikeout leader with 188. Dealt to the San Francisco Giants in 1959 (he was with them until 1965), he went 24-7 in 1962. Also played with the Angels and Kansas City A's. In 12 years he was 137-101 with a 3.69 ERA in 388 contests.

Mac Scarce, p (#44, 1972-74) – He went 5-18 in 141 games over three seasons. A reliever, he notched 21 saves and had a 3.65 ERA.

Ted Taylor

Carl Sawatski, c (#47, 1958-59) – Journeyman catcher spent two seasons with the Phils appeared in 134 games, batted .262. Broke in with Cubs in 1948, with White Sox, Milwaukee Braves and Cardinals. In 11 years, 633 games, batted .242.

Roman "Ray" Semproch, p (#48, 1958-59) – He was 16-21 with a 4.44 ERA in 66 games (48 of which he started). Appeared with Angels and Tigers after leaving the Phillies. Career four years, 19-21.

Jim "Rawhide" Tabor, if (#5, 1946-47) – Broke in with the Red Sox in 1938 and was with them until 1944 (in the service in 1945). With the Phillies for 199 games over two seasons, batted .256. With Boston he averaged 15 homers-a-year and drove in 101 runs in 1941.

Antonio "Tony" Taylor, if/coach (#8, 1960-71; #12, 1974-76, 1988-89) – One of the most popular men to wear a Phillies uniform in the second half of the 20th Century. His Phils stats include 1669 games and a .261 batting average. Broke in with the Cubs in 1958, swapped to the Phils in 1960. Traded to Detroit in 1971 he spent three years there and then returned to Philadelphia for his final three years as a player. Over 19 seasons he was in 2195 games and batted .261.

20th Century Phillies by the Numbers

Al Todd, c-of (#9, 1932; #10, 1933; #11, 1934-35) – Got in to 304 games, batted .281. Best year for the club was 1934 when he batted .318 in 91 games. Also played for Dodgers and Cubs. In 11 years 863 games and a .276 batting average.

John "Jocko" Thompson, p (#9, 1948; #33, 1950-51; #37, 1949) – A "Whiz Kid" Jocko's whole career was as a Phillie. In 41 games he was 6-11 with a 4.24 ERA.

Clifford "Earl" Torgeson, 1b (#9, 1953-55) – The bespectacled one anchored first base in 293 games for the Phils, batting .272. Broke in with the Boston Braves in 1947, also played for the Tigers, White Sox and Yankees. In his 15-year-career batted .265 in 1668 games and stroked 149 homeruns.

Gus Triandos, c (#9, 1964-65) – Some wags tagged him "Gus Tremendous" and while he really wasn't tremendous he was a decent big league catcher for a number of teams. Originally a Yankee (came up in 1953), then swapped to the Orioles, to Detroit in 1963 and to the ill-fated '64 Phillies. In mid-1965 he was swapped to Houston. Spent 13 seasons, in 1206 games, batted .244 with 167 homeruns.

Manny Trillo, 2b (#9, 1979-82) – Smooth as silk second baseman. Logged 17 years in the majors and was on the Phils 1980 World Championship team (batting .292). Broke in with Oakland in 1973, swapped to the Cubs in 1975 and to the Phillies in 1979. He opened 1983 with the Indians, was dealt to Montreal in mid-season. Also played with the Giants, Cubs (again) and finished with the Reds in 1989. In 1780 games he batted .263.

Ted Taylor

Frank Torre, 1b (#16, 1962; #14, 1963) – Another example of the Phillies having the wrong brother, though Frank was a decent player he wasn't his All-Star/Hall of Fame brother Joe. Came up with the Braves in 1956 and was them until 1960. Best year was 1958 when he batted .309 in 138 games. Hit .310 in a part-time role (108 games) for the 1962 Phils. Total of seven seasons, 714 games .273 batting average.

Ken Trinkle, p (#22, 1949) – Finished his big league career with the Phils in 1949. A reliever, he got in to 40 games, was 1-1 with a 4.00 ERA and two saves. Broke in with the New York Giants in 1943, then spent the next two years in the service. With the Giants again 1946-48, going 20-28 with 19 saves. Phils farmed him out to Toronto in 1950 where he want 5-11 in 40 games with 13 saves – but it didn't get him back to the majors. He spent seven years in the minors (five seasons with the Baltimore Orioles AAA). Career in the minors 50-63.

Milt Thompson, of (#24, 1986-88; #25, 1994; #28, 1986) – Hit .302 in 150 games for the 1987 Phils, batted .307 for the 1991 Cardinals. Broke in with Atlanta in 1984. Career 980 games, .281 batting average. He was Phils batting coach for a number of years in the 2000's.

Kent "Teke" Tekulve, p (#27, 1985-88) – Longtime Pirates reliever lead the league in games three times (91 in '78, 94 in '79 and 85 in '82). With the Bucs from 1974 until dealt to the Phils in 1985 where he stayed through 1988 (best mark 11-5 in 1986). Finished up

20th Century Phillies by the Numbers

with the Reds in 1989. Lifetime 94-90 with a 2.85 ERA in 1050 games – never started a game in the big leagues. Longtime Pirates broadcaster after he retired.

Bobby Tolan, of (#28, 1976-77) – Spent 13 years in the majors one full year and part of another one with the Phils. Broke in with the Cardinals in 1965, finished up with the Padres in 1979. Also played for the Reds and Pirates. 1282 games, batted .265. Lead the league in stolen bases with 57 in 1970.

Wayne Twitchell, p (#33, 1971-77) – Had a 10-year-career (seven with the Phils). Came up with Milwaukee in 1970. After he left the Phils he saw service with the Montreal, the Mets and Seattle. In 282 games he was 48-65 with a 3.98 ERA.

Bob Uecker, c (#9, 1966-67) – One of baseball's funniest men and, after his playing career ended, he was a longtime broadcaster for the Milwaukee Brewers. Made the most of his playing days (1962-67) playing for the Milwaukee and Atlanta Braves, the Phils and the St. Louis Cardinals. In 1966 was in 78 games batting .208 and in 1967 saw action in 18 games (.171) before they dealt him to Atlanta.

John Vukovich, if / coach / manager (#3, 1996; #7, 1988; #18, 1979-81, 1990-95, 97; #22, 1976; #26, 1971; #28, 1977; #30, 1970-71) – He did about everything they asked him and was still doing it when he succumbed to Cancer. He was very popular with the players and the fans. If there was a place in the Hall of Fame for "great people" he'd be a lock for admission. Played in the majors for ten years as a utility infielder. Broke in with the Phils in 1970 and finished with them in 1981. In between he had stints with the Brewers and the Reds. In just 277 games he hit .161 lifetime (batted over .200 just twice).

Emil "The Antelope" Verban, 2b (#9, 1946-48; #50, 1946) – The Glenside Kid's first baseball card (at least his first Phillie) was Verban and he never forgot that. Of course the Phillies quickly dealt him to the Cubs. Spent just seven years in the majors (broke in with the Cardinals in 1944, finished with the Braves in 1950. Career 853 games, .272 batting average.

Elmer Valo, of (#15, 1956; #18, 1961) – Broke in with the Philadelphia A's and was a longtime Phillies scout after his playing career ended. Spent 20 years in the majors (parts of 1956 and 1961 with the Phillies) got in to 1806 games and batted .282. Was with the A's from 1940 to 1956 (by then the Kansas City A's). Was with Dodgers when they moved from Brooklyn to Los Angeles, was with Washington when they moved to Minnesota. Three times Valo's teams left town. Imagine. Batted over .300 seven times.

Ozzie Virgil Jr. c (#17, 1982-85; #24, 1980; #11, 1981-82) – His father played nine years in the majors, Ozzie Jr. came up with the Phils in 1980 (one game) but by 1984 he was their regular catcher. Dealt to Atlanta in 1986, he finished up with Toronto in 1990. He hit 18 homers for the Phils in '84, 19 in '85.

20th Century Phillies by the Numbers

Al Verdel, p (#18, 1944; #30, 1944) – One game, one inning, nothing else. Came to the Phils out of the Army where he was 20-4 in 1943 at Fort Dix.

Johnny Vergez, 3b (#23, 1935-36) – Broke in with the Giants in 1931 finished with the Cardinals in 1936. Lifetime 672 games, batted .255.

George Vuckovich, of (#29, 1980-82) – Split his six-year-career between the Phillies and the Indians. In 628 games he crafted a .268 lifetime batting mark.

Freddy Van Dusen, of (#45, 1955) – In one game but never got to the plate.

Bobby Wine, ss/coach (#1, 1960, 71; #7, 1963-64, 66-68, 72-83; #13, 1965; #42, 1962) – Badly wanted to become Phillies manager, but it never happened. He did manage the Braves for awhile.

Johnny Wyrostek, of (#1, 1946-47; #17, 1952-54) – When Johnny returned to the Phillies in 1952 his son, Johnny Jr., ended up in my homeroom at Thomas Williams junior High in Wyncote PA. He was the second off-spring of a big leaguer in the homeroom, Carolyn Walters, whose dad Bucky was a pretty fair player for the Phils and Reds was, at that time, a Braves coach. Pretty heady stuff for a baseball nut kid like your author. In the majors eleven seasons with Phils, Pirates and Reds. In 1221 games batted .271.

Ted Taylor

Jim Wasdell, of (#3, 1943-46; #28, 1943-44) – Spent 11 years in the majors, broke in with Washington in 1937, finished up with Cleveland in 1947. Also played for Brooklyn and Pittsburgh. In 888 games he batted .273.

Harry "The Hat" Walker, of (#4, 1947-48) – He was the defending NL batting king (he batted .363 in 1947) and he lost his job to a rookie in spring training – a kid named Richie Ashburn. Brother of Fred "Dixie" Walker. Walker batted .296 lifetime over an eleven-year-career. Began and ended his playing days with the Cardinals – also saw service with the Cubs and Reds. Harry managed in the big leagues after his playing days for the Cardinals, Pirates and Astros.

Eddie Waitkus, 1b (#4, 1949-53; #44, 1955) – Waitkus had the dubious honor of being the inspiration for the book/film "The Natural" when a deranged fan lured him to her Chicago hotel room in 1949 and then proceeded to shoot him. She had this crush 'from afar" on him and when the Cubs traded him to the Phillies in 1949 it apparently sent her around the bend. Eddie survived the gunshot wounds but he was never the same player again. Swapped to the Orioles in 1954, they swapped him back to the Phils in 1955. Career eleven years, .285 batting mark. Before the shooting he was at or close to .300 each year, after he was not the same hitter.

20th Century Phillies by the Numbers

Arthur "Pinky" Whitney, if (#5, 1928-33, 38; #20, 1939; #25, 1936-37) – Batted over .300 four times in his career, 12 years .295 lifetime batting average and 93 homeruns. Broke in with the Phils in 1928, dealt to Boston Braves in 1933 and then swapped back to them in 1936. For Phils 1157 games, .307 batting average, 69 homeruns. Never quite got the recognition he deserved.

Bennie Warren, c (#5, 1942; #24, 1942; #26, 1939-41) – Spent four of his six year big league career with the Phils. In 335 games batted .224 with 29 homeruns. After four-years out the majors came back with the New York Giants 196-47 as a backup catcher. Career six years, 377 games, .219, 33 homers.

Del "Babe" Wilber, c (#10, 1951-52) – Broke in with the Cardinals in 1946 and stayed with them to 1949. In the minors in 1950, Phils acquired him in 1951 and then, early in 1952, dealt him to the Red Sox where he remained until 1954. Eight year career as backup catcher, 299 games, .242, 19 homers.

Bill White, 1b (#10, 1966-68) – Fine big league first baseman and eventually became President of the National League. Broke in with the New York Giants in 1956, missed 1957 for military service and when he came back to the San Francisco Giants. Dealt to the Cardinals he was a fixture at first base from 1959-65, and then back in 1969 at the end of his career. Spent three years with the Phillies 1966-68 appeared in 396 games, batted .258 with 39 homeruns. Career spanned 13 years, 1673 games, 202 homers and a .286 lifetime batting average.

Ted Taylor

The Glenside Kid Remembers...

When Bill retired from baseball he took a job as a sportscaster for a Philadelphia TV station. At that time, I was working for Widener College (as PR director) and met Bill at several press luncheons, usually with our ace football running back Billy "White Shoes" Johnson. A couple of years later Bill moved on to do New York Yankees broadcasts with Phil Rizzuto. I was in Chicago attending a two week seminar at the Ambassador Hotel and sitting in the hotel lobby one Friday when, who comes over to say hello, but Bill White. It turns out that the Yankees were in Chicago for a three-game weekend series with the White Sox. Bill asked what I was doing that weekend and I said, "Nothing". He replied "You have something to do now". For the whole weekend I rode the team bus to and from Comiskey Park, ate meals with the players and hung out in the press box. I even signed a few baseballs as I was walking in with the team because Bill said, "If you don't sign they'll think the Yankees are snubbing them". Somewhere in Chicago there are signed Yankee baseballs with "Ted Taylor" signed on them as well.

Jimmy "Ace" Wilson, c/manager (#12, 1923-28, 1934-38) – Broke in with the Phillies in 1923 and stayed with them until1928 when he was dealt to the Cardinals. Returned in 1934 as player-manager and piloted the club until 1938. As a player 18 years, 1525 games, .284 and 32 homeruns. Played with the Reds in 1939 and 40 and then moved over to the Cubs where he was named manager in 1941 (fired in 1944 with his club losers of nine of his first ten games). With the Phils he spent eleven seasons, batted .288 and hit 22 homers.

20th Century Phillies by the Numbers

Glenn Wilson, of (#12, 1985-87; #27, 1984) – The popular, hard-nosed, Texan broke in with the Tigers in 1982 and was dealt to the Phils in 1984. He was in 602 games for the locals, batted .265 and stroked 49 homers. Also played with Seattle, Houston and the Pirates. Ten years, 1201 games, .267, 98 homers.

Wally Westlake, of (#15, 1956) – He's on a 1956 Topps baseball card as a Phillies outfielder. Truth of the matter is that he appeared in just five games and, in May, got released. No hits, no batting average. Signed originally by the Brooklyn Dodgers he ended up arriving in the big leagues with the Pirates thanks to some confusing minor league transactions. Stayed with the Bucs until 1952 when he was swapped to the Cardinals. From there it was the Reds, Indians and the Orioles – before the Phils signed him in November 1955. Career 10 years, .272 batting average, 127 homers.

William "Bucky" Walters, if/p (#17, 1938; #20, 1935; #35, 1943; #40, 1936-37) – Longtime resident of Glenside PA (home of the "Kid"), native of Germantown where he attended high school. Son Billy, a pretty good player himself, and daughter Carolyn went to Cheltenham High. Some say Bucky should be in the Hall of Fame – and a case can be made. Began in 1931-32 with Boston Braves, stayed in Boston but switched to the Red Sox in 1933, who, in turn dealt him to the Phillies. An infielder up until then, Bucky pitched in 29 Phils games that year and 24 in 1935, but he was still seen primarily as a hitter (which he did quite well). Full-time pitcher in 1936 and went 11-21. Dealt to the Reds in 1938 and he was a fixture for them for the next decade. As a hurler he won 27, 22 and 23 games for

Ted Taylor

them. In 1950, as a Braves coach, Walters pitched one more game. As a batter Bucky owns a lifetime .286 average in 715 games with 23 homeruns. He was often used as a pinch-hitter when pitching became his fulltime occupation. Walters managed the Reds in 1938 (part of season) and 1939.

Hal Wagner, c (#17, 1948; #26, 1949) – A backup catcher at the end of the road when he joined the Phillies. Over two seasons, just four games, no hits, no nothing. Broke in with the Philadelphia A's in 1937 and stayed with them for eight years (339 games, .248). Also played with Red Sox and Tigers. Career spanned 12 years, batted 248 with 15 homers in 672 games.

Rick Wise, p (#18, 1964; #28, 1966; #38, 1966-71; #62, 1964) – Rick will always be remembered as the pitcher traded to St. Louis for Steve Carlton – and when it happened Phillies fans were not very happy. Rick was always a fan favorite and a pretty good pitcher (who could also hit a bit). Phils (1964-71), Cardinals (1972-73), Red Sox (1974-77), Cleveland 1978-79), Padres (1980-82). Career spanned 18 years, 188-181, 3.69 ERA in 506 games. Won 19 for Boston in 1975, lost a league-leading 19 for Indians in 1978.

Herman Wehmeier, p (#22, 1954-56) – Won 20 games for the Phils (lost 22) but it took three seasons to do it. Starter in 49 of his 59 games, had a 4.17 ERA. Came over from Cincinnati where he had been a mainstay on their staff since 1948. With Columbia in the Sally League in 1946 he went 17-6.

Billy Wilson, p (#24, 1969-70; #37, 1970-73) – Got in to 179 games, all in relief, went 9-15 had a 4.23 ERA, saved 17.

Mitch "The Wild Thing" Williams, p (#28, 1991-92; #99, 1993) – Not a Phillies closer for too long, but will probably always be remembered for serving up the walk-off homerun that made the Toronto Blue Jays 1993 World's Champions. Broke in with Texas in 1986, also played with Cubs, Astros, Angels. Out of baseball for a year he tried a comeback with Kansas City in 1997 and that lasted seven games, 0-1, with a 10.80 ERA. With the Phils he was 20-20 overall, 102 saves, 3.11 ERA. Best year was 1991 when he went 12-5 with a 2.34 ERA.

Gary Wagner, p (#31, 1965-69; #64, 1965) – Mostly a reliever, Wags appeared in 118 games, posted a career ERA here of 3.59, had 15 saves.

Hack Wilson, of (#34, 1943) – Not much left in the tank when he got to the Phils. But a Hall of Famer with the Cubs. Only made it in to seven games, went 2-for-20 (.100) and was done. Career included 244 homers in 12 seasons.

Lloyd Waner, of (#34, 1942) – See above (Hack Wilson). A Hall of Famer with the Pirates he was spent by the time he hit Shibe Park. Played in 100 games that one season, batted .261 and then retired.

Ted Taylor

Dick Whitman, of (#37, 1950-51) – The Phils got him from the Dodgers and he was a member of the Whiz Kids team that beat Brooklyn in '50 for the NL pennant. Batted .235 over 94 games in two years with the club. Dodgers (1946-49) then to the Phils until 1951 – six years, 285 games, .259.

Bob Walk, p (#41, 1980) – Better known in baseball as a Pittsburgh Pirates announcer. A member of the World's Champs, he went 11-7 with a 4.56 ERA in 27 contests all as a starter.

Jim Westlake, of (#48, 1955) – Another wrong brother (one game, 0-for-1). Wally, who did play briefly with the Phils in 1956, had a solid - if unspectacular - big league career. Jim had a very small cup of coffee, probably "to go".

Randy Wolf, p (#54, 1999) – Sparked a group of zany fans who donned wolf masks, called themselves "The Wolf Pack" and haunted the upper regions of "The Vet" each time Randy pitched. Was still pitching in 2014 (1-3 with Miami). Broke in with Phillies in 1999, then to the Dodgers in 2007 following by appearances with San Diego, Houston, Dodgers (again), Milwaukee, Baltimore and Miami. In 15 seasons he was 133-120 with a 4.21 ERA.

Dick Young, 2b (#5, 1952; #9, 1951) – 20 games and cups-of-coffee in parts of two big league seasons, .234 average. At Schenectady in 1951 batted .301 with a league-leading 166 base hits.

Del Young, if (#7, 1938; #17, 1939-40) – Played in 309 games for the Phils, batted .224 lifetime.

Floyd Youmans, p (#33, 1990) – 1-5 in 10 games, 5.70 ERA. Broke in with Expos (1985-99) and then dealt to Phils. Career five seasons, 30-34 in 94 games.

Bobby Young, 2b (#37, 1958) – 32 games, 233 batting average.

Chapter 8
Unlisted Numbers..
they came, they went

The following players show up on rosters, in season statistics and in news and magazine stories about a coming season but we cannot find a number for them. In a time when apparently numbers weren't all that important, these men were clearly given a uniform with a number on it, but nobody bothered to keep track. They must have been good players if you think about it...they got a shot.

Doug "Poco" Taitt, of (1932) – Came up in 1931, .222 in 40 games over two seasons.

Charlie Butler, p (1933) – 11 games, no record, 9.00 ERA.

Tommy Thomas, p (1935) – Four games, 0-1, 5.25 ERA.

Lefty Bertrand, p (1936) – One game, no record, 9.00 ERA.

Leon "Lefty" Pettit, p (1937) – 0-1, three games, 11.25 ERA.

Ted Taylor

Charley "Nipper" Knapp, c (1937) – Signed out of college and a protégé of then Phils manager Jimmy Wilson, Nipper was a Drexel graduate (and three sport letterman). Enjoyed same birthday as Skipper Wilson too. None of that helped.

Duce De Weese, of (1938) – Batted .314 at Montgomery in 1937, leading the club in all offensive categories. Phillies Manager Doc Prothro said "I like the way he swings the bat" but, clearly, he didn't like it well enough to keep him on the club.

Eddie "Itzy" Feinberg, if (1938, 39) – Appeared in 16 Phillies games over two seasons, but batted just .184. A local boy and a graduate of South Philadelphia High School. Could play any infield position, but liked shortstop the most.

Tom Lanning, p (1938) – Three games, 0-1, 6.43 ERA.

Alex "Spunk" Pitko, of (1938) – Lifetime batting average of .316 but his whole career was just seven games (6-for-19). Wonder why? Had a 19-game hitting streak at Montgomery in 1937 and was homerun champ of the Eastern Shore League with 20.

Joe Dickinson, p (1939) – Was 21-9 in the Class C Canadian-American League pitching for the Cornwall Bisons in 1938. The year before that he was 20-7 in the same league. But obviously the move up didn't work.

20th Century Phillies by the Numbers

Gordy Troy, of (1940) – Played with Moultrie in 1939 and was from the Pennsylvania coal regions (where he had been a football star). No clue as to why he was on the roster for spring training.

Roy Clark, p (1940) – 20-game-winner in Class B Piedmont League in 1939. Not enough, obviously.

Tom Pullig, p (1940) – Worked 22 scoreless innings in-a-row for the Texarkana Liners in 1939 (Class C) and had an ERA of 3.10. Other than that, he didn't make the club.

Paul Schoen, if (1940) – A protégé of Goose Goslin (Trenton manager), Schoen had once had a trial as a pitcher with the Cincinnati Reds. As a converted first baseman he batted .360 in the Interstate League in 1939. The Phils became the second club to pass on his talents.

Dill Dillingham, if (1941) – Invited to spring training right out of semi-pro ball. The jump was too long, they revoked his invitation.

Stan Stuka, c (1941) – Batted .297 at Martinsville in 1940 in 113 games. Didn't make the club.

Dan "The Squirrel" Reynolds, if (1942) – Came to the Phils from Martinsville where he was the best fielding second baseman in the Bi-State League. That didn't get him to Philly. He did finally make it to the majors in 1945 with the White Sox appearing in 29 games and batting, a less than robust, .167. He wore #2 for the Chisox.

Bill Anske, c (1943) – Back in the day a lot of big league clubs employed players who would join them when they took on semi-pro teams in the not-so-uncommon in season exhibition games (those games helped pay the bills). Anske was one such player. He was bullpen catcher for the Phils and played for their "Main Line" semi-pro club. He did play pro ball in 1940 and 1941, but never actually made the roster.

Manny Salvo, p (1943) – One game as a reliever, no record but a 27.00 ERA.

Karl "Hap" Winsch, p (1944) – A 10-9 record at Trenton in 1943 got him a "look" in the big league camp that spring. A right-hander, he spent 1944 at Utica (where he was 4-4) and that was it. But it wasn't "it" for his baseball career. As manager of the South Bend Blue Sox (AAGPBL) 1951-54 Karl's women's teams won two league championships (1952 and 1953). He was born in Allentown, PA. The Phillies had two other AAGPBL managers, too. Dave "Beauty" Bancroft managed three seasons (South Bend, 1949-50 and the Battle Creek Belles,1951) and Jimmie Foxx managed the Fort Wayne Daisies in 1952. (In "A League of their own" Tom Hanks played an AAAGPBL manager named Jimmie Dugan who was supposed to be modeled after Foxx. His daughter, Nanci, who was a bat girl for the '52 Daisies said it was a lie that her Dad was not like that.)

Warren "Moose" Fralick, p-of (1944) – How desperate were the war-years Phillies for players? They signed Fralick who had gone 8-0 (with a no-hitter) in "independent ball" in 1943. Not sure of his age but he had kicked around pro ball for, at least, eight years and was 114-70 lifetime.

Julius Homokay, p (1944) – Desperate times? He was 5-6 at Utica in 1943 and still got an invite to spring training.

Cecil "Turkey" Tyson, 1b (1944) – 6'6 and thin as a rail, he had kicked around in the minors for a lot of years – MVP at Tallahassee in '39, Martinsville '40, Hagerstown '42 and hit .324 at Trenton in 1943. He got in to one game for the Phillies in 1944, got one at-bat...nothing else happened.

Wilbur Reeser, p (1944, 45) – A lefty who, despite his 15-9 record at Utica in 1944, never made it to the show. He got his first invite to camp off a 6-3 record at Trenton.

Les Scarsella, 1b, of, p (1945) – The 34-year-old MVP (batted .329) in the Pacific Coast League in 1944, the big veteran fly chaser cost the Phillies $40,000 and two players to secure his services. Turns out they wasted their money, he never made the club. He had been in the majors 1935-40 with the Reds and Braves. Lifetime batting mark of .284 in 262 games. Wore #'s 24, 11, 16 for the Reds, #3 for the Braves. (Les is pictured here on his '49 Bowman PCL card).

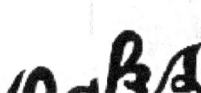

Ted Taylor

John O'Neil, ss (1946) – Hit .314 for Portland in the PCL in '46 and Phils paid $30,000 for his contract. He was supposed to take Skeeter Newsome's job – he didn't.

George Estock, p (1946) – Went 22-6 as the ace of Inter-State League Wilmington's staff. That didn't get him a slot on the Phillies roster. In 1951, though, he made it with the Boston Braves, appeared in 37 games, was 0-1 and had a 4.33 ERA. He wasn't back in 1952. With the Braves he wore #22.

Bill Pless, p (1947) – His one asset as a pitcher was that he stood 6'4. That wasn't enough.

Joe Scheldt, of (1947) – At Wilmington in 1946 he stole 47 bases, walked 124 times and was a good fielder. None of that was enough, he never made the club.

Jesse Levan, of (1947, 48) – Whole career, two games, 4-for-9, .444.

Al "Broadway" Flair, 1b (1948) – The experts said he'd be the Phillies regular first baseman in 1948 off a .308 batting mark with New Orleans and leading the Southern Association with 128 RBI's in 1947. I didn't happen. Al had logged time in 10 big league games with the '41 Red Sox batting just .200.

John Werner, c (1949) – Batting .321 at Wilmington in '48 didn't help him make the big club the following year.

20th Century Phillies by the Numbers

Charles Bowers, p (1950, 51) – Invited to spring training in '51 after going 2-5 with AAA Toronto. Scouting report said, "Last season was his first in organized ball and his record was not impressive. But his fast ball is a hummer." End of story. Signed as a free agent in late 1949 off the Massachusetts sandlots.

Alex Garbowski, ss (1950) – A shortstop who had batted .266 at AAA Toronto in 1949. Who's Who said "He's a man to watch" but they didn't tell us where we should look. He surfaced in Detroit in 1952 for two games, never got an at-bat.

Lou Heyman, c (1950) – A big catcher (6'3, 255) who never made the big show. They said he was big enough to stop anything and could hit the ball a mile – problem was he seldom hit it at all.

Charlie Hood, c-if-of (1950) – Perennial prospect – they tried him as a catcher, third baseman and outfielder. Batted .307 with 103 RBI's in the minors in '49 but he didn't get out of spring training.

Bill Koszarek, p (1950) – Right handed hurler failed to make the club in '50 after going 2-7 at Utica, then 14-2 at Terre Haute.

Elmer Sexauer, p (1950) – 6'4 righty spent 1949 on the DL at Wilmington.

Ted Taylor

Walt Derucki, 3b (1951) – Spring training invitee off a .284 year (33 doubles, ten homers) at Utica. That's as close as he got.

Bill Fogg, p (1951) – He got a look off a 11-16 record at Utica. Scouts said "he lost close ones because of wildness". That said it all.

Buddy Hicks, if (1951) – Picked up from Hollywood PCL. Had three strong seasons 1947-49, not so hot in 1950, but the Phils took a look. Batted .239 in the minors in 1950. Were the Phillies desperate? Why? They had just won the NL pennant.

Bill Loos, of (1950, 51) – Frequently considered a prospect – but usually done in because he was a slow starter. At Wilmington in 1950 he batted .318 for the Blue Rocks after batting .318 at Portland in 1949.

John Walz, p (1949, 1951) – Got some spring looks, never hooked on. Was 8-4 in 1950 with Wilmington in 1950 and a 2.52 ERA.

Con Dempsey, p (1952) – Was with the Phils in spring training (and even, left, on a 1952 Topps card as a Phillie) but didn't go north. In 1951 he started the year with the Pirates but developed arm problems. Next thing he knew he was in the PCL with San Francisco where he went 7-7. He wore #30 for the Buccos.

Chapter 9
The Front Office

The Phillies have employed 15 team presidents since their move to Philadelphia in 1883, beginning with baseball pioneer Alfred J. Reach and right up to the current leader, Dave Montgomery.

They had some odd ducks in the top post, including two men who ended up being banned for life from baseball and one who also was the manager though the only ball he ever played in his life was on the sandlots. They had a president who disliked Philadelphia so much that, for a long while, he commuted to town daily from New York.

The longest-tenured president was Robert R. M. "Bob" Carpenter, Jr., who oversaw the club for 30 years and made them the dominant Philadelphia team at a time when Connie Mack's Athletics were in turmoil – eventually causing that club to be sold and moved.

Ownership groups have often included the team president, but at other times, such as the tenure of Charles Phelps Taft, others were simply appointed to fill the president's role.

Ted Taylor

The Big Whigs

Alfred J. Reach (1883-02) - (May 25, 1840 – January 14, 1928) who was one of the early stars of baseball in the National Association, went on to become an influential executive, publisher, sporting goods manufacturer and spokesman for the sport.

Born in London Reach was a regular for the champion Eckford club of Brooklyn in the early 1860s before moving to the (original, pre-Connie Mack) Philadelphia Athletics in 1865. When the National Association began, he helped the A's win the first professional baseball pennant in 1871. He retired as a player in 1875, and helped found the Philadelphia Phillies franchise (which had been transplanted from Worcester, MA). Reach served as team president from 1883 to 1899. Later Reach formed a sporting goods company and earned millions. He later sold his company to Albert Spalding in 1889.

Reach kept his interest in the Phillies franchise, selling out in 1899 to his longtime partner, John Rogers. Reach died at age 87 in Atlantic City and is interred at West Laurel Hill Cemetery in Bala Cynwyd.

20th Century Phillies by the Numbers

John I. Rogers (1883-1902, President & owner) - was part-owner of the Phillies from 1883 to 1899, and majority owner from 1899 to 1903. He also owned the Philadelphia Phillies of the short-lived National Football League of 1902. (Connie Mack fielded a Philadelphia Athletics team in the same football conference.)

A prominent attorney and politician in Philadelphia, Rogers came to the baseball business when former player and sporting goods magnate Al Reach consulted with him on a patent for a baseball. Rogers and Reach later teamed up to acquire the remnants of the Worcester baseball club in 1883, winning the rights to the franchise via drawing of lots. Reach and Rogers relocated the franchise to Philadelphia, where they became known as the Quakers (they would later become the Phillies), entering the team as an expansion franchise in the National League in 1883. During these early days, Rogers was involved in creating baseball's reserve clause which would remain in effect until the era of free agency. Reach sold his interest to Rogers due to repeated disagreements about the direction of the club.

Reach and Rogers sold the Phillies to a group led by James Potter in February 1903, but retained the rights to the team's stadium, National League Park (which eventually became Baker Bowl). On August 8, a balcony collapsed at the park, killing 12 people and injuring hundreds more. Rogers was nearly ruined by the resulting avalanche of lawsuits, and was forced to sell the stadium to Potter as well. Eventually, both Rogers and Reach were absolved of blame and financial responsibility for the accident by the U.S. Supreme Court.

James Potter (1903-1904, owner) - He was the owner of the Phillies from 1903 through 1904. In 1903, Porter purchased the club from John Rogers. He sold the club to Billy Shettsline in 1905.

William J. "Billy" Shettsline (1905-08, President) – Billy wore lots of hats with the Phillies, and though he never played pro baseball his five-year term as club manager was highly successful (1898-1902). He posted a 367-302 record. He got the job when George Stallings was fired. At the time he was club secretary. After the end of his term as manager, Shettsline owned the team from 1905 to 1909. Shettsline also spent some time as the team's business manager after he sold the club.

Charles P. Taft (1905-13, owner) – Strictly an owner, was never involved in club operation, though he did become embroiled in a dispute with Horace Fogel over the potential sale of the club.

Israel W. Durham (1909, President & owner) – Part of a group of investors that bought the team in February 1909 – he died in June 1909 in Atlantic City NJ.

20th Century Phillies by the Numbers

Horace S. Fogel (1909-12, President) – An odd duck if ever there was one. First thing he did was suggest abandoning the Phillies name and calling them "The Live Wires". (The logo he envisioned was an Eagle holding lightning bolts in his talons.) Fogel had been a sportswriter who was a manager for two years (1887;1902) and team owner/president for four years (1909-1912). He first became a manager at age 48 with the Indianapolis Hoosiers on July 11, 1887. He then managed the New York Giants from the start of the 1902 season until June 10, 1902 and then was owner/president of the Phillies (1909-1912). Fogel himself, however, had doubts about what was the best team. After one too many drunken accusations that the Giants had beaten the Chicago Cubs in 1912 mainly because St. Louis Cardinals manager Roger Bresnahan had not fielded his best nine against his former Giants teammates and because league umpires were pro-New York, he was summoned to a league meeting to back up his charges. When he couldn't, he was banished for having "undermined the integrity of the game". Bresnahan was also ill advisedly removed from his position. After his baseball days were over, Fogel ran for Congress as a Democrat and lost.

Albert D. Wiler (1912-13, Interim President) – Occupied the spot for just three months between Fogel's ouster and Locke's acquisition of the team.

Ted Taylor

William H. Locke (1913, President and owner) - Youthful owner of the Philles (with cousin) William F. Baker, he was a "baseball man" and worked hard and was full of ambition and interesting ideas. He died six months to the day after he took over the team - on July 15, 1913 – and then Baker took over. Two years later, 1915, his vision of a Phillies pennant came true.

William F. Baker (1913-30, President and owner) – The Phillies ball park (Philadelphia Park) came under increasing criticism just about the time that it started to be called Baker Bowl. William F. Baker, who assumed the presidency and ownership, was a former New York Police Commissioner who did not really like Philadelphia and commuted back and forth every day for quite some time. To say that he was thrifty was an understatement.

Lewis C. Ruch (President, 1931-32) – Got a job he neither sought or wanted when William Baker died. He and Baker were actually partners and when he died there was speculation that the club would be sold to a syndicate – one of them including Ty Cobb. Baker's will specified that the club could not be sold. Ruch, by all accounts a nice man, served, in ill health, for two years. Gerald Nugent would succeed him in a most unusual set of circumstances.

Gerald P. Nugent (President, 1932-43) - A leather goods and shoe merchant, Nugent married longtime Phillies secretary Mae Mallen in 1925. Phillies owner William Baker died in 1930, leaving half of his estate to Mallen and half to his wife. With the support of Baker's widow, Nugent became team president. Baker's widow

20th Century Phillies by the Numbers

died in 1932, leaving Nugent in full control – nothing like being in the right place at the right time.

Unlike Baker, Nugent cared more about winning than saving money. However, even with his income from his other businesses, he didn't have the financial means to get the Phillies out of the National League basement. After saying he'd do no such thing, he was forced to trade what little talent the team had to make ends meet and had to use some creative financial methods to be able to even field a team. His 1932 club finished with a 78-76 record in 1932, it was, incredibly, the only time that the Phillies finished with a winning record between 1918 and 1948. (The two Philadelphia franchises were both being run on a shoestring and the fans had little to be excited about for a long, long time. As a result, a lot of them never showed up.)

Nugent finally gave up in 1942. A year after posting a 43-111 record, the worst in franchise history, the Phillies needed an advance from the league just to be able to conduct spring training. Realizing that there was no way he could operate the team in 1943, he reached an agreement in principle that February to sell the team to consummate baseball promoter Bill Veeck, who planned to either move the team to Milwaukee (home of the successful American Association franchise) or bring in Negro League stars in an effort to turn the moribund franchise around. (Imagine a lineup with Satchel Paige, Josh Gibson and other stars.) However, when Baseball Commissioner Kenesaw Mountain Landis, an intractable opponent of integration, got wind of it, he pressured National League President Ford Frick to quash the deal and take over the team. A week later, the league sold the Phillies to lumber broker

William B. Cox. Roy Campanella, a native Philadelphian who grew up in the same neighborhood as my step-father, often said his desire was always to play his hometown Phillies.

William D. Cox (President and owner, 1943) - In 1943, Cox bought the Phillies. Financially strapped Gerald Nugent had barely survived the 1942 season and the league sold the franchise to Cox (they should have gone with Veeck). Judge Landis and League president Ford Frick engineered the sale. At the age of 33 at the time, he was the youngest owner in the league. Ironically Cox would fire his manager and then the manager who would get him banned from baseball.

At the time Cox took over, the Phillies had been the worst team in the National League for a quarter century; at least in part because the team's owners had been unwilling (mostly unable) to spend the money necessary to build a winner. Cox, however, was not afraid to spend what it would take to get the Phillies out of the cellar. He significantly increased the team's payroll and devoted significant resources to player development (including the farm system). His downfall, as it turned out was when he hired future Hall of Fame manager Bucky Harris, who had won two pennants and one World Series with the Washington Senators.

Cox was a hands-on owner. He thought of himself as a star athlete; believing the team needed to be better conditioned, he hired his high school track coach, Harold Bruce, as team trainer.

Cox even suited up for workouts, and frequently showed up at the clubhouse before and after games.

All of this annoyed the daylights out of Harris, and when he protested against the boss's interference, Cox fired him on July 27 at a press conference, without bothering to even let him know. (He then hired "Fat Freddie" FitzSimmons as Harris' replacement.) The players threatened to go on strike, but Harris urged them to drop those plans after Cox threatened legal action.

Despite this, the Phillies finished 64-90, a healthy 22-game improvement from 1942, to get out of the cellar for the first time in five years. The long-suffering Phillies fans appreciated what Cox was trying to do, as the Phillies had their best attendance since 1916. At the time of Harris' firing, the Phillies were doing much better and had already won 38 games, just four fewer than they had won in the previous season.

A day after he was fired Harris, no shrinking violet, dropped a bombshell at his hotel room in Philadelphia: he told the press that he had evidence that Cox was betting on his own team. When Judge Landis got wind of Harris' charges, he launched an immediate investigation. Initially, Cox denied any wrongdoing, but then conceded that some of his business associates bet on the Phillies. Cox eventually changed his story again and admitted making some bets on the Phillies, and he claimed that he didn't know it was against the rules. This made no difference to Landis, who suspended Cox indefinitely on November 23. Cox immediately resigned as team president, but appealed Landis' ruling 11 days later.

At a December 4 hearing, Harris testified that he'd heard Cox's secretary asking about the odds for a game between the Phillies and Brooklyn Dodgers; when Harris asked, "*Do you mean to tell me Mr. Cox is betting on baseball?*" the secretary replied that it was common knowledge in the Phillies office. On the basis of this and other evidence, Landis ordered that Cox be suspended for life, thus making Cox the first non-player to be banned from baseball by Landis (but the second Phillies owner to gain this dubious distinction); he is the last owner to be banned for life as of this writing.

Robert R. M. Carpenter Jr. (President and owner, 1943-72) - He took command of the Phils, in November 1943 after his father (Robert R. M. Carpenter Sr.) purchased the franchise, Carpenter became the youngest club president in baseball history. Unlike his predecessors, money was not a problem (thanks to solid investments and being part of the DuPont family.) He became principal owner upon his father's death in 1949. Under his leadership and successful management, it was the more-successful Connie Mack Athletics that left town and Carpenter even bought their ballpark. "Bob" Carpenter, as he was known in baseball, would serve as president of the Phillies until 1972, when his son, Ruly, succeeded him.

The Carpenter family owned the Phillies from 1943–81, winning National League championships in 1950 and 1980, National League East Division titles in 1976, 1977, 1978, and 1980, and the team's first World Series title in 1980. Distressed by the free-spending, free-agent era of the day, and anticipating the 1981

20th Century Phillies by the Numbers

baseball strike, the Carpenters sold the Phils months after their World Series triumph. The team made the 1981 playoffs, and won the 1983 NL pennant under Bill Giles and the new owners.

Robert R. M. "Ruly" Carpenter III (President and owner, 1972-81) - Carpenter was born in Wilmington, Delaware. He was three years old when his grandfather, Robert Carpenter, Sr. bought the Phillies in 1943 and gave control of the team to his father, Bob, Jr. He graduated from Yale University in 1962, and joined his father in the Phillies' front office in 1963. In 1965, he suggested that his father hire Paul Owens, a young scout, as farm system director. Owens would eventually become general manager in 1972 – and a two-time Phils manager, even taking them to the '83 World Series.

Ruly became team president at 32, when his father stepped down in the 1972 season. From 1976 to 1981, the Phillies won their division five times, including the team's first World Series win in 1980.

Soon after that first-time title, however, Carpenter decided to sell the team. I remember well that the Philadelphia baseball community was stunned. He explained that with the advent of free agency salaries were already starting to spiral upward, and he believed that even with his considerable wealth he needed to take on minority investors in order to stay afloat. Unwilling to have to get permission from partners in order to make major decisions, he sold the Phillies to a group headed by Bill Giles for $32.5 million in 1981. By comparison, his grandfather had bought the team in 1943 for $400,000.

Ted Taylor

Carpenter's great-grandmother, Margaretta Carpenter, was the sister of Pierre S. du Pont, president of DuPont from 1915 to 1919.

William Y. Giles (President and owner, 1981-97) - He is the son of former National League president Warren Giles, a baseball "lifer". His baseball career began in his father's former organization, the Cincinnati Reds, during the 1950s and he was among a group of Reds executives (including former Cincinnati general manager Gabe Paul and MLB executive Tal Smith) who helped to found the Houston Astros when they debuted as the *Colt .45s* in 1962. The Sporting News' *1962 Official Baseball Guide and Record Book,* published in the Colt .45s' initial season, lists Giles as the club's traveling secretary and publicity director – he was known during his entire baseball career as a promoter. Subsequently, he became promotions director, and focused on that role after the renamed team moved into the Astrodome in 1965.

Giles started with the Phillies as the vice president of business operations in 1969. He worked his way up in the organization, with stops as executive vice president and president, before becoming the chairman in 1997.

Giles was also part of the ownership group that bought the Phillies from the Carpenter family in 1981. The group was composed of Giles, David Montgomery, Claire S. Betz, Tri-Play Associates (Alexander K. Buck, J. Mahlon Buck Jr. William C. Buck), & Double Play

Inc. (John S. Middleton). The group reportedly purchased the team for $30 million.

Giles holds the title of honorary president of the National League—the same job his father held on an official full-time basis. The honorary president's only task for the season is to present the Warren C. Giles Trophy—which is named after his father, Warren—to the NLCS winner.

David P. Montgomery (President and part owner, 1997-2015) – Montgomery, a Penn Wharton School grad, served as line coach for the Germantown Academy football team while in college and reached out to former Phillies ace Robin Roberts, whose son he coached, about a job with the baseball club. Montgomery was hired as a member of the Phillies' sales department in 1971, becoming director of sales and marketing in the mid-1970s and the head of the business department by 1980. During the early 1970s, he was also the team's scoreboard operator. The only thing he never did was to be the "Phillie Phanatic" at least so it would seem.

Montgomery, along with co-owner Bill Giles, purchased the team in 1981 for $30,000,000; Giles, the primary owner, named Montgomery the executive vice president of the team. In 1997, when Giles left the team presidency to become the chairman and focus on winning a new stadium for the team, he recommended Montgomery to replace him as team president. In so doing, Montgomery became the first native of Philadelphia to head the team in over 60 years.

Ted Taylor

After taking a medical leave from the post in summer, 2014, Montgomery was replaced on an "interim" basis by Hall of Fame GM Pat Gillick for the rest of the year.

Pat Gillick (Interim President, 2014; President, 2015-) In January, 2015, the Phillies removed the "interim" tag from the title of the 77-year-old Hall of Famer and made him President. Montgomery was named chairman of the board and Bill Giles was made chairman emeritus. Gillick, a long-time and highly successful general manager with several big league clubs, was the architect of the Phillies second World's Championship (2008) and retired from the post in favor of his assistant, Ruben Amaro Jr., in 2011. Gillick had remained with the club as an "advisor".

The General Managers

The first Phillies GM was Herb Pennock, hired by the youthful Bob Carpenter to oversee the operation of the team as he served in the Army during World War II.

Prior to Pennock's appointment the role of GM was usually assumed by the owner, sometimes in concert with the field manager. When Pennock died in 1948 Carpenter, again, took over the GM's job through the '53 season, naming former Yankee GM H. Roy Hamey to succeed him in 1954.

When Paul Owens stepped down as GM after the 1983 season, Bill Giles assumed the duties (in addition to being President) and kept the post until 1987 when he tabbed Woody Woodward.

Herb Pennock (1944-48) – Seen as the architect of the "Whiz Kids", he died January 30, 1948 just as the Ashburn-Ennis-Roberts-Hamner juggernaut was taking hold. A Hall of Fame pitcher, Herb came on board and immediately started building the club. Herb spent the first four seasons of his 22 year career with the Philadelphia Athletics, he was then traded to the Red Sox, but it was with the Yankees (1923-33) that he made his mark, twice winning 20 games, twice winning 19 on his way to a career 240-162 record. He was elected to the Hall in 1948, the year he died. He was known as "The Knight of Kennett Square", his Pennsylvania hometown.

Bob Carpenter (1948-53) – It was only fitting that Carpenter would step in to Pennock's role and continue to build toward the second NL pennant in club history.

H. Roy Hamey (1954-58) – Managed to keep the Phillies mediocre. Had some success prior to this job with the Yankees (asst. GM, farm posts) and little success as GM of the Pirates. He got there the year the club finished third, the year he left they were dead last.

Ted Taylor

John J. Quinn (1959-72) – A baseball lifer and longtime exec. He was GM of the Boston Braves in 1945 and enjoyed success there and when the club moved to Milwaukee. His 1964 team "almost" won the NL flag, but he will be long remembered as the man who traded Rick Wise to St. Louis for Steve Carlton. He "retired" shortly after that and was replaced by Paul Owens.

Paul F. "The Pope" Owens (1972-83) – Ruly Carpenter recommended Owens for a farm post, he had been a scout, and soon he was one of the most integral members of the club hierarchy.

Bill Giles (1984-87) – There really wasn't a job in baseball front office management that Giles couldn't do – he just did some of them better than others.

Woody Woodward (1987-1988) – A journeyman infielder over eight seasons, got in to management with the Reds. Short stay, not much happened on his watch other than a lot of unhappiness. Apparently he couldn't get along with anybody and Giles fired him on June 8 (along with farm director Jim Baumer). Six weeks later Thomas was named VP of baseball operations by the Seattle Mariners.

Lee Thomas (1988-97) – Pretty good player in his day, a decade of lots of trades and a solid working knowledge of baseball. His daring acquisitions were rewarded when the unlikely '93 Phils ran off with the NL pennant.

20th Century Phillies by the Numbers

Ed Wade (1998-2005) – Wade became a lightening rod for all that was wrong with the Phillies and he got fired for his troubles. Shortly after he was canned a lot of the players he brought on board began to play well and began a successful run that included a World's Championship in 2008. Became GM of Houston Astros and they were pretty bad, too. He got fired again. The Phillies rehired him as a special (albeit low profile) assistant.

It should be noted here that Hall of Famer **Pat Gillick** assumed the Phils GM role in 2006 (kept it until 2008) and is credited with the Phils second World' Championship (2008) and the dynasty of the first decade of the 21st Century. Ruben Amaro Jr., a Phillies farm system graduate, took the GM job in 2008.

The Glenside Kid Remembers...

Bill Giles could always spot a good promotion and it didn't take him long to notice that the twice-yearly Philadelphia Baseball Card & Sports Memorabilia Shows that my partner Bob Schmierer and I were running at the George Washington Motor Lodge were drawing big weekend crowds. This was 1968-70 and our weekend count was usually in the 12,000-to14,000 range – more than once the local Fire Marshall made us stop selling tickets.

Giles contacted me (it was Spring 1969 after we had gotten great press and a large turnout of buyers and sellers for our March show) and invited me to Veteran's Stadium to discuss how we could move the show from Willow Grove to South Philly and how we'd both benefit. I brought lots of photos, floor/table layouts,

Ted Taylor

roster of dealers (from all over the United States) with me.

Bill envisioned holding the show on the weekend when the Phillies were home, thus having a full weekend (Friday, Saturday, Sunday) exposure. As he walked me around the mezzanine behind the first level he said that's where he envisioned putting the dealer tables. He also said, and I'll never forget it, "The wrong team left Philadelphia, it was always an American League town." He said that by way of explaining why attendance wasn't all that hot.

I was interested but he flinched when I asked him how much he was going to pay us to move the show (obviously we had to compensate for the 12,000 admission fees we wouldn't be able to charge), but then he killed the deal when he said, "of course the tables would have to shut down during the game and the existing concessionaires would have final say over what your dealers sold." In other words if a dealer of ours wanted to sell pennants, caps, almost anything souvenir oriented they couldn't do it. I told him, thanks but no thanks and the idea went no further. It was flattering, though, to be recognized by one of baseball's most prolific promoters.

In 1979 I approached Bill about a job with the Phillies. I got the usual, nothing available story (still have the letter), but he did suggest that I contact Reading Phillies owner Joe Buzas – I did and never heard a word from him. One can dream, can't one?

Chapter 10
About the Phils

Sports Illustrated Magazine in their April 15, 2013 edition listed writer Mark Bechtel's "Eight worst Major League team" and Philadelphia claimed two of them.

Bechtel listed the 1899 Cleveland Spiders (20-134) as the worst team ever – and he gets no argument from me. In eighth place is the 2003 Detroit Tigers (43-119), again no argument here. The '62 Mets (40-120) are second worst and were simply awful, Connie Mack's 1916 Philadelphia A's were third worst (36-117), the 1988 Baltimore Orioles were fourth (54-107) and the 1942 Phillies (42-109) were his choice for fifth. Others included 2004 Arizona (51-111) at sixth and Babe Ruth's 1935 Boston Braves (38-115) as seventh.

I'm going to disagree with Mr. Bechtel on the worst Phillies team. I think he missed it by a year, but I'll concede it is close. The 1941 team was truly dreadful, going 43-111, finishing 57 games out. (So, okay, the '42 club won one less and lost two less and finished just 62 ½ games out, they were both bad.) Doc Prothro was the '41 skipper, Hans Lobert managed the '42 club.

Ted Taylor

The '41 club lost more games than any team in Phillies history – going back to 1883 and including some pretty awful teams.

PHILADELPHIA PHILLIES 1941

First row—Mueller, Blanton, Rizzo, Warren, Pearson, Johnson, Livingston, Marty. Second row—Miller, trainer; Klein, Murtaugh, Lobert, coach; Marnie, Lambert, Etten, Bragan. Third row—Benjamin, Litwhiler, May, Hughes, Hoerst, Melton, Harmon, Podgajny, Beck.

The ace of their pitching staff, Hugh "Losing Pitcher" Mulcahy (he was 13-22 in 1940) was the first player drafted in to the military. That left them a staff that included Walter "Boom Boom" Beck (he went 1-9) and not a single pitcher who won more than nine games (Tom Hughes, John Podgajny notched that many). Lee Grissom was 2-13, Cy Blanton 6-12, Ike Pearson 4-14, Frank Hoerst 3-10 and they were the good pitchers.

Their offense included a promising rookie, Danny Litwhiler, who hit .305 with 18 homeruns and 66 RBI's and Nick Etten who batted .311 with 14 homers and 79 RBI's. That was pretty much it. Chuck Klein, now a shadow of his prime, batted just .123 in 50 games. Two future big league managers, Bobby Bragan (ss) and

20th Century Phillies by the Numbers

Danny Murtaugh (2b) had decent, if not spectacular years.

The futile Phils put one stretch of 28 scoreless innings together (good if you are a pitcher, not so hot if that's the output of your offense) and drew a whopping 231,401 fans to Shibe Park.

The Phils finished fourth in 1932 and then began lurking in the depths of the league until 1949. The team was seventh for three straight years, 1933 (60-92), 1934 (56-93), 1935 (64-89); last in 1936 (54-100), seventh again in 1937 (61-92) and then last in 1938 (45-105), 1939 (45-106), 1940 (50-103), 1941 (43-111), 1942 (42-109), seventh in 1943 (64-90) and then eighth again in 1944 (61-92), 1945 (46-108) and then things began looking up in 1946 when they finished fifth albeit 16 games below .500 (69-85). Back to seventh they went in 1947 (62-92), sixth in 1948 (66-88), third in 1949 (81-73) their first plus .500 year since 1932 and then, of course, the pennant in 1950 (91-63), it had been a long climb.

Ted Taylor

Chapter 11
Strictly by the Numbers

Here's a breakdown of the players who wore the following numbers (and the order in which the players wore them, i.e., Hamner wore #1 before Ashburn, Dark wore it after) – many players wore multiple numbers. Names in bold indicate that the number was retired for that player.

#00 - Omar Olivares

#1 – Kiddo Davis, Chuck Fullis, Chuck Klein, Doc Prothro, Hans Lobert, Danny Murtaugh (left on his 1950 Bowman card), Charlie Letchas, Bitsy Mott, Johnny Wyrostek, Granny Hamner, **Rich Ashburn (number retired),** Alvin Dark, Joe Morgan, Bobby Wine, Al Vincent, George Myatt, Bob Skinner, Frank Lucchesi, Carroll Berringer, Jose Cardenal.

#2 – Dick Bartell, Hersh Martin, Hans Lobert, Pinky May, Bill Killefer, Moon Mullin, Buster Adams, Benny Culp, John Antonelli, Ken Richardson, Rollie Hemsley, Ralph Caballero, Sparky Anderson, Bobby Malkmus, Bob Lemon, Al Widmar, Cal McLish, Andy Seminick, Dave Watkins, George Myatt, Brandy Davis, Billy

Ted Taylor

DeMars, Deron Johnson, Lee Elia, Jim Davenport, Dave Bristol, Larry Bowa, Rico Brogna.

#3 – Chuck Klein, Morrie Arnovich, Sylvester Johnson, Mickey Livingston, Babe Dahlgren, Rogers McKee, Jim Wasdell, Andy Karl, Eli Hodkey, Charlie Gelbert, Bert Haas, Ralph Caballero, Tom Glaviano **(left on his '53 Topps card)**, Bobby Morgan, Peanuts Lowrey, Bobby Del Greco, Don Hoak, Al Widmar, Ron Stone, Billy DeMars, Danny Ozark, Lee Elia, Claude Osteen, Darold Knowles, Dale Murphy, Todd Pratt, Billy Hatcher, Kevin Elster, John Vukovich, Chuck Cottier.

#4 – Don Hurst, Gus Dugas, Ray Stoviak, Spud Davis, Art Mahan, Danny Litwhiler, Coaker Triplett, Ron Northey, Jimmie Foxx, Harry Walker, Eddie Waitkus, Bobby Morgan, Solly Hemus, Gene Freese, Ted Lepcio, Gene Mauch, Larry Hisle, Ray Ripplemayer, Herm Starrette, Dave Bristol, Lee Elia, Denis Menke, Lenny Dykstra, Torey Lovullo.

#5 – Pinky Whitney, Fritz Knothe, Mickey Haslin, Ike Pearson, Bill Atwood, Lefty Watwood, Bill Burch, Johnny Rizzo, Bennie Warren, Earl Naylor, Buster Adams, Coaker Triplett, Vance Dinges, Jim Tabor, Eddie Miller, Jimmy Bloodworth, Tommy Brown **(at left on a 1952 Bowman baseball card)**, Dick Young, Mickey Micelotta, Jim Command, Ed Bouchee, Cal Neeman, Bob Sadowski, George Williams, Roy

20th Century Phillies by the Numbers

Seivers, Bob Oldis, Larry Shepard, Don Money, Doc Edwards, Larry Cox, Billy Grabarkewicz, Ron Clark, Fred Andrews, Tim Blackwell, Carroll Berringer, Bob Tiefenauer, Mike Ryan, Pat Corrales, Paul Owens, Kim Batiste, Gary Varsho, Mike Benjamin, Gene Schall, Rob Butler, Mark Lewis, Ron Gant.

#6 – Sheriff Lee, Wes Schulmerich, George Scharien, Gus Suhr, Cy Blanton, Sam File, Bill Crouch, Paul Busby, Mickey Livingston, Lefty Gerheauser, Andy Karl, Charlie Letchas, Fred Daniels, Granny Hamner, Roy Hughes, Skeeter Newsome, Dick Sisler, Willie Jones, Jim Bolger, Johnny Callison, Tim McCarver, John Bateman, Jim Essian, Johnny Oates, Ted Sizemore, Dave Rader, Keith Moreland, Bob Diaz, Alan Knicely, John Russell, Dwayne Murphy, Sil Campusano, Wally Backman, Todd Pratt, Gene Schall, Scott Rolen, Doug Glanville.

#7 – Spud Davis, Mickey Finn, Jim McLeod, Del Young, Joe Kracher, Al Hollingsworth, Bud Hafey, Stan Benjamin, George Jumonville, Cy Blanton, Wally Berger **(at left on a 1930's National Chicle card)**, Danny Litwhiler, Hal Marnie, Walter "Boom Boom" Beck, Mickey Livingston, Ken Raffensberger, Ted Cieslak, Nick Picciuto, Vince DiMaggio, Ben Chapman, Eddie Sawyer, Bud Blattner, Jack Lohrke, Ted Kazanski, Joe Lonnett, Tony Curry, Pancho Hererra, Ted Savage, Bobby Wine, Dick Stuart, Vic Roznovsky, Mike Compton, John Felske, Ken Dowell, Ken Jackson, John Vukovich, Kim Batiste, Mariano Duncan, Glenn Murray, Terry Francona.

Ted Taylor

#8 – Hank McCurdy, Spud Davis, Earl Brown, Justin Stein, Buck Jordan, Max Butcher, Wally Millies, Mel Mazzera, Ed Levy, Frank Hoerst, Rube Melton, Si Johnson, Hilly Flitcraft, Paul Masterson, Chuck Klein, Glen Stewart, Garvin Hamner, Ed Walczak, Wally Flagler, Charlie Ripple, Don Padgett, Dick Sisler, Connie Ryan, Terry Moore, Bob Bowman, John Kennedy, Joe Lonnett, Valmy Thomas, Tony Taylor, Paul Owens, Bob Boone, Pat Corrales, Joe Morgan, Juan Samuel, Charlie Hayes, Dale Sveum, Jim Eisenreich, Mark Parent, Desi Relaford.

#9 – Al Todd, Hank McCurdy, Heinie Mueller, Hugh Mulcahy, Gene Lambert, Bill Nagel, Hal Marnie, Paul Busby, Bob Finley, Gus Mancuso, Emil Verban **(pictured at left on the first baseball card ever purchased by the author – a 1948 Bowman),** Jocko Thompson, Mike Goliat, Ralph Caballero, Dick Young, Nippy Jones, Earl Torgeson, Glen Gorbous, Harry Anderson, Lee Walls, Sammy White, Mickey Harrington, Cal Emery, Gus Triandos, Bob Uecker, Gene Oliver, Mike Ryan, John Stearns, Bill Nahorodny, Barry Foote, Manny Trillo, Juan Samuel, Von Hayes, Dale Sveum, Tom Marsh, Mike Ryan, Pete Incaviglia, Brad Mills.

#10 – Eddie Delker, Al Todd, Joe Holden, Bubber Jonnard, Earl Grace, Cap Clark, Charlie Letchas, Dave Coble, Ham Schulte, Vito Tamulis, Lee Grissom, Walter "Boom Boom" Beck, Andy Lapihuska, Si Johnson, Dee Moore, Harry Shuman, Chet Covington, Charlie Ripple, Johnny Peacock, Hal Spindel, Whitlow

20th Century Phillies by the Numbers

Wyatt, Dick Mulligan, Buck McCormick, Howie Schulz, Del Wilbur, Danny Schell, Jim Greengrass, Bob Bowman, Jim Coker, Cal Neeman, Darrell Johnson, Al Kenders, Bob Oldis, Danny Cater, Pat Corrales, Bill White, Gene Stone, Larry Bowa, Dave Roberts, Mike Lavalliere, Darren Daulton

#11 – Bernie Friberg, Eddie Delker, Al Todd, Bill Atwood, Jinx Poindexter, Bill Kersieck, Frank Hoerst, Danny Litwhiler, Cy Blanton, Walter "Boom Boom" Beck, Al Gerheauser, Vern Kennedy, Whitlow Wyatt, Andy Karl, Benny Bengough, Clay Dalrymple, Deron Johnson **(pictured on his 1971 ARCO 8x10 pin-up card)**, Jerry Martin, Tim McCarver, Ozzie Virgil, Ivan DeJesus, Tom Foley, Gregg Legg, John Kruk, Keith Miller, Sil Campusano, Jim Fregosi, Kevin Sefcik

#12 – Les Mallon, Jack Warner, Jimmie Wilson, Jim Henry, Ray Harrell, Ike Pearson, Bill Peterman, Ernie Koy, Charlie Fuchs, Dale Mathewson, Deacon Donahue, Dick Barrett, Eli Hodkey, Lou Finney, Willie Jones, Howie Schulz, Lou Possehl, Bill Nicholson **(pictured on his 1950 Phila. Evening Bulletin Pin-Up)**, Stan Jok, Bob Kuzava, Marv Blaylock, Dave Philley, Clarence "Choo Choo" Coleman, Tony Gonzalez, Don Hoak, Johnny Briggs, Pete Koegel, Cesar Tovar, Tony Taylor, Ruben Amaro Sr., Len Matuszek, Glenn Wilson, Mickey Morandini

Ted Taylor

#13 – Claude Passeau, Eddie Pellagrini, Bobby Wine, Lance Parrish, Roger Mc Dowell, Charlie Hayes.

#14 – Fred Brickell, Schoolboy Cohen, Mickey Weintraub, Swede Burkhart, Al Smith, Kirby Higbe, Cy Blanton, Ed Murphy, Lefty Hoerst, Ron Northey, Fred FitzSimmons, Del Ennis, Rip Repulski, Wally Post, Don Ferrarese, Bobby Locke, Ted Savage, Frank Torre, **Jim Bunning (number retired),** Woodie Fryman, Tommy Hutton, Bud Harrelson, Pete Rose, John Wockenfuss, Jeff Stone, Tom Barrett, Denis Menke, Rex Hudler, Gary Bennett.

#15 – Cliff Heathcote, Don Hurst, Hugh Mulcahy, Tom Hughes, Hal Marnie, Walter "Boom Boom" Beck, Bob Finley, Andy Seminick, Ken Raffensberger, Dick Mauney, Bama Rowell, Jackie Mayo, Ed Sanicki, Stan Palys, Wally Westlake, Elmer Valo, Rip Repulski, Joe Koppe, Charlie Smith, Billy Consolo, Dick Allen **(pictured left on his 1964 Topps card),** Denny Doyle, Alan Bannister, Jim Morrison, Davey Johnson, Bud Harrelson, Ramon Aviles, Julio Franco, Larry Milbourne, Steve Jeltz, Rick Schu, Jackie Gutierrez, Bill Almon, Floyd Youmans, Dave Hollins, Gary Bennett, Rick Otero, Dave Doster.

#16 – Ray Benge, Phil Collins, Tom Reis, Tuck Stainback, Gib Brack, Max Butcher, Stan Benjamin, Les Powers, Roy Hughes, Lefty Smoll, George Jumonville, Danny Murtaugh, Hilly Flitcraft, Si Johnson, Jack Kraus, Charley Schanz, Ken Raffensberger,

20th Century Phillies by the Numbers

Johnny Blatnick, Ken Johnson, Lou Possehl, Mel Clark, Frank Baumholtz, Warren Hacker, Chico Fernandez, John Easton, Bobby Gene Smith, Frank Torre, Cookie Rojas, Don Money, Jose Pagan, Alan Bannister, Fred Andrews, Jim Morrison, Todd Cruz, Luis Aguayo, Juan Samuel, Nick Leyva, Braulio Castillo, Tony Longmire, Midre Cummings, Marlon Anderson.

#17 – Jack Berely, Jumbo Jim Elliott, Bucky Walters, Al Hollingsworth, Del Young, Charlie Frye, John Podgajny, Rube Melton, Rogers McKee, Dutch Deitz, Moon Mullen, Bill Lee, Hugh Mulcahy, Oscar Judd, Granny Hamner, Hal Wagner, Stan Hollmig, Johnny Wyrostek, Roy Smalley, Chico Fernandez, Kenny Walters, Jim Coker, Jack Davis, Earl Averill Jr., Costen Shockley, Ed Roebuck, Doug Clemens, Terry Harmon, Orlando Gonzalez, Pete Mackanin, Don McCormack, Ozzie Virgil **(left on his Topps baseball card),** Ron Roenicke, Ricky Jordan, Dave Gallagher, J. R. Phillips, Desi Relaford, Scott Rolen.

Ted Taylor

#18 – Phil Collins, Mickey Haslin, Reggie Grabowski, Clarence Pickrell, Al Smith, George Scharien, Hal Marnie, Sam Nahem, Tom Padden, George Eyrich, Al Verdel, Charlie Sproull, Charley Schanz, Jackie Mayo **(picture above in a 1950 Philadelphia Bulletin photo),** Milo Candini, Howie Fox, Johnny Lindell, Jim Owens, Jim Command, Pancho Hererra, Chris Short, Elmer Valo, Frank Sullivan, Ryne Duren, Rick Wise, Phil Linz, Doug Clemens, Rick Joseph, Bobby Pfeil, Craig Robinson, Bill Grabarkewitz, Richie Hebner, John Vukovich, Ivan DeJesus, Pat Corrales, Kiko Garcia, Derrel Thomas, Francisco Melendez, Chris James, Jim Adduci, Andy Van Slyke, Benito Santiago.

#19 – Clise Dudley. Snipe Hansen, Wild Bill Hallahan, Pinky May, Ike Pearson, Glen Stewart, Deacon Donahue, Johnny Peacock, Vern Kennedy, Jack Kraus, Schoolboy Rowe **(left on his '49 Bowman card),** Bob Miller, Bobby Malkmus, John Boozer, Terry Fox, Bob Skinner, Terry Harmon, Del Bates, Greg

20th Century Phillies by the Numbers

Luzinski, Dave Roberts, Al Holland, Keith Hughes, Mike Young, Tom Nieto, John Kruk, Jim Lindeman, Kevin Stocker, Domingo Cedeno.

#20 – Hal Elliott, Jack Berely, Dick Bartell, Bucky Walters, Charlie Scheerin, George Scharein, Pete Sivess, Pinky Whitney, Jim Shilling, Bobby Bragan, John Podgajny, Bill Webb, Roy Hamrick, Charlie Brewster, Benny Culp, Dale Mathewson, Ralph Caballero, Dick Coffman, Si Johnson, Dutch Leonard, Hank Borowy, Steve Ridzik, Andy Hansen, Murry Dickson, Harvey Haddix, Harry Hannebrink, Ruben Amaro Sr., Jackie Brandt, Rick Joseph, Jim Hutto, Roger Freed, **Mike Schmidt (number retired),** Ron Jones.

#21 – Jumbo Jim Elliott, Ed Holley, Lou Chiozza, Leo Norris, Ed Heusser, Wayne Lamaster, Heinie Mueller, Andy Lapihuska, Dick Conger, Nick Goulish, Heinie Hetzel, Granny Hamner, Don Hassenmayer, Ike Pearson, Charlie Gelbert, Al Jurisch, Andy Seminick, Smokey burgess, Dick Carter, Peanuts Lowrey **(left on a Phillies media photo),** John Herrnstein, Jim Lemon, Ray Herbert, Pete Ramos, Jim Schaffer, Larry Colton, John Boozer, Ron Stone, Bill Robinson, Ron Diorio, Jay Johnstone, Bake McBride, Sid Monge, Greg Gross, Dickie Thon, Pat Combs, Tom Marsh, Jon Zuber, Paul Blazier, Mark Portugal.

#22 – Snipe Hansen, Ad Liska, Mickey Haslin, Dino Chiozza, Blondy Ryan, Chile Gomez, Gene Corbett,

Ted Taylor

Walt Stephenson, Syl Johnson, Jack Bolling, John Podgajny, Wally Millies, Nick Etten, Schoolboy Rowe, Turkey Tyson, Charley Schanz, Chet Covington, Rene Monteagudo, Frank Hoerst, Jack Albright, Ralph LaPointe, Don Padgett, Ken Trinkle, Karl Drews, Herman Wehmeier, Ben Flowers, Jim Hearn, Ruben Gomez, Tony Gonzalez, John Hernnstein, Woodie Fryman, Larry Hisle, Mike Anderson, Mike Schmidt, John Vukovich, Dane Iorg, Bake McBride, Jay Loviglio, Bob Dernier, Ed Farmer, Tim Corcoran, Gary Redus, Hal Lanier, Stan Javier, Pete Incaviglia, Mark Whiten, Gary Bennett, Ron Blazier.

#23 – George Knothe, Cy Moore, Andy High, Bud Clancy, Johnny Vergez, Stan Sperry, Ray Benge, Del Young, Gene Corbett, Howie Gorman, Wally Millies, Bud Bates, Jinx Poindexter, Earl Whitehill, Benny Culp, John Fick, Ted Cieslak, Lee Riley, Andy Karl, Hal Spindell, Charlie Letchas, Ralph LaPointe, Bubba Church, Stan Palys, Jim Greengrass, Johnny Buzhardt, Paul Brown, Dennis Bennett, Morrie Stevens, Adolfo Phillips, Don Lock **(pictured),** Rich Barry, LeRoy Reams, Oscar Gamble, Ollie Brown, Greg Gross, Jeff Stone, Joe Lefebvre, Eric Bullock, Randy Ready, Brad Brink, Todd Pratt, Doug Jones, Kevin Jordan.

#24 – Ed Holley, Flint Rehm, Dolph Camilli, Earl Brown, Hal Kelleher, Max Butcher, Morris Arnovich, Maxie Wilson, Hal Marnie, Bennie Warren, Bill Nagel, Al Glossup, Bucky Harris, Lefty Gearhauser, Andy Seminick, Eddie Sawyer, Steve O'Neill, Mayo Smith,

20th Century Phillies by the Numbers

Don Demeter, Frank Thomas, Billy Sorrell, Dick Groat, Billy Cowan, Larry Hisle, Billy Wilson, Byron Browne, Bill Robinson, John Montague, Pete Mackanin, Keith Moreland, Ozzie Virgil, Ryne Sandberg, Len Matuszek, Bob Dernier, Tony Perez, Jerry Koosman, Milt Thompson, Curt Ford, Carmelo Martinez, Darrin Fletcher, Steve Searcy, Juan Bell, Joe Millette, Mike Leiberthal.

#25 – Flint Rehm, Frank Pearce, Irv Jeffries, Art Bramhall, Pinky Whitney, Hans Lobert, Hersh Martin, Al Monchak, Neb Stewart, Nick Etten, Bennie Culp, Bert Hodge, Garton De Salvo, Dale Mathewson, Bill Lee, Merv Shea, Al Lakeman, Ken Silvestri, Gus Niarhos, Stu Miller, Don Erickson, Ken Lehman, Tony Gonzalez, Al Raffo, Scott Reid, Joe Lis, Del Unser, Don Hahn, Jerry Martin, John Montague, Willie Montanez, Bob Molinaro, Mike Ryan, Shane Turner, Steve Lake, Milt Thompson, Gregg Jefferies, Rob Ducey.

#26 – Burt Shotton, Newt Hunter, Bill Andrus, Elmer Burkhart, Chuck Klein, Bennie Warren, Pinky May, Dick Barrett, Frank McCormick, Howie Schultz, Al Lakeman, Dick Koecher, Jim Konstanty, Hal Wagner, Bob Greenwood, Saul Rogovin, Ron Northey, Paul Brown, Bobby Del Greco, Cal McLish, Alex Johnson, Joe Verbanic, Dallas Green, Lowell Palmer, John Vukovich, Gene Garber, Fred Andrews, Kerry Dineen, John Poff, Len Matuszek, Dick Davis, Bill Robinson, Von Hayes, Bob Molinaro, Jeff Stone, Chris James, Ron Jones, Mel Roberts, Lee Tinsley, David Doster, Alex Arias.

#27 – Jack Onslow, Burt Shotton, Newt Hunter, Dolph Camilli, Gib Brack, Paul Masterson, Danny Murtaugh, Newt Kimball, Barney Mussill, Coaker Triplett, John

Ted Taylor

O'Neill, Freddy Schmidt, Ken Heintzelman, Ralph Caballero, Ron Mrozinski, Jim Coker, Jack Baldschun, Ed Roebuck, Steve Ridzik, John Morris, Dick Hall, Sam Parilla, Dick Selma, Willie Montanez, Lonnie Smith, Alex Sanchez, Glenn Wilson, Kent Tekulve, Randy O'Neal, Curt Ford, Rick Schu, Joe Millette, Danny Jackson, Lenny Webster, Todd Zeile, Bobby Estallela.

#28 – Reggie Grabowski, John Jackson, Spud Davis, Lee Grant Scott, Bill Hoffman, Roy Hughes, Danny Litwhiler, Lloyd Brown, Bill Burich, Tom Hughes, Jimmy Wasdell, Andy Karl, Nick Goulish, Ralph Caballero, Glenn Crawford, Curt Simmons (left), Art Mahaffey, Rick Wise, Roger Craig, John Boozer, Pedro Ramos, Lou Peraza, Bobby Pfeil, Mike Rogodzinski, Rick Bosetti, Bobby Tolan, John Vukovich, Orlando Isales, Sparky Lyle, Bill Robinson, Sexto Lezcano, Tim Corcoran, Milt Thompson, Shane Rawley, Tommy Herr, John Kruk, Mitch Williams, Tyler Green.

#29 – Bob Adams, Chuck Klein, Benny Culp, Barney Mussill, Tony Lupien, Oscar Judd, Skeeter Newsome, Lou Possehl, Stan Lopata, Gene Conley, Frank Sullivan, John Boozer, Bobby Del Greco, Grant Jackson, Manny Muniz, Mike Rogodzinski, Garry Maddox, Cy Acosta, Rick Bosetti, Orlando Isales, George Vukovich, Bob Dernier, Darren Daulton, Bill Campbell, John Russell, Ronn Reynolds, Willie Hernandez, Phil Bradley, Tommy Barrett, Louie Meadows, John Kruk, Steve Frey, Wendell Magee.

20th Century Phillies by the Numbers

#30 – Ad Liska, Ethan Allen, Hersh Martin, Bill Harman, Stan Benjamin, Ed Freed, Al Verdel, Joe Antolick, Ron Northey, Blix Donnelly, Bob Ross, Jim Woods, Ryne Duren, Lew Burdette, Ferguson Jenkins, Bob Buhl, Jeff James, John Vuckovich, Darrell Brandon, Dave Cash, Mike Buskey, Jim Morrison, Bob Dernier, Porfirio Altamirano, Steve Jeltz, Dennis Cook, Joe Boever, Steve Lake, Jeff Manto, Tom Quinlan, Kevin Flora, Desi Relaford, Scott Aldred.

#31 – Hugh Willingham, Chuck Fullis, Kiddo Davis, George Watkins, Heinie Mueller, Danny Litwhiler, Bob Finley, Benny Culp, Izzy Leon, Cy Perkins, Earl Combs, Whitlow Wyatt, Bill Posedel, Ken Silvestri, Mel Roach, Costen Shockley, Gary Wagner, Billy Champion, Ken Brett, Frank Linzy, Cy Acosta, Garry Maddox, Jeff Calhoun, Mark Ryal, Al Pardo, Jim Vatcher, Wes Chamberlain, Steve Scarsone, Brad Brink, Randy Ready, Kevin Sefcik, Mark Leiter, Robert Person.

#32 – Harvey Hendrick, Orville Jorgens, Gene Corbett, Earl Naylor, Stan Andrews, Art Lopatka, Rollie Hemsley, Curt Simmons, Dusty Cooke, Eddie Mayo, Wally Moses, Gene Mauch, Billy Klaus, Dick Allen, Gary Sutherland, Darold Knowles, Ruben Gomez, Dick Farrell, Fred Wenz, Darrell Brandon, **Steve Carlton (number retired).**

#33 – Prince Oana, Johnny Moore, Roy Bruner, Dale Jones, Ron Northey, Fred FitzSimmons, Andy Karl, Wally Flagler, Freddy Schmidt, Gran Hamner, Ed Sanicki, Jocko Thompson, Kent Peterson, Tommy Qualters, Duane Pillette, Al Schroll, Bo Belinsky, Paul Brown, Jerry Johnson, Willie Montanez, Mike Jackson,

Ted Taylor

Wayne Twitchell, Kevin Saucier, Tim Corcoran, Dave Wehrmeister, Dave Shipanoff, Tom Gorman, Mike Jackson, Greg Harris, Floyd Youmans, Darold Knowles, John Morris, Ruben Amaro Jr., Fernando Valenzuela, Gene Harris, Russ Springer, Scott Ruffcorn, Chad Ogea.

#34 – Freddie Frink, Art Ruble, Hack Wilson, Ed Boland, Fred Lucas, Lou Chiozza, Morris Arnovich, Gene Schott, Bill Atwood, Len Gabrielsion, Si Johnson, Lloyd Waner, Mitch Chetkovich, Ben Chapman, Vince DiMaggio, Hugh Poland, Frank Hoerst, Freddy Schmidt, Walt Dubiel, Russ Meyer, Paul Stuffel, Thornton Kipper, Mack Burke, Humberto Robinson, Bobby Locke, Wayne Graham, Bob Oldis, Costen Shockley, Terry Fox, Jimmie Schaffer, Terry Harmon, Roberto Pena, Barry Lersch, Tom Underwood, Keith Moreland, Jack Kucek, Scott Munninghoff, Gary Matthews, Chris James, Jeff Bittiger, Mike Easler, Doug Bair, Alex Madrid, Bill Scherer, Dickie Noles, Danny Cox, Ben Rivera, Andy Van Slyke, Howard Battle, Manny Martinez, Glenn Dishman, Derrick May, Mike Robertson, Paul Byrd.

#35 – Wes Schulmerich, Bucky Walters, Elmer Burkhart, Joe Marty, Charlie Ripple, Lee Handley, Granny Hamner (left), Charlie Bicknell, Jim Konstanty, Joe Lonnett, Solly Drake, Bobby Shantz, Roger Craig, Dick Hall, Gary Sutherland, Woodie Fryman, Dave Downs, George Culver, Tom

20th Century Phillies by the Numbers

Hilgendorf, Manny Seoane, Horacio Pina, Nino Espinoza, Jerry Reed, Tony Ghelfi, Dan Schatzeder, Dan Clay, Al Pardo, Darrel Akerfelds, Doug Lindsey, Don Robinson, Bobby Munoz, Ryan Nye, Cliff Politte.

#36 – Chuck Klein, Lou Lucier, Lefty Scott, Jake Powell, Nick Etten, Al Porto, Nick Strincevich, **Robin Roberts (number retired).**

#37 – George Watkins, Ernie Sulik, Fred Tauby, Howie Gorman, Nick Goulish, Don Grate, Ray Hamrick, Granny Hamner, Homer Spragins, Lou Grosmick, Lou Possehl, Willie Jones, Jocko Thompson, Dick Whitman, Tom Brown, Jimmy Bloodworth, Mel Clark, Steve Ridzik, Glen Gorbous, Chuck Essegian, Bobby Young, Hank Mason, Ray Culp, Dick Ellsworth, John Sullivan, Howie Bedell, Billy Wilson, Ron Schueler.

#38 – Bill Lee, Al Jurisich, George Earnshaw, Leo Cristante, Floyd Baker, Ron Negray, John Gray, Jim Hegan, Rick Wise, Bob Terlecki, Larry Christenson, Pat Zachry, Dave Stewart, Wally Ritchie, Bob Sebra, Brad Moore, Pat Combs, Curt Schilling.

#39 – Lou Novikoff, Al Milnar, Lou Possehl, Charlie Bicknell, Paul Stuffel, Ken Johnson, Jim Owens, Ed Bouchee, Jack Sanford, Johnny Riddle, Andy Cohen, Paul Brown, Dick Farrell, Dick Selma, Dave Wallace, Eddie Watt, Marty Bystrom, Sparky Lyle, Lerrin Lagrow, Mike Kurkow, Don Carmen, Dave Rucker, Joe Cowley, Scott Service, Dennis Cook, Wally Ritchie, Donn Pall, Kyle Abbott, Rich Hunter, Ryan Nye, Toby Borland.

Ted Taylor

#40 – Phil Collins, Hugh Mulcahy, Bucky Walters, Johnny Humphries, Don Hassemayer, Maje McDonnell, Ruben Gomez, Lowell Palmer, Bob Boone, Dick Ruthven, Warren Brusstar, John Denny, Steve Bedrosian, Andy Ashby, Don Robinson, David West, Reggie Harris, Jon Zuber.

#41 – George Darrow, Pretzel Pezzulo, Pete Sivess, Tom Zachary, Larry Crawford, Bob Allen, Vance Dinges, Stan Lopata, Paul Erickson, Bob Miller, Jack Brittin, Niles Jordan, Lou Possehl, Paul Stuffel, Bob Conley, Freddy Rodriguez, Chris Short, Jim Lonborg, Bob Walk, Jay Baller, Steve Fireovid, Tom Hume, Steve Ontiveros, Darrin Chapin, Mike Williams, Erik Plantenberg, Billy McMillan.

#42 – Curt Davis, Mickey Haslin, Hugh Mulcahy, Hal Kelleher, Charley Stanceau, Jack Meyer, Bobby Wine, Steve Ridzik, John Boozer, Greg Luzinski, Ken Reynolds, Jim Nash, Ron Reed, Don Carman, Dave LaPoint, Mike Hartley, Toby Borland, Galen Cisco. **This number was retired throughout baseball in 1998 to honor the memory and achievements of Jackie Robinson.**

#43 – Jumbo Jim Elliott, Chief Moore, Herb Harris, Hal Kelleher, Glenn Crawford, Don Grate, Lynn Lovenguth, Dick Farrell, Wes Covington, Roger Craig, Dick Thoenen, Joe Hoerner, Ed Farmer, Mike Buskey, Doug Bird, Mark Davis, Charlie Hudson, Willie Hernandez, Sixto, Lezcano, Fred Tolliver, Bill Dawley, Ken Howell, Jeff Juden, Dave Leiper, Rafael Quilrico, Bronson Heflin, Jon Zuber, Galen Cisco.

20th Century Phillies by the Numbers

#44 – Reggie Grabowski, Orville Jorgens, Andy Karl, Dave Cole, Eddie Waitkus, Dick Farrell, Seth Morehead, Taylor Phillips, John Herrnstein, Mac Scarce, Wayne Simpson, Larry Fritz, Dick Ruthven, Steve Comer, Steve Fireovid, Mike Maddux, Amalio Carreno, Wes Chamberlain, Jim Deshaies, Mike Grace.

#45 – Snipe Hansen, Ray Prim, Chief Moore, Lefty Burke, Wayne Lamaster, Jack Spring, Fed Van Dusen, Angelo LiPetri, Chico Fernandez, Sparky Anderson, John Kippstein, Bill Laxton, Ron Diorio, Pete Richert, Tug McGraw, Greg Jelks, David Palmer, Terry Mulholland, Shawn Boskie, Tom Edens, Michael Mimbs, Danny Tartabull, Yorkis Perez, Jeff Brantley.

#46 – Ed Holley, Joe Bowman, Lefty Burke, Wayne Lamaster, Jack Spring, Angelo LiPetri, Don Cardwell, Dallas Green, Ferguson Jenkins, Larry Jackson, Billy DeMars, Joe Lis, John Montague, Dan Boitano, Ed Farmer, Kevin Gross, Larry McWilliams, Brad Moore, Johnny Podres, Carlton Loewer.

#47 – Ted Kleinhaus, Sylvester Johnson, Walt Stephenson, Rollie Hemsley, Vance Dinges, Marv Blaylock, Carl Sawatski, Bill Smith, Morrie Stevens, Larry Loughlin, Dallas Green, George Myatt, Ken Reynolds, Jesus Hernaiz, Randy Lerch, Tony Ghelfi, Larry Anderson, Bruce Ruffin, Kyle Abbott, Dennis Springer, Michael Mimbs, Amaury Telemaco, Mike Welch.

#48 – Cy Moore, Jim Bevin, Claude Passeau, Hugh Mulcahy, Jim Westlake, Ray Semproch, Jack Sanford, Jack Hamilton, Andy Seminick, Dan Larson, Dickie

Ted Taylor

Noles, Kevin Gross, Willie Hernandez, Shane Rawley, Marvin Freeman, Brad Moore, Jason Grimsley, Jose Deleon, Mark Davis, Roger Mason, Paul Quantrill, Ricky Jordan, Jerry Sprawling, Yorkis Perez.

#49 – Cy Mails, Bill Harman, Frank Pearce, Walt Masters, Warren Hacker, Jim Owens, Al Widmar, Mike Wallace, Crawly East wick, Dan Larson, Sid Monge, Charlie Hudson, Jeff Parrott, Tommy Greene, Edgar Ramos, Billy Brewer.

#50 – Hans Lobert, Emil Verban, Angelo LiPetri, Chuck Harmon, Ed Keegan, Jim Essian, Dan Larson, Marty Bystrom, Rocky Childress, Tom Newell, Gordon Dillard, Steve Searcy, Jose Deleon, Andy Carter, Sid Fernandez, Calvin Mauro, Joe Graze, Paul Solaris.

#51 – Dick Spalding, Tom Ferrick, Chuck McElroy, Cliff Brantley, Heathcliffe Slocumb, Ken Ryan.

#52 – Francisco Melendez, Todd Frohwirth, Tim Mauser, Keith Shepherd, Mickey Weston, Ricky Botallico, Ryan Karp, Steve Schrenk.

#53 – Bobby Shantz, Rick Schu, Chuck Malone, Greg Mathews, Tony Barron, Bobby Abreu.

#54 – Adolfo Phillips, Ed Roebuck, Jason Grimsley, Jose DeJesus, Carlos Crawford, Garrett Stephenson, Randy Wolf.

#55 – Gary Kroll, Bob Ayrault, Matt Beech.

20th Century Phillies by the Numbers

#56 – Dave Wehrmeister, Rick Surhoff, Jay Baller, Bob Wells, Calvin Maduro, Hal McCrea.

#57 – Porfirio Altamarino, Kevin Foster, Larry Mitchell, Ryan Karp, Robert Dodd.

#58 – Morrie Stevens, Johnny Briggs, Paul Fletcher, Jim Wright, Darrin Winston.

#59 – Dave Bennett, Joe Rigoli, Ramon Henderson.

#60 – Alex Johnson, Dickie Noles.

#61 – Wayne Gomes.

#62 – Rick Wise, Vic Power.

#64 – Gary Wagner.

#99 – Mitch Williams.

Ted Taylor

HOOPSTERS... In the 50's, perhaps even later, the Phillies would play charity exhibition baseball games each winter at local high schools and colleges. Here are a bunch of the Phils players prior to a game at, I believe, Abington High School. Top row Del Ennis (14), Robert Roberts (#36, who actually played college basketball), Al Lakeman (#25). Bottom row, Curt Simmons (#28), Ralph LaPointe (#23), Don Padgett (#22) and Maje McDonnell (#40). The young man in front is not identified.

Chapter 12
The Roster Evolves

Over the 100 years a lot of players played the eight basic starting positions and a lot of pitchers took the mound as the stopper. What follows is a look at the regular players (i.e., those who started the most games at a position) and top-two starting pitchers (most wins) by the decades. By tracing this evolution you will be able to see how the good teams developed and how some player moves set the stage for the bad years.

1900-09

1b – Ed Delahanty (00), Hughie Jennings (01, 02), Klondike Douglas (03) Jack Doyle (04) Kitty Bransfield (05, 06, 07, 08, 09)

2b – Nap Lajoie (00), Billy Hallman (01), Pete Childs (02), Kid Gleason (03, 04, 05, 06) Otto Knabe (07, 08, 09)

SS – Monte Cross (00-01). Rudy Hullswit (02, 03, 04), Mickey Doolan (05, 06, 07, 08, 09)

3b – Harry Wolverton (00. 01, 03, 04), Barry Hallman (02), Ernie Courtney (05, 06, 07) Eddie Grant (08, 09)

Ted Taylor

Of – Elmer Flick (00, 01), Shad Barry (02, 03), Sherry Magee (04, 05, 06, 07, 08, 09)

Of – Roy Thomas (00, 01, 02, 03, 04, 05, 06, 07) Ossie Osbom (08), Johnny Bates (09)

Of – Jimmy Slagle (00), Ed Delahanty (01), George Brown (02), Bill Keister (03), John Titus (04, 05, 06, 07, 08, 09)

C – Ed McFarland (00), Chief Zimmer (01), Red Dooin (02, 04, 05, 06, 07, 08, 09), Frank Roth (03)

SP – Al Orth (00, 01), Don White (02), Bill Dugglesby (03, 04, 05), Tuffy Sparks (06, 07, 08), Earl Moore (09)

SP – Red Donahue (01), Chick Fraser (00, 02, 03, 04), Togie Pittinger (05) Johnny Lush (06), Frank Comdon (07), George McQuillan (08), Lew Moran (09)

Manager – Billy Shettsline (00, 01, 02), Chief Zimmer (03), Hugh Duffy (04, 05, 06), Billy Murray (07, 08, 09)

Earl Moore was an 18 game winner (against 12 losses) for the 1909 Phillies and came back the following year to win 22 (against 15 losses). Moore broke in to the big leagues with Cleveland in 1901 (16-14) and finished out his career with Buffalo of the Federal League in 1914. He was with the Phils from 1908-1913. He saw action in 388 games and was 161-153 for his career. He played with the Yankees (1907), Cubs (1913) in addition to his time with Cleveland and the Phillies. Nickname was "Crossfire". He was born (1879) in Pickerington, OH and died in Columbus, OH (1961).

1910-19

1b – Kitty Bransfield (10), Fred Luderus (11, 12, 13, 14, **15,** 16, 17, 18, 19)

2b – Otto Knabe (10, 11, 12, 13), Bobby Byrne (14), **Bert Niehoff (15,** 16, 17**),** Patsy McGaffigan (18), Gene Paulette (19)

SS – Mickey Doolan (10, 11, 12, 13), Jack Martin (14), **Dave Bancroft (15**, 16, 17, 18, 19**)**

3b – Eddie Grant (00), Hans Lobert (11, 12, 13, 14), **Bobby Byrne (15),** Milt Stock (16, 17, 18), Lena Blackburne (19)

Of – John Titus (10, 11), Gavvy Cravath (12, 13, 14, **15,** 16, 17, 18), Leo Callahan (19)

Of – Johnny Bates (10), Dode Paskert (11, 12, 13, 14, **15,** 16, 17), Cy Williams (18, 19)

Of – Sherry Magee (10, 11, 12, 13), Beals Becker (14), **Possum Whitted (15,** 16, 17**),** Irish Meusel (18, 19)

C - Red Dooin (10, 11), Bill Killefer (12, 13, 14, **15,** 16, 17), Jack Adams (18, 19)

Ted Taylor

SP – Earl Moore (10, 11), Tom Seaton (12, 13), Erskine Mayer (14, **15**), Eppa Rixey (16, 17), Brad Hogg (18), Lee Meadows (19)

SP – Bob Ewing (10), Grover C. Alexander (11, 12, 13, 14, **15**, 16, 17), Mike Pendergast (18), Jack Packard (19)

Mgr – Red Dooin (10, 11, 12, 13, 14), **Pat Moran (15, 16, 17, 18)**, Jack Coombs (19) & Gavvy Cravath (19)

*1915 NL Pennant winning players in bold

Bert Niehoff was the second baseman on the pennant winning '15 Phillies. He broke in with the Reds in 1913 and a broken leg ended his career in 1918 while a member of the New York Giants. Never a hitter for average, Bert did lead the NL in doubles in 1916 with 42 of them. The Phils finished second in '16. He was active in baseball for 50 years as a coach and manager in the minors, a coach with the Giants in '29 and a longtime scout for the Angels and the Yankees. Born 1884 in Louisville, CO, he died in 1974 in Inglewood, CA.

20th Century Phillies by the Numbers

1920-29

1b – Gene Paulette (20), Ed Konetchy (21), Roy Lesley (22), Walter Holke (23, 24), Chicken Hawks (25), Jack Bentley (26), Russ Wrightstone (27), Don Hurst (28, 29)

2b – Johnny Rawlings (20), Jimmy Smith (21), Frank Parkinson (22), Cotton Tierney (23), Hod Ford (24), Bernie Friberg (25, 26), Fresco Thompson (27, 28, 29)

SS – Art Fletcher (20, 22), Frank Parkinson (21), Heine Sand (23, 24, 25, 26, 27, 28), Tommy Thevenow (29)

3b – Ralph Miller (20), Russ Wrightstone (21, 23, 24), Goldie Rapp (22), Clarence Huber (25, 26), Bernie Friberg (27), Pinky Whitney (28, 29)

Of – Casey Stengel (20), Bevo LeBourveau (21), Curt Walker (22, 23), George Harper (24. 25), Freddy Leach (26, 27, 28), Lefty O'Doul (29)

Of – Cy Williams (20, 21, 22, 23, 24, 25, 26, 27), Chuck Klein (28, 29)

Of – Irish Meusel (20, 21), Cliff Lee (22), Johnny Mokan (23, 24, 26), George Burns (25), Dick Spalding (27), Denny Sothern (28, 29)

C – Mark Wheat (20), Frank Bruggy (21), Butch Henline (22, 23, 24), Jimmie Wilson (25, 26, 27), Walt Lerian (28, 29)

Ted Taylor

SP – Lee Meadows (20, 21, 22), Clarence Mitchell (23), Bill Hubbell (24), Hal Carlson (25, 26), Jack Scott (27), Ray Benge (28), Claude Willoughby (29)

SP – George Smith (20), Johnny Ring (21, 22, 23, 24, 25), C. Mitchell (above, 26), Dutch Ulrich (27), Bob McGraw (28), Lee Sweetland (29)

Mgr – Gavvy Cravath (20), Wild Bill Donovan (21) & Kaiser Wilhelm (21, 22), Art Fletcher (23, 24, 25, 26), Stuffy McInnis (27), Burt Shotton (28, 29)

Don Hurst was the Phillies regular first baseman from 1928 to 1933. Hurst could hit the long ball and fielded his position well. In his rookie campaign he banged out 19 homeruns and then came back the following year to bash 31 round trippers and drive in 125 runs. He began the year with the Phils and was dealt to Cincinnati in 1934, his last season and batted a disappointing .199 for the Reds. For his career he appeared in 905 games, batted .298 and had 115 homeruns. Born in Maysville KY in 1905, he died in Los Angeles in 1952.

1930-39

1b – Don Hurst (30, 31, 32, 33), Dolph Camilli (34, 35, 36, 37), Phil Weintraub (38), Gus Suhr (39)

20th Century Phillies by the Numbers

2b – Fresco Thompson (30), Lee Mallon (31, 32), Jack Warner (33), Lou Chiozza (34, 35), Chile Gomez (36), Del Young (37), Emmett Mueller (38), Roy Hughes (39)

SS – Tommy Thevenow (30), Dick Bartel (31, 32, 33, 34), Mickey Haslin (35), Leo Norris (36), George Scharein (37, 39), Del Young (38)

3b – Pinky Whitney (30, 31, 32, 36, 37, 38), Jim McLeod (33), Bucky Walters (34), Johnny Vergez (35), Pinky May (39)

Of – Chuck Klein (30, 31, 32, 33, 36, 37, 38), Johnny Moore (34, 35, 36), Joe Marty (39)

Of – Denny Sothern (30), Buzz Arlett (31), Kiddo Davis (32, 34), Chuck Fullis (33), George Watkins (35), Lou Chiozza (36), Hersh Martin (37, 38, 39)

Of – Lefty O'Doul (30), Fred Brickell (31), Hal Lee (32), Wes Schulmerich (33), Ethan Allen (34, 35), Morrie Arnovich (37, 38, 39)

C – Spud Davis (30, 31, 32, 33, 39), Al Todd (34, 35), Earl Grace (36), Bill Atwood (37, 38)

SP – Phil Collins (30, 32, 34), Jumbo Jim Elliott (31), Ed Holley (33), Syl Johnson (35), Claude Passeau (36, 38), Wayne LeMaster (37), Kirby Higbe (39)

SP – Ray Benge (30, 31, 32), Cy Moore (33), Curt Davis (34, 35), Bucky Walters (36, 37), Hugh Mulcahy (38, 39)

Ted Taylor

Mgr – Burt Shotton (30, 31, 32, 33), Jimmie Wilson (34, 35, 36, 37, 38), Hans Lobert (38), Doc Prothro (39)

1940-49

1b – Art Mahan (40), Nick Etten (41, 42), Jimmy Wasdell (43, 45), Tony Lupien (44), Frank McCormick (46), Howie Schultz (47), Dick Sisler (48, 49)

2b – Ham Schulte (40), Danny Murtaugh (41, 43), Al Glossop (42), Moon Mullen (44), Fred Daniels (45), Emil Verban (46, 47), Granny Hamner (48), Eddie Miller (49)

SS – Bobby Bragan (40, 41, 42), Glen Stewart (43), Ray Hamrick (44), Bitsy Mott (45), Skeeter Newsome (46, 47), Eddie Miller (48), Granny Hamner (49)

3b – Pinky May (40, 41, 42, 43), Glen Stewart (44), John Antonelli (45), Jim Tabor (46), Lee Handley (47), Ralph Caballero (48), Willie Jones (49)

Of – Chuck Klein (40), Stan Benjamin (41), Ron Northey (42, 43, 44, 46), Vance Dinges (45), Harry Walker (47), Richie Ashburn (48, 49). **Harry "The Hat" Walker** (left) had the dubious distinction of winning the NL batting title in 1947 and then losing his job to a kid, Richie Ashburn, the following spring. The 6'2 outfielder always played with is cap, hence the nickname "The Hat".

20th Century Phillies by the Numbers

Of – Joe Marty (40, 41), Lloyd Waner (42), Buster Adams (43, 44), Vince DiMaggio (45), Johnny Wyrostek (46, 47), Johnny Blatnick (48), Bill Nicholson (49)

Of – Johnny Rizzo (40), Danny Litwhiler (41, 42), Coaker Triplett (43, 45), Jimmy Wasdell (44), Del Ennis (46, 47, 48, 49)

C – Bennie Warren (40, 41, 42), Mickey Livingston (43), Bob Finley (44), Andy Seminick (45, 46, 47, 48, 49)

SP – Kirby Higbe (40), Johnny Padjajny (41), Rube Melton (42), Schoolboy Rowe (43, 46, 47, 48), Charlie Schanz (44), Andy Karl (45), Russ Meyer (49)

SP – Hugh Mulcahy (40), Tommy Hughes (41, 42), Dick Barrett (43, 45), Ken Raffensberger (44), Oscar Judd (46), Dutch Leonard (47, 48), Ken Heintzelman (49)

Mgr – Doc Prothro (40, 41), Hans Lobert (42), Bucky Harris (43), Freddie FitzSimmons (43, 44, 45), Ben Chapman (45, 46, 47), Dusty Cooke (47), Eddie Sawyer (47, 48, 49)

1950-59

1b – **Eddie Waitkus (50**, 51, 52**)**, Earl Torgeson (53, 54), Marv Blaylock (55, 56), Ed Bouchee (57, 58, 59)

Ted Taylor

2b – **Mike Goliat (50)**, Ralph Caballero (51), Connie Ryan (52), Granny Hamner (53, 54, 57), Bobby Morgan (55), Ted Kazanski (56), Solly Hemus (58), Sparky Anderson (59)

SS – **Granny Hamner (50,** 51, 52, 56**)**, Ted Kazanski (53), Bobby Morgan (54), Roy Smalley (55), Chico Fernandez (57, 58), Joe Koppe (59)

3B – **Willie Jones (50**, 51, 52, 53, 54, 55, 56, 57, 58**)**, Gene Freese (59)

Of – **Del Ennis (50,** 51, 52, 53, 54, 55, 56**)**, Rip Repulski (57), Wally Post (58, 59)

Of – **Richie Ashburn (50**, 51, 52, 53, 54, 55, 56, 57, 58, 59**)**

Of – **Dick Sisler (50,** 51**)**, Johnny Wyrostek (52, 53), Danny Schell (54), Jim Greengrass (55), Elmer Valo (56), Harry Anderson (57, 58, 59)

C – **Andy Seminick (50,** 51, 55**)**, Smoky Burgess (52, 53, 54), **Stan Lopata** (56, 57, 58), Carl Sawatski (59)

SP – **Robin Roberts (50,** 51, 52, 53, 54, 55, 56, 58, 59**)**, Jack Sanford (57)

SP – **Curt Simmons (50,** 52, 53, 54, 56, 57**)**, Bubba Church (51), Murry Dickson (55), Ray Semproch (58), Gene Conley (59)

20th Century Phillies by the Numbers

(**Note: Jim Konstanty** went 16-7 with 22 saves as a reliever for the Whiz Kids)

Mgr – **Eddie Sawyer (50,** 51, 52, 58, 59**)**, Steve O'Neill (52, 53, 54), Terry Moore (54), Mayo Smith (55, 56, 57, 58)

Members of the 1950 NL Champions in Bold

(**Note:** Rich Ashburn became the first Phillies player in fifty years to be a starter at his position for an entire decade. Ashburn's run actually began in 1948, ended in 1959, he was traded to the Chicago Cubs for the '60 season)

1960-69

1b – Pancho Herrera (60, 61), Roy Sievers (62, 63), John Hernnstein (64), Dick Stuart (65), Bill White (66, 67, 68), Dick Allen (69)

2b – Tony Taylor (60, 61, 62, 63, 64, 65), Cookie Rojas (66, 67, 68, 69)

SS – Ruben Amaro Sr. (60, 61), Bobby Wine (62, 63, 64, 65, 67), Dick Groat (65), Roberto Pena (68), Don Money (69)

3b – Al Dark (60), Charlie Smith (61), Don Demeter (62), Don Hoak (63), Dick Allen (64, 65, 66, 67), Tony Taylor (68, 69)

Ted Taylor

Of – Ken Walters (60), Don Demeter (61), Ted Savage (62), Wes Covington (63, 64), Alex Johnson (65), Johnny Briggs (66, 67, 69), Dick Allen (68)

Of – Bobby Del Greco (60), Tony Gonzalez (61, 62, 63, 64, 65, 66, 67, 68), Larry Hisle (69)

Of – Johnny Callison (60, 61, 62, 63, 64, 65, 66, 67, 68, 69)

C – Jimmie Coker (60), Clay Dalrymple (61, 62, 63, 64, 65, 66, 67), Mike Ryan (68, 69)

SP – Robin Roberts (60), Art Mahaffey (61, 62), Ray Culp (63), Jim Bunning (64, 65, 66, 67), Rick Wise (69)

SP – Dick Farrell (60), Chris Short (61, 64, 65, 66, 68), Jack Baldschun (62), Cal McLish (63), Larry Jackson (68), Grant Jackson (69)

Mgr – Eddie Sawyer (60), Andy Cohen (60), Gene Mauch (60, 61, 62, 63, 64, 65, 66, 67, 68), George Myatt (68, 69), Bob Skinner (68, 69)

Notes: By managing in the opening game, losing it and then resigning, Eddie Sawyer became the only Phillies manager to pilot the team in three decades. Johnny Callison became the second player in Phillies history to maintain his starting position for an entire decade (Ashburn was the first).

20th Century Phillies by the Numbers

1970-79

1b – Deron Johnson (70, 71), Tommy Hutton (72), Willie Montanez (73, 74), Dick Allen (75, 76), Richie Hebner (77, 78), Pete Rose (79)

2b – Denny Doyle (70, 71, 72, 73), Dave Cash (74, 75, 76), Ted Sizemore (77, 78), Manny Trillo (79)

SS – Larry Bowa (70, 71, 72, 73, 74, 75, 76, 77, 78, 79)

3b – Don Money (70, 72), John Vukovich (71), Mike Schmidt (73, 74, 75, 76, 77, 78, 79)

Of – Ron Stone (70), Roger Freed (71), Bill Robinson (72, 73), Mike Anderson (74), Jay Johnstone (75, 76, 77), Bake McBride (78, 79)

Of – Larry Hisle (70), Willie Montanez (71, 72), Del Unser (73, 74), Garry Maddox (75, 76, 77, 78, 79)

Of – Johnny Briggs (70), Oscar Gamble (71), Greg Luzkinski (72, 73, 74, 75, 76, 77, 78, 79)

C – Tim McCarver (70, 71), John Bateman (72), Bob Boone (73, 74, 75, 76, 77, 78, 79)

SP – Rick Wise (70, 71), Steve Carlton (72, 74, 75, 76, 77, 78, 79), Wayne Twitchell (73)

SP – Jim Bunning (70), Woody Fryman (71). Darrell Brandon (72), Ken Brett (73), Jim Lonborg (74, 76), Tommy Underwood (75), Larry Christenson (77), Dick Ruthven (78), Nino Espinosa (79)

Ted Taylor

Mgr – Frank Lucchesi (70, 71, 72), Paul Owens (72), Danny Ozark (73, 74, 75, 76, 77, 78, 79), Dallas Green (79)

Note: Shortstop Larry Bowa became the first infielder (and third Phillie overall) to start at his position for an entire decade. Bowa's run would end after the 1981 season when he was traded to the Cubs.

1980-89

1b – **Pete Rose (80,** 81, 82, **83),** Len Matuszek (84), Mike Schmidt (85), Von Hayes (86, 87, 88), Ricky Jordan (89)

2b – **Manny Trillo (80,** 81, 82**), Joe Morgan (83),** Juan Samuel (84, 85, 86, 87, 88), Tommy Herr (89)

SS – **Larry Bowa (80,** 81**), Ivan DeJesus** (82, **83**. 84**),** Steve Jeltz (85, 86, 87, 88), Dickie Thon (89)

3b – **Mike Schmidt (80,** 81, 82, **83**, 84, 86, 87, 88**),** Rick Schu (85), Charlie Hayes (89)

Of – **Bake McBride (80,** 81**),** George Vukovich (82), **Von Hayes (83**, 84, 85, 89**),** Milt Thompson (86, 87, 88)

Of – **Garry Maddox (80,** 81, 82, **83**, 84**),** Jeff Stone (85), Gary Redus (86), Chris James (87, 88), Lenny Dykstra (89)

20th Century Phillies by the Numbers

Of – **Greg Luzinski (80)**, **Gary Mathews** (81, 82, **83**), Glenn Wilson (84, 85, 86, 87), Phil Bradley (88). John Kruk (89)

C – **Bob Boone (80,** 81**)**, **Bo Diaz** (82, **83**), Ozzie Virgil (84, 85), John Russell (86), Lance Parrish (87, 88), Darren Daulton (89)

SP – **Steve Carlton (80,** 81, 82, **83,** 84**),** Kevin Gross (85, 86, 88), Don Carman (87, 88), Jeff Parrett (89)

SP – **Dick Ruthven (80,** 81**)**, Mike Krukow (82), **John Denny (83),** Jerry Koosman (84), Shane Rawly (85, 87), Kent Tekulve (86), Ken Howell (89)

Mgr – **Dallas Green (80,** 81**)**, **Pat Corrales** (82, **83**), **Paul Owens (83,** 84**) (left),** John Felske (85, 86, 87), Lee Elia (87, 88), John Vukovich (88), Nick Leyva (89). Paul Owens, left, was known as "The Pope" and was a key figure in the evolution of the ball club from all aspects.

Notes: All starters names from the 1980 & 1983 NL Champions and World Champion 1980 club are in bold. 42 games in to the '89 season Mike Schmidt retired from baseball. With the exception of the 1985 (when he played first base) Schmidt had been the Phil's regular third sacker since 1973 – the longest run of any Phillies player, ever.

Ted Taylor

1990-99

1b - Ricky Jordan (90), **John Kruk** (91, 92, **93,** 94), Gregg Jefferies (95, 96), Rico Brogna (97, 98, 99)

2b – Tommy Herr (90), **Mickey Morandini** (91, 92, **93,** 94, 95, 96, 97), Mark Lewis (98), Marlon Anderson (99)

SS – Dickie Thon (90, 91), Juan Bell (92), **Kevin Stocker (93,** 94, 95, 96, 97**)**, Desi Relaford (98), Alex Arias (99)

3b – Charlie Hayes (90, 91, 95), **Dave Hollins** (92, **93,** 94), Todd Zeile (96), Scott Rolen (97, 98, 99)

Of – Von Hayes (90, 91), Wes Chamberlain (92), **Jim Eisenreich (93,** 94, 95, 96**),** Darren Daulton (97), Bobby Abreu (98, 99)

Of – **Lenny Dykstra** (90, 91, 92, **93,** 94, 95, 96), Greg Jefferies (97, 98), Ron Gant (99)

Of – John Kruk (90), Dale Murphy (91), Mariano Duncan (92), **Milt Thompson (93,** 94**),** Mark Whitten (95), Pete Incaviglia (96), Midre Cummings (97), Doug Glanville (98, 99)

C – **Darren Daulton** (90, 91, 92, **93,** 94, 95), Benito Santiago (96), Mike Leiberthal (97, 98, 99)

SP – Pat Combs (90), **Tommy Greene** (91, **93**), **Curt Schilling** (92, **93,** 96, 97, 98, 99), Danny Jackson (94), Paul Quantrill (95)

20th Century Phillies by the Numbers

SP – Terry Mulholland (90, 91, 92, 96), Bobby Munoz (94), Michael Mimbs (95), Mark Leiter (97), Mark Portugal (98), Paul Byrd (99)

Mgr - Nick Leyva (90, 91), **Jim Fregosi** (91, 92, **93,** 94, 95, 96), Terry Francona (97, 98, 99)

Note: Starters from 1993 NL Champions will be in bold. Outfielder **Pete Incaviglia** (left) shared the team homerun crown with 24, but played in just 96 games as a fielder, ten games less than Milt Thompson who was regarded as the third outfield "regular".

Chapter 13
Player Awards ... things they won

The Phillies weren't blessed with a lot of great players all at once, but when they managed to get one, the entire City embraced their talents. Here, then, is a rundown of awards won by Phillies players, 1900-1999.

Most Valuable Player –

Baseball writers – **Chuck Klein** (1932); **Jim Konstanty** (1950); **Mike Schmidt** (1980, 1981, 1986)

Sporting News – **Chuck Klein** (1931, 1932)

Major League Player of the Year –

Sporting News – **Robin Roberts** (1952); **Mike Schmidt** (1980, 1986)

Manager of the Year –

Sporting News – **Gene Mauch** (1962); **Danny Ozark** (1976)

Ted Taylor

National League Manager of the Year –

Associated Press/United Press International – **Eddie Sawyer** (1950); **Gene Mauch** (1962, 1964); **Danny Ozark** (1976).

Rookie of the Year –

Sporting News - **Del Ennis** (left), 1946; **Richie Ashburn**, 1948; 1957 – **Ed Bouchee**, 1957; **Dick Allen,** 1964; **Lonnie Smith**, 1980; **Juan Samuel**, 1984. Rookie Pitcher of the year – **Jack Sanford**, 1957; **Ray Culp**, 1963.

Baseball Writers – **Jack Sanford**, 1957; **Dick Allen**, 1964.

Cy Young Award –

Steve Carlton - 1972, 1977, 1980, 1982; **John Denny** - 1983; – **Steve Bedrosian** – 1987.

No-Hitters –

1903 – **Chick Fraser** vs. Cubs; 1906 – **John Lush** vs. Brooklyn; 1964 – **Jim Bunning** vs. NY Mets (perfect game); 1971 – **Rick Wise** vs. Cincinnati; 1990 – **Terry**

20th Century Phillies by the Numbers

Mulholland vs. San Francisco; 1991 – **Tommy Green** vs. Montreal.

Most wins by pitcher –

Grover C. Alexander – 1911 (28); 1914 (27); 1915 (31); 1916 (33); 1917 (30); 1920 (27); **Tom Seaton** – 1913 (27); **Robin Roberts** – 1952 (28); 1953 (23, tied); 1954 (23); 1955 (23); **Steve Carlton** – 1972 (27); 1977 (23); 1980 (24); 1982 (23); **John Denny** – 1983 (19).

Most strikeouts by a pitcher –

Earl Moore – 1910 (185); **Grover C. Alexander** – 1912 (195); 1914 (214); 1915 (241); 1916 (167); 1917 (201); 1920 (173); **Tom Seaton** – 1913 (168); **Claude Passeau** – 1939 (137, tied); **Robin Roberts** – 1953 (198); 1954 (185); **Jack Sanford** – 1957 (188); **Jim Bunning** – 1967 (253); **Steve Carlton** – 1972 (310); 1974 (240); 1980 (286); 1982 (286); 1983 (275); **Curt Schilling** – 1997 (319); 1998 (300).

ERA Leader –

George McQuillan – 1910 (1.60); **Grover C. Alexander** – 1915 (.1.22); 1916 (1.55); 1917 (1.86); 1919 (1.72); 1920 (1.91); **Steve Carlton** – 1972 (1.98).

Ted Taylor

Saves Leader –

Joe Oeschger – 1918 (3, tied); **Phil Collins**, 1933 (6); **Andy Karl** – 1945 (15, tied); **Ken Raffensberger** (pictured left) – 1946 (6); **Jim Konstanty** – 1950 (22); **Russ Meyer** – 1955 (16); **Steve Bedrosian** – 1987 (40).

Pitcher's winning percentage –

Grover C. Alexander – 1915 (.756); **John Denny** – 1983 (.760).

Homerun Champions –

Gavvy Cravath – 1913 (19); 1914 (19); 1915 (24); 1917 (12, tied); 1918 (8); 1919 (12); **Cy Williams** – 1920 (15); 1923 (41); 1927 (30, tied); **Chuck Klein** – 1929 (43); 1931 (31); 1932 (38, tied); 1933 (28); **Mike Schmidt** – 1974 (36); 1975 (38), 1976 (38); 1980 (48); 1981 (31); 1983 (40); 1984 (36, tied); 1985 (37).

Batting Average Leader –

Sherry Magee – 1910 (.331); **Lefty O'Doul** – 1929 (.396); **Chuck Klein** – 1933 (.368); **Harry Walker** – 1947 (.363); **Richie Ashburn** – 1955 (.338); 1958 (.350).

20th Century Phillies by the Numbers

RBJ Leader –

GAVVY CRAVATH, Outfield
Phillies, 1912-20

Sherry Magee – 1907 (85); 1910 (123); 1914 (103); **Gavvy Cravath** (pictured left on his 1977 Philly Favorites card) – 1913 (128); 1915 (115); **Chuck Klein** – 1931 (121); 1933 (120); **Don Hurst** – 1932 (143); **Del Ennis** – 1950 (126); **Greg Luzinski** – 1975 (120); **Mike Schmidt** – 1980 (121); 1981 (91); 1984 (106, tied); 1986 (119); **Darren Daulton** – 1992 (109).

Base hits Leader –

Gavvy Cravath – 1913 (179); **Sherry Magee** – 1914 (171); **Lefty O'Doul** – 1929 (254); **Chuck Klein** – 1932 (226); 1933 (223); **Richie Ashburn** – 1951 (221); 1953 (205); 1958 (215); **Dave Cash** – 1975 (213); **Pete Rose** – 1981 (140); **Lenny Dykstra** – 1990 (192, tied); 1993 (194).

Stolen Bases –

Chuck Klein – 1932 (20); Danny Murtaugh – 1941 (18); Richie Ashburn – 1948 (32).

Chapter 14
The Phillies Trade
That Changed Baseball

Outfielder Curt Flood never played for the Phillies, so you might wonder what a story about him is doing in this book. But Flood should have played for the Phillies and if he had, well, the whole history of baseball as we know it today, might have changed.

Flood was a very good player, not great, not a Hall of Famer, but he had a solid career. He played 15 years (1956-71) batted .293 and was a three-time All-Star. He played centerfield for the St. Louis Cardinals and won seven consecutive Gold Gloves. He was on three pennant-winning teams with the Cardinals and earned two World Series rings.

At the end of the 1969 season, the Cardinals traded him, along with Tim McCarver, Byron Browne, and Joe Hoerner, to the Phillies for Dick Allen, Jerry Johnson, and Cookie Rojas. But this trade was turned out to be different from all other trades.

Flood refused to report to the Phils citing the team's poor record and the dilapidated Connie Mack Stadium (a year later they would move to a brand new park), and for (what he thought were) belligerent—and,

Ted Taylor

racist—fans. Some reports say he was also irritated that he had learned of the trade from a reporter; but Flood wrote in his autobiography that he was told by midlevel Cardinals management and was angry that the call did not come from the general manager. He met with Phillies general manager John Quinn, who left the meeting believing that he had persuaded Flood to report to the team. Flood stood to forfeit a lucrative $100,000 contract. *(Topps included this baseball card of Flood in their 1970 set even though he was never a Phils player.)*

Flood sat out the entire 1970 season. The Cardinals sent two minor leaguers to the Phillies in compensation for Flood's refusal to report. One of them—centerfielder Willie Montañez, (left) who became known as "Willie the Phillie"—went on to a 14-year major league career. The other, Jim Browning, never made the club. In November 1970 the Phillies traded the rights to Flood (and four other players) to the Washington Senators. He signed a $110,000 contract with Washington but played only 13 games of the 1971 season, with a .200 batting average and lackluster play in center field. It was reported that Flood once returned to his locker to find a funeral wreath on it. Despite manager Ted Williams' vote of confidence, Flood retired.

So adamant was he that he went to his personal lawyer and then to Marvin Miller, founder and executive director of the Players Association, and told them he wanted to sue Major League Baseball. The decision sent shock through all professional sports. Flood was, in essence, saying that his career no longer mattered and that he was fighting for his principles.

At the time of this trade, baseball's reserve clause bound a player to a team for life. He was, in basic terms, the team's property. Unless the team chose to trade him or release him, his first big-league team would be his only big-league team for his entire career. A player's only recourse was retirement. (The owners argued that they spent money finding, training and developing their players, hence had a right to their talents.)

Oddly enough, the language of the reserve clause was ambiguous. It merely said that if you played for a team, you must play for that team the next season as well. Two players before Flood had challenged the reserve clause and failed because baseball was exempt from Federal antitrust laws. This was based on a verdict handed down in 1921 by Supreme Court justice Oliver Wendell Holmes.

Miller said that the exemption was irrational. Miller once said, "The courts were saying 'Yes, you're an American and have the right to seek employment anywhere you like, but this right does not apply to baseball players.'"

When Flood came to Miller, his mind was already made up. Miller said "I told him that he didn't have a chance in hell of winning. More important than that, I told him even if he won, he'd never get anything out of it—he'd never get a job in baseball again."

Flood asked Miller if it would benefit other players and was told it would. Flood understood the odds and replied "That's good enough for me." Miller told Flood "You're a union-leader's dream."

Born in Houston in 1938, Flood was raised in Oakland, California. His mother, who had fled the racial bigotry of the pre-World War II South, never let him forget what things had been like where she grew up. In 1962, having little idea of what he was about to encounter, the 24-year-old Flood went to Mississippi to join his idols Dr. Martin Luther King and Jackie Robinson to support the non-violent protests organized by the NAACP.

Less than two years later, racial prejudice pursued him to the suburbs of his own home town when he rented a house for his pregnant wife and four small children only to be denied entrance by the owner, who didn't know they were black when they signed the lease. The man barred their way with a loaded shotgun. Flood sued and won, but it left him without illusions about what it was like to be a black man in America in 1964—even an affluent one who had just helped a major league baseball team win the World Series.

Most black baseball stars were all but invisible during the Civil Rights movement, so Flood's activism was years ahead of its time. When it came time for him to take a stand on being traded to Philadelphia, he was ready. "I do not regard myself as a piece of property to be bought or sold," he told Commissioner of Baseball

Bowie Kuhn in a letter in which he requested the right to be a free agent. Kuhn, echoing the court decisions of previous years, replied that he was sympathetic to Flood's feelings but "simply did not see how that applied to Major League Baseball."

Flood's teammates and colleagues were skeptical of his suit and did not support him; on the day he testified only two former players, Jackie Robinson and Hank Greenberg (left), stood by him. No active players were there all fearful of retaliation from the owners.

What Miller thought was an impossible goal turned out to be within reach. When the decision was announced in 1972, Flood lost 5-3, but only after Judge Lewis Powell, who was sympathetic to Flood, withdrew from the case because of what he called conflict of interest. Powell owned stock in Anheuser-Busch, whose owner, Augie Busch, owned the St. Louis Cardinals. If Powell had remained, Flood may have won a 5-4 decision, but his withdrawal, combined with Chief Justice Warren Berger's 11th-hour switch from Flood's side to baseball's, killed Flood's case.

In effect, the court ruled that yes, Flood should have the right be a free agent, but that baseball's antitrust exemption could only be removed by an act of Congress and that free agency for players should be attained through collective bargaining and that's precisely what happened.

Ted Taylor

Because of the pressure that Flood's suit brought to the baseball owners, Miller and the union were able to bargain for binding arbitration on grievances. And, finally, in 1976, when pitchers Andy Messersmith and Dave McNally agreed to play a season without a contract, arbitrator Peter Seitz ruled them free agents. Overnight, the system that had ruled baseball virtually since its professional organs, collapsed.

Prophets of doom and gloom about the future of the game could be seen on every sports page, but in the end, the Players Association worked out things with management, and salaries sky-rocketed—along with profits, it turned out, as fans liked the exciting new era of free agency and the players it brought to their teams.

As Miller had predicted, Flood never benefited from the revolution he helped begin. Flood had been a heavy drinker practically since the time he became a professional ballplayer, and by the early 1970s he was an alcoholic. His first marriage fell apart in the mid-1960s from the combination of alcohol abuse, long stretches away from home, and the animosities his unwavering Civil Rights stance inspired. After the Supreme Court decision, he was bombarded with hate mail from fans who accused him of trying to destroy baseball; his teammate Bob Gibson said "He got four or five death threats a day."

Flood left the country and opened a bar in Majorca, Spain, frequented by American sailors. Plagued by increasing debt, including unpaid child support, and guilt that he had been a bad father, Flood was finally admitted into a Barcelona psychiatric hospital. His sister sent him the money to return to the U.S. And yet,

Flood managed to pull some strands of his life back together. He married a former girlfriend and reestablished contact with his children.

Recognition came late. In 1992 Flood was given the NAACP Jackie Robinson Award for contributions to black athletes, and in 1994, in perhaps the most satisfying moment of his life, he gave a speech on solidarity to the players as they prepared to go on strike. The players gave him a standing ovation.

Decades of smoking and drinking finally caught up to him. Early in 1995, he was diagnosed with throat cancer. The Players Associating, urged by former legal counsel Dick Moss, paid his medical bills. He died on January 20, 1997, two days after his 59th birthday. The Rev. Jesse Jackson's funeral eulogy stands as his epitaph: "Baseball didn't change Curt Flood. Curt Flood changed baseball. He fought the good fight."

Chapter 15
They took my team away...
A's left town 61 Years ago

In the spirit of true confession, I have to come clean about my initial childhood baseball allegiance.

Sixty-one years ago on a Spring Tuesday (April 13) the Philadelphia Athletics (aka, The A's) opened their final season in town by besting the Red Sox 5-4 behind Bobby Shantz. Just 16, 331 fans showed up. A sorry crowd for any opening day.

Since 1901 Philadelphia fans had the luxury of rooting for teams in both the National and American Leagues. The Athletics were the more successful of the two clubs, winning nine pennants and five world's championships. The Phillies, usually described in print

Ted Taylor

"as the lowly", won but two pennants since they came to town in the 1880's – one in 1915, the other in 1950. The A's last championship (an AL pennant) came in 1931. It wasn't easy being a baseball fan in the Quaker City.

The handwriting was on the wall when the 1954 season began. All winter rumors of a pending sale of the ball club had filled the sports sections of the local newspapers. The Boston Braves had abruptly left town for Milwaukee in spring training 1953, the St. Louis Browns abandoned the Midwest for Baltimore for the 1954 season.

The longtime owner – and manager for 50 years – Connie Mack was old and ill. It was suggested that he was senile (Alzheimer's didn't exist then). A power struggle for control of the club in late 1949 ended up with Connie Jr. losing out to his older brothers Earle and Roy for control of the club. The younger Mack, clearly the brightest of the trio, was exiled to Florida. Mr. Mack was exiled to his tower office and given no power at all.

Roy and Earle were not the sharpest knives in the drawer and soon were in hock up to their ears. First they mortgaged the ballpark to the hilt, then they sold it to the Phillies. The A's had played there since 1909. It's doubtful the senior Mr. Mack knew.

What was the baseball landscape for fans in 1954? First of all, not many showed up for A's games. The

20th Century Phillies by the Numbers

Phillies Whiz Kids were the town's darlings since 1950's flag.

The A's had no giveaways to entice fans. Not even any fireworks shows. Typical souvenirs included A's caps, pennants, buttons, small souvenir bats, pre-printed autographed baseballs. Typical ball park fare included hot dogs (I recall them as being great), peanuts, pop corn, cracker jacks, soda and yummy orange drinks in a carton. The smell of the hot doggies cooking was pure ecstasy. I'm sure you could have purchased cigarettes and cigars, but you couldn't buy a beer.

Simply making the payroll had first dibs on the Mack Family money. Roy and Earle were running the club and they were even bigger penny pinchers than their father. Plus, they hated each other. The team traveled by train. The furthest outpost was St. Louis. I'm sure if they thought they could get away with it they'd have gone by bus to closer opponents.

All the games were on the radio – WFIL (560 AM) - with Byrum Saam as the play-by-play man and Claude Haring as his sidekick. Saam and Haring also did TV, the few games (weekends, usually) that were telecast.

Someone once asked me if the Phillies and A's ever played in Shibe Park the same day – the schedule makers always had one club on the road when the other was home. This meant that there was always baseball at 21st & Lehigh. They did play an annual City Series (1903-54) with the A's winning 22, the Phils 16

Ted Taylor

and there were ten ties. They played nine times one year (1928) and the A's won seven of them.

There were both a team yearbook and game programs. The A's produced yearbooks between 1949 and 1954. They A's also produced a regular newsletter called "Along the Elephant Trail" that kept fans up-to-date on the club. These are collector's items to this day. I have the 1949 yearbook that my Uncle Ernie bought me at a game.

The largest home crowd for the '54 A's came on April 25. They drew 19,930 fans for a doubleheader with the Yankees. The A's lost the first game, won the second.

The smallest home crowd was on June 5 when they beat Baltimore 7-6 before 1,092 fans. The final A's home game drew just 1,715 fans on September 19. But the smallest crowd they played before all season was in Washington DC in a 5-4 loss before 460 people. Imagine. A's 1954 manager Eddie Joost, pictured left, told me (at an A's Society function in the 1990's) "that was one long season". As I recall, the day games started at 1 PM, night games at 8 PM. Sunday doubleheaders could not continue after 6.59 PM thanks to Pennsylvania's Blue Laws.

The A's won the last game they played as a Philadelphia team – September 26 at Yankee Stadium.

20th Century Phillies by the Numbers

They topped the Yanks 8-6 recording 16 hits. The game meant little to the New Yorkers who played Mickey Mantle at short, Yogi Berra at third, Bill Skowron at second. Art Ditmar was the winning pitcher. In between opening day and last day wins, however, they managed to drop 103 games.

The local citizenry organized "Save the A's" campaigns but the league owners (bullied by the New York Yankees) wanted them gone. So all efforts failed (the Philly Mayor didn't want to get involved) even one headed by Connie Mack Jr. It was a daily soap opera

I was just 13 that year and saw just a few games. The last one was Sunday August 22 when they beat the Senators 3-2 in twelve innings. I got a foul ball at that game and it landed two sections away from where my mother, Helen, and I were seated. I casually walked over and picked it up. No one else even bothered going after it. When the club left town I was heart broken. They had taken my team away!

Ted Taylor

Chapter 16
The Phillies new stadium almost ended up in the Suburbs

In Chapter 15 we established that in 1954 the Philadelphia Athletics were allowed to leave the city. Some say it was a conspiracy, and pointed out that the Phillies wanted them gone from here so they'd have no competition for ticket sales. Others say the conspiracy centered on the all powerful New York Yankees who wanted to be rid of their long time East Coast rival – and the would-be buyer (Arnold Johnson) was deeply entwined with the Yankees (in fact he owned Yankee Stadium). Others blame the city's Democrat Mayor, Joe Clark, who simply didn't seem to care.

Phillies owner Bob Carpenter bought the A's ballpark when they left (the two teams had shared it) but knew he needed to move to a newer stadium. Located in North Philly, Connie Mack Stadium was in a declining (dangerous, even) neighborhood and offered no parking.

And so Carpenter looked to a new area – the suburbs – and found a willing accomplice in Montco real estate developer Paul C. Yerger who had an option on 150 acres (Cedarbrook Country Club in Wyncote) and was prepared to build a baseball stadium there. Carpenter was anxious to sign a long term lease. It was 1958 and the stuff hit the fan in Cheltenham. Despite the fact that no one actually lived in that immediate area a large NIMBY (not in my back yard contingent) quickly mustered a 5,000 signature petition in opposition, presented it to the township commissioners and that was the end of that. To this day most of that ground remains empty, save for an aging apartment complex called "The Towers".

But suppose Yerger had built the ballpark, suppose the Phillies agreed to play there. Had that happened the area would, of course, look and feel different. Perhaps Cheltenham's outrageous school taxes would have been supplemented by significant businesses taxes generated by the ballpark. That would have allowed young people to afford homes there and the elderly to keep the ones they already had. It's not far fetched to envision restaurants, hotels, other enterprises thriving in the ballpark region.

Moving a pro franchise outside of the city was an idea that resulted in the Meadowlands (Giants and Jets), Foxboro (New England Patriots) and Fed Ex Field (Redskins) in Landover, MD. And of course there are others. Convenience for the fans and ample parking made those moves sensible ones.

The infrastructure was already in place to handle worries about our city residents getting to the park. Route 6 SEPTA buses ran right by Cedarbrook, trolley

20th Century Phillies by the Numbers

cars ran nearby too (until 1968). The Reading Railroad station was not that far away – you could walk it or, perhaps, take a shuttle. The 309 Expressway opened on-ramps at Cedarbrook in 1961. And, of course, Broad Street ran in to Cheltenham Avenue that passed just below the potential stadium site.

Less than a mile away stood Temple Stadium (built in 1928 it was an oval, lighted and with 34,000 seats – one end zone was sans seats, more could have been added) and the university had played football there for decades (for a time, big-time opponents were on the schedule there). The Eagles had even played some games there and in 1952 actually offered to buy it from the university. Maybe, had the Phillies moved to Cedarbrook the Eagles might have taken another look at the Owls' gridiron, upped the offer, and considered expanding the seating there for pro football – there was plenty of room, and ample parking space to do it. The two stadiums would have been close – not quite as close as in South Philly, but reasonably so to allow other entertainment venues to set up in between.

I wrote two columns about this idea in April and May, 2012, in five of the Montgomery Newspapers. Reaction was swift. Some people really let me have it – using mostly lame ideas about lack of transportation (false),

Ted Taylor

the timing (1948, wrong), it would be inconvenient for city fans (right now South Philly isn't exactly convenient to a lot of suburban fans). Others strongly favored the idea, wished it had happened because they could see a whole different future for their area. But the NIMBY's won out, most of the 150 acres still remain empty and weed infested (the golf club moved long ago) and in discussing Cheltenham Township School taxes most comments are usually preceded by the word onerous.

Chapter 17
Cy Williams, Dick Allen, Del Ennis – Why the Hall Not?

As I near the end of this book up, let's consider that in November of last year (2014) Dick Allen's name was added to the list of "Golden Era" players to be considered for Hall of Fame inclusion by the Veteran's Committee. I was pleased for Dick, but believed that he has about as much chance of being named to the Hall this time as I do. (In an incredibly close tally, however, Allen failed to be elected by just one vote.)

Missing from that list, for a long, long time, are two other Phillies favorites, Fred "Cy" Williams (left) and Olney's own Del Ennis. It mystifies me how Williams has been overlooked over the decades and, yes, I know that he played from 1912 to 1930, but for him to have been skipped over all these years should be an embarrassment to Cooperstown. And, yes, I've been hammering away at Del Ennis' inclusion for a long time. There are men in the Hall no where the equal of Williams and who couldn't carry Del's jockstrap. Of late it has become the "Hall of who

Ted Taylor

you know", rather than a player being elected on actual merit. If the hall can include Red Schoendienst, Bobby Doerr, Travis Jackson and, yes, even Phil Rizzuto, then it should deal Cy, Del and Dick in as well.

You counter with the fact that even his own club, the Phillies, don't give Del his due. And that's true. Elsewhere in this book you have read my feelings about the fact that they retired Del's #14, but awarded that honor to Jim Bunning – whose total contribution to the club was pretty insignificant (no post season, no 20 win seasons). Ironically, Allen wore #15. He broke in as a third baseman. Some believe that Allen's number should also be retired by the Phillies. I've had this "discussion" with Larry Shenk of the Phillies who counters that they only retire the numbers worn by Hall of Famers. He and I strongly disagree.

That all considered, let's compare Cy, Dick and Del, as this book suggests, strictly "By the Numbers". Williams played 19 seasons (13 with the Phillies), Allen, with 15 total, played one more season than Ennis (but only 10 games in his first campaign, 1963), Del, however, got in to 154 more games (when he played that's the equivalent of one season more). Williams, in his career played in 2002, more than either of them. Williams and Allen batted .292 lifetime, Ennis' .284 is pretty comparable. Del, however had more at-bats, more hits than Allen (215 more).

Allen batted over .300 seven times, Williams six (over .285 twice and .471 in 20 games his last season), Del only twice (but he was over .285 four times).

20th Century Phillies by the Numbers

In the dead ball era, Williams stroked 251 homers (but that got him four homerun titles) – his best year was 1923 when he hit 41. Allen had more homeruns then either of them, his best year was 40 (he hit over 24-or-more 7 times). Del's best was 31 (but he hit 24-or-more 8 times). Del drove in 165 more runs than Allen – and had seven seasons with 100 or more RBI's, Allen had just three. Ennis had 38 more doubles, Allen ten more triples. Williams drove in 1005 runs.

Allen played in the post season once (NL playoffs, 1976) but the Phillies wouldn't have gotten to the one World's Series without his breakout 1950 season, 153 games (missed one all year), .311 batting average, 31 homeruns and a league leading 126 RBI's. Playing with the Cubs (with whom he broke in) and the Phillies meant that Williams never made it to the post season.

Cy (real name Fred) was born in Wadena, Indiana on January 31, 1882, he died April 23, 1974 in Eagle River, Wisconsin, April 23, 1974. He stood 6'2, weight 180 and batted and threw left.

Del was born June 8, 1925 in Philadelphia. He died February 8, 1996 in Huntingdon Valley PA. He was 6', 195, batted and threw right.

Dick was born March 8, 1942 in Wampum, PA. He was 5'11, 187, batted and threw right.

Check out these career stats and you'll see how close each man is to the other, and why all three of them belong in the Hall of Fame.

Ted Taylor

Category	Cy Williams	Dick Allen	Del Ennis
Years in the majors	**19**	15	14
Games played	**2002**	1749	1903
Lifetime batting average	**.292**	**.292**	.284
Years batting over .300	6	**7**	2
At bats, hits	6780-1981	6332-1848	**7254-2063**
Homeruns	251	**351**	288
RBI's	1005	1119	**1284**
Doubles	306	320	**358**
Triples	74	**79**	69
Yrs. Over 25 HR's	3	**7**	**7**
Yrs. Over 100 RBI's	1	3	**7**
Struck out	721	1556	**719**
Over 100 K's in a season	**0**	10	**0**
Walked	690	**894**	597

20th Century Phillies by the Numbers

Years with Phillies	13/19	9/15	12/14
Homerun Championships	**4**	2	0
RBI championships	0	1 (113)	1 (126)
Post Season	0	1, 2-for-9, 0 HR	1, 2-for-14, 0 HR
Position	Of	Of-3b, inf.	Of

Note: Bold indicates best of the three

Chapter 18
Philadelphia's Third
"Big League" team – The Stars

If I could gain access to a time machine I'd like to go back to the period when Philadelphia had three major league teams (1934-52). Of course I'm including the Philadelphia Stars in this mix.

I was too young to ever see them, heck I didn't even know they existed until much later in my life. In fact it wasn't until one of the early Philadelphia Baseball Card & Sports Memorabilia Shows that I co-chaired in the early 1960's when I met Gene Benson, onetime centerfielder for the Stars and acknowledged inventor of "the basket catch" (made famous by Willie Mays). On a whim, partner Bob Schmierer and I invited Benson to be a celebrity signer at the show (along with Dick Sisler) and we were amazed at how many people knew about Benson, The Stars and about the Negro Leagues. As an aside, I found Benson to be a charming man and our friendship remained until he died.

One of my goals as founding President of the Philadelphia Athletics Historical Society (in 1995) was to eventually expand the society to include all aspects of professional baseball in the organization. The

Ted Taylor

museum, the library, the publications would have been a perfect forum for the inclusion of all professional baseball in the region. As it turned out my vision and that of a number of board members were in conflict. I saw it as an educational/historical organization, others saw it more for the social aspects. In 1999 I stepped aside and my vision remained unmet until the organization, itself, closed the shop and museum and, like the A's, faded in to the past.

The Stars were a professional Negro league baseball team that called Philadelphia home. They were founded in 1933 when African-American entrepreneur Ed Bolden returned to professional black baseball after being idle since early 1930. The Stars were an independent ball club in 1933, a member of the Negro National League from 1934 until the League's collapse following the 1948 season, and affiliated with the Negro American League from 1949 to 1952. So Philadelphia lost the Stars at the end of the '52 season and, two years later, said goodbye to the Athletics after the '54 season.

20th Century Phillies by the Numbers

In 1934, led by 20-year-old left-hander Slim Jones, the Stars defeated the Chicago American Giants four games to three, for the Negro National League pennant. Like the Phillies, the Stars didn't win many titles. At their high point in mid-1930s, the team starred such greats as Biz Mackey, Jud Wilson, and Dick Lundy. I was amazed to learn, while researching this that after Cleveland released him, Satchel Paige signed with the Stars in July 1950. Later he'd return to the Majors with Bill Veeck and the St. Louis Browns. (Paige also played for the Stars in 1946.)

History

1933: **Independent**

Ed Bolden organized the Philadelphia Stars who played their first season in 1933. The Negro National League was composed primarily of mid-western teams in 1933 and many east-coast clubs were independent making the record keeping difficult. What games counted? What ones didn't?. The Stars were originally one such unaffiliated club and primarily played against local white semi-professional and professional teams. For example, by June 1933, the Stars' only games against black teams had been against the Philadelphia Bacharach Giants and the Pittsburgh Crawfords.

1934-1948: **Negro National League**

The Negro National League used a split-season playoff system in 1934 with the season's first-half winner playing the second-half winner for the championship.

Ted Taylor

The Chicago American Giants won the first-half. The Stars won the second-half with a record of 11-4.

The Stars finished in fourth place in 1945 and 1946, fifth in 1947, and finished in fourth place again in 1948 with a 27 and 29 record. (Record keeping was, at best, informal and though their league record showed 56 games they likely played a similar number of games as exhibitions.)

1949-1952: **Negro American League**

Ownership

The Stars were founded and organized by Ed Bolden. Bolden had owned the Hilldale Club Negro league ballclub that won the Eastern Colored League pennant in 1923, 1924, and 1925, and which beat the Kansas City Monarchs in the Negro League World Series in 1925. Bolden was also a founder of the ECL. Bolden was instrumental in building the Stars' 1934 championship club and ran the team until his death in 1950. After Bolden's death, his ownership passed to his daughter, Hilda Bolden Shorter. Shorter ran the club through 1952.

The team was financed, and owned in part by sports promoter Eddie Gottlieb who also owned the Philadelphia Sphas and Philadelphia Warriors basketball teams. Gottlieb leased Penmar Park from the Pennsylvania Railroad for use by the Stars. In addition to the Stars, Gottlieb was the booking agent for all the Negro league teams in the Northeast, taking 10-percent of gate receipts for his work.

20th Century Phillies by the Numbers

Home Ballparks

The team played at Passon Field during the 1934 and 1935 seasons. Passon Field was located at the current site of West Philadelphia High School's athletic field (baseball and football) now called Pollock Field and was the former home of the Philadelphia Bacharach Giants. In 1936, the Stars moved to 44th and Parkside Ballpark where they played the majority of their home games through 1947 when they lost their lease. The Stars often played on Monday nights at Shibe Park which had a higher seating capacity. The *New York Times* reported that the Stars had their largest crowd at Shibe Park in June 1943 when they beat the Kansas City Monarchs in front of 24,165.

After 1947, the Stars played home games at several area ballparks including Wilmington Park in Delaware, home of the Wilmington Blue Rocks minor-league team.

Logos and Uniforms

The Stars did not have an official team logo, that wasn't important in those days. The Stars wore uniforms with red and navy blue decoration. The cap most commonly associated today with the Stars is their 1938 cap which has a navy crown, red brim, and white star with a red sanserif P. For most of their history, they wore a white cap with a red brim, and red sanserif P as seen to the left. Another style cap worn by the Stars was an all navy cap with a red P. **(From the Cooperstown Ball Cap baseball card collection of Negro League uniforms.)**

Brief Bios of Selected Players/Managers

Jimmie Armstead – He was a pitcher (1938-40). **Frank "Pee Wee" Austin** – Native of Panama, fine shortstop, fashioned a .330 lifetime Negro League batting average.

Pepper Bassett – Noted for catching from a rocking chair, Basset succeeded Josh Gibson as catcher for the Pittsburgh Crawfords. Had a 17-year-career. **Bill Bea** – Played with the NY Black Yankees and Stars in 1940. **Gene Benson** – Noted as the inventor of "the basket catch" – made famous by Willie Mays. Benson was a centerfielder. Broke in with the Atlantic City Bacharach Giants in 1934. Played 13 years had a .319 lifetime batting average. **Archie Braithwaite** – Outfielder with Newark and the Stars, 1944-47. **Barney Brown** – pitcher with Stars, Cuban Stars and New York Black Yankees. **Chet Brewer** – A pitcher for several teams 1925-48. Lifetime 88-61. **Larry Brown** – Catcher and manager in the Negro Leagues. Career spanned 1932-49. **Ralph Burgin** – Career spanned 1917-40. Mostly a second baseman, also played with Hilldale and the NY Black Yankees.

Walter "Rev" Cannady – Played about every position, including pitcher. Also was a manager. Broke in with Columbus Buckeyes, career spanned 1921-45. **George "Tank" Carr** – Infielder, outfielder, catcher between 1921 and 1934. **Ernest "Spoon" Carter** – Pitcher in a career that stretched from 1932-1949. **Jimmy Carter** – Two years, 1938-39, as a Stars pitcher. **William "Mickey" Casey** – Catcher and a manager between 1931-43. **Bill "Ready" Cash** – Versatile player, mostly a catcher. Caught entire 1949 East-West All-Star game. Finished his career in the Chicago White Sox organization. **Oscar Charleston** – Baseball Hall of Fame, career spanned 1915-50. A total of 26 seasons saw him bat a lifetime .350 with 150 homers. An outfielder, he managed the Stars 1941044, 46-50. **Joe Chestnut** – Pitcher, 1950 with Stars and Indianapolis Clowns. **Buster Clarkson** – A good hitting infielder, Satchel Paige once issued an intentional walk to him with the bases loaded. Said Paige, "I'd rather give up one run than four". **Phil Cockrell** – A pitcher, his career spanned 1913-1946. Started out with the Havana Red Sox. **Ron Coder** – No information available. **A. D. "Dewey" Creacy** – Third baseman with numerous clubs between 1924-40. Broke in with the Kansas City Monarchs. **Homer "Goose" Curry** – Outfielder, manager in a career that spanned 1930-50. Broke in with Memphis Red Sox.

Nathaniel Davis – First baseman for NY Black Yankees and Stars, 1947-50. **Wesley Dennis** – Baltimore Elite Giants and Stars, 1944-48 was a first baseman/outfielder. **Herbert "Rap" Dixon** – Big league pitchers brought out the best in him, he had a .362 average in exhibition games against them. An outfielder he had a .304 lifetime batting average (1924-37). **Mahlon Duckett** – Negro National League rookie of the Year, 1940. Broke in at age 17, finished his career with the Homestead Grays in 1950. **Bill**

Ted Taylor

Dumpson – Pitched for the Stars in 1950. **Jake Dunn** – infielder, manager in a career spanning 1930-41.

Rocky Ellis – Pitcher, 1934-42. Broke in with Hilldale also played with the Homestead Grays.

Joe Fillmore – Pitched for the Stars for seven seasons, also spent considerable time playing winter ball in Mexico.

Jonas Gaines – A pitcher, 1937-50 with the Stars, Newark Eagles and Baltimore Elite Giants. **Willie Gaines** – Pitcher for the Stars in 1950. **Walter Lee Gibbons** – A pitcher, had a cup of coffee with the Stars in 1941. **George Giles** – 15 year Negro League career, played first base. Lifetime .313 batting average. **Stanley Glenn** – Six year catcher for the Stars, also played in the Boston Braves organization. **Harold Gould** – He was a pitcher, no other information available. **Bob Griffith** – Pitcher from 1934-49 with a number of teams including the NY Black Yankees and the Washington Elite Giants.

Wilmer Harris – Pitched for the Stars for five seasons 1945-50. **Bill Harvey** – Shortstop for Stars 1937. **Charles "Gabby" Hayes** – Infielder for 1940 Stars. **Curt Henderson** – Infielder, 1936-41. **Bill Holland** – A pitcher and then a manager during his career (1920-41). **Frank Holmes** – Pitcher, 1931-34, broke in with Bacharach Giants (Atlantic City). **Leniel Hooker** – Pitched mostly for the Newark Eagles. Career spanned 1940-48.

Eddie Jefferson – Pitcher, 1946. **Clarence "Fats" Jenkins** – A lifetime .331 batting outfielder, played for the Renaissance basketball team inducted in to the Basketball Hall of Fame. Broke in to Negro ball in 1920 with the New York Lincoln Giants. Ended in 1938 with him splitting the year between the Pittsburgh Crawfords and the NY Black Yankees. **Stuart "Slim" Jones** – Went 32-4 in 1934 for the championship Stars. Career spanned 1933-38.

Steve "Youngie" Keyes – Pitched 1941-48 for Stars and Memphis Red Sox. **Larry "Schoolboy" Kimbrough** – Because of a childhood injury to his right arm, Larry learned to pitch with his left. When he injured that arm a year later, he discovered, upon recovery, that he could pitch with either arm. Career spanned ten years as both a pitcher and slugging outfielder. An outstanding high school athlete he refused to sign a Negro League contract until he graduated, hence the nickname "Schoolboy".

Holsey "Scrip" Lee – Did it all. Played infield, outfield but was mostly a pitcher, 1943. When his playing days ended he became a Negro National League umpire. **Ben Little** – Outfielder, 1947-50, with Homestead Grays, NY Black Yankees and the Stars. **Lester Lockett** – Infielder, career spanned 1939-50. **Dick "King Richard" Lundy** – mostly a shortstop, later a manager in a career that spanned 1916-48. Lifetime .324 batter. **Granville Lyons** – Played first base and pitched, career 1931-37, broke in with Nashville Elite Giants.

Webster McDonald – A pitcher, later a manager in a career that began in 1918 and ended in 1945. Lifetime 93-60 mark on the hill. He also played for the Hilldale, Darby and Philadelphia Giants teams in the city. **Henry**

Ted Taylor

McHenry – Twenty years a pitcher (1930-50). **Biz Mackey** – Baseball Hall of Fame; A switch-hitting catcher, batted .335 lifetime. Had a 30-year career. **Ulysses Mahoney** – A pitcher for the Stars in 1944. **Max Manning** – A pitcher, 1939-49 also played for Newark Eagles and Houston Eagles. **Jack "Boisy" Marshall** – Mostly a second baseman, played for several clubs breaking in with the Dayton Marcos in 1926, last year was 1944. **Fran Matthews** – First baseman, played five years (1940-45). **Verdell Mathis** – Mostly a pitcher, but also saw action at first base and in the outfield. On the mound he was 61-68 lifetime. **Cy Morton** – Had a nine year career, mostly as a shortstop.

Robert LeRoy "Satchel" Paige – Baseball Hall of Fame, a big league rookie at age 42 with the '48 World Champion Cleveland Indians (he was 6-1 for them). In the games they kept track of, Paige was 124-80 in the Negro Leagues. Pitched for the Stars in 1946 and 1950. His best big league season was 1952 when he went 12-10 for the St. Louis Browns (he was 46 years old). Paige returned to the major leagues in 1965 with the Kansas City A's (he was 59) appearing one game. Total big league career 179 games, 28-31 with a 3.29 ERA. **Ted Page** – Played for two of the greatest teams in Negro League history, 1931 Homestead Grays, 1932 Pittsburgh Crawfords. Career ended with the Stars in 1935. **Clarence "Spoony" Palm** – A catcher, 1927-46, began with Birmingham Black Barons. **Roy "Red" Parnell** – Mostly an outfielder, but also played first base, pitched one season (1932) and went 5-1. He was also a league manager. Career spanned 1926-50. Lifetime .309 batter. **Andy "Pat" Patterson** – Career spanned 1934-49, played third base. **Roy Partlow** – Sixteen years as a pitcher in the NNL (1934-50). **Lennie Pearson** – Outfielder, infielder and manager over the 13 years he was in the league. **Bill Perkins** – Satchel Paige's battery mate when they both joined the Birmingham Black Barons. A constant .300 hitter, he also caught Paige with the Pittsburgh Crawford.

Joe Reynolds – Pitched for the Stars in 1935. **Bill Ricks** – Six years as a Stars hurler, 1944-50. **Leon Ruffin** – Career spanned 1936-50. He was a catcher, later a manager.

Sammy Samuels – Pitched for the Stars in 1940. **George Scales** – He was versatile, played most infield slots and the outfield, later a manager. Career spanned 1921-48, started with the St. Louis Giants. Lifetime .309 batting average. **Dick Seay** – Infielder, 1925-47, with many clubs starting out with the Pennsylvania Red Caps. **Harry "Suitcase" Simpson** – An outfielder who went from two years with the Stars to the Cleveland Indians for whom he batted .266 during an 8-year-career. **Milt Smith** – Just one season, a pitcher, with the Stars (1950). **John "Neck" Stanley** – Broke in with Atlantic City's Bacharach Giants in 1928, finished with the Stars twenty years later. **Norman "Turkey" Stearnes** - Baseball Hall of Fame; played the outfield 1921-42, broke in with Montgomery Grey Sox. Batting average for his career was .352. **Jim Stevens** – Second baseman for the 1933 Stars. **Paul "Jake" Stephens** – Shortstop, played with several clubs 1921-37.

Ted Taylor

Clint Thomas – A lifetime .333 hitter, hit .373 in 1923, his rookie year for the Hilldale Giants, another Philadelphia team.

Edsall "Big" Walker – Pitched, mostly, for the Homestead Greys. **Pete Washington** – Outfielder, 1923-35. Started out with the Washington Potomacs. **Murray Watkins** – Third baseman played for the Newark Eagles and the Stars. **Roy Welmaker** – Pitcher, 1932-45, broke in with the Atlanta Black Crackers. Jim West – A first baseman for the entire 17 years he played in the Negro Leagues (1930-47). **Charles "Chaney" White** – An outfielder, also played locally with the Darby Daisies. Career spanned 1921-35. Lifetime batting average .308. **Don Whittington** – No record available. **Chester Williams** – Infielder for numerous clubs, 1930-43. **Marvin Williams** – Outstanding second baseman for the Stars, had a tryout in 1945 with the Boston Red Sox, of course they didn't sign him. **Jud "Boojum" Wilson** – Baseball Hall of Fame; Lifetime .347 batter, career spanned 1922-45. **Jesse "Nip" Winters** – Pitched from 1919-33 also played locally with Hilldale and the Darby Daisies. Lifetime he was 94-55.

Bill "Yank" Yancey – Part of the Renaissance five Basketball team inducted as a unit by the Basketball Hall of Fame. He was a good hitting shortstop in his baseball career (1923-36).

Author's Note: Negro League record keeping was, at best, casual. The information preceding this is the best we could gather from a number of sources including, but not limited to, the book "Only The Ball Was White" © 1970 by Robert Peterson; The Baseball Encyclopedia (9th edition); Baseball-Reference.com; Wikipedia; Larry

20th Century Phillies by the Numbers

Fritsch Cards, "Negro League Baseball Stars" (1986) and personal recollections from many of the players I have met over the years.

Negro National League Championships

- *1934*

All-Star Team Selections

The Negro League Baseball All-Star Game was called the East-West Game. Players were not divided by league, but by geographical location; Stars players played for the East. Players were voted to the teams by the fans with votes tallied by the Chicago Defender and the Pittsburgh Courier newspapers.

These Philadelphia Stars appeared in the All-Star game for the East team. For some reason – no explanation available - only players from the Pittsburgh Crawfords and Washington Elite Giants played for the East in the 1936 game. Two games were played in 1939, 1942, and 1946-1948.

- 1933 – Rap Dixon (RF), Dick Lundy (SS), Biz Mackey (C), Jud Wilson (3B)
- 1934 – Slim Jones (P), Jud Wilson (3B)
- 1935 – Slim Jones (P), Biz Mackey (C), Webster McDonald (MGR), Dick Seay (2B), Paul Stephens (SS), Jud Wilson (3B)
- 1936 – *no Stars on team*
- 1937 – Jake Dunn (2B)
- 1938 – Jake Dunn (PH)
- 1939 – Red Parnell (LF), Andy Patterson (3B)
- 1940 – Gene Benson (CF), Henry McHenry (P)

Ted Taylor

- 1941 – Henry McHenry (P)
- 1942 – Barney Brown (P), Andy Patterson (3B), Jim West (1B)
- 1943 – *no Stars on team*
- 1944 – Barney Brown (*did not appear in game*), Marvin Williams (P)
- 1945 – Frank Austin (SS), Gene Benson (LF), Bill Ricks (P)
- 1946 – Frank Austin (PH), Gene Benson (RF), Barney Brown (P), Murray Watkins (PH)
- 1947 – Frank Austin (SS), Henry Miller (P)
- 1948 – Frank Austin (SS), Bill Cash (C)
- 1949 – Bill Cash (C), Oscar Charleston (MGR), Buster Clarkson (RF), Bob Griffith (P)
- 1950 – Jonas Gaines (P), Ben Littles (RF), Charles White (3B)
- 1951 – Wilmer Harris (P), Ben Littles (PH), Milt Smith (3B)
- 1952 – Wilmer Harris (P), Jimmy Jones (RF), Ted Washington (SS), Don Whittingdon (3B)

Negro National League Rookie of the Year

- 1940 **Mahlon Duckett**

Hall of Famers

While none of these players were enshrined in Cooperstown with a Stars cap, each of them was a part of the Philadelphia Stars franchise at one point in his career.

Oscar Charleston, Player 1942, manager 1942-44, 46-50

Biz Mackey, 1933-35

Satchel Paige, 1946, 1950

Turkey Stearns, 1936

Jud Wilson, Player 1933-39, manager 1937

Stars co-owner **Eddie Gottlieb** was inducted into the Basketball Hall of Fame in 1972.

Today at 44th and Parkside is a Negro leagues memorial park. In 2004, West Philadelphia's Business Association of West Parkside led a coalition of local groups in building the park. The Philadelphia Building Trades Council donated $150,000 in labor to help build the park in which the memorial statue, Pennsylvania historical marker, and the very attractive Stars mural – which adorns the side of a building - are now located.

A Negro Leagues Memorial Statue also stands at 44th and Parkside in tribute to the ballplayers that played at the site. The Phillies hosted the dedication of the statue on June 18, 2003 at Veterans Stadium. Mayor John

Ted Taylor

Street and Phillies shortstop Jimmy Rollins attended the unveiling of the statue, along with the then living members of the Stars, Bill Cash, Mahlon Duckett, Stanley Glenn, Harold Gould, and Wilmer Harris.

In 1998, Philadelphia's West Parkside community, established a historical marker at the southwest corner of Belmont and Parkside Avenues, site of the former YMCA Athletic Field, which became home to the Philadelphia Stars and known as the 44th and Parkside Ballpark. The historical marker recognizes the history of African-American baseball there and in greater Philadelphia.

Prior to its 2008 First-Year Player Draft, Major League Baseball held a ceremonial draft of surviving players from the Negro leagues to honor those players excluded from organized professional baseball. Every team in Major League Baseball selected a player whose career encompassed the Negro leagues. Former Stars players who participated in the draft were **Walter Lee Gibbons**, a pitcher who pitched briefly for the Stars in 1941 and was selected by the Tampa Bay Rays, pitcher **Harold Gould** selected by the Toronto Blue Jays, and infielder **Mahlon Duckett** who was selected by the Phillies.

Negro league players who had signed with Major League organizations were not eligible for the ceremonial Draft. Former Stars players **Bill Cash** had played in the organization of the Chicago White Sox and **Stanley Glenn** had played in the Boston Braves' minor-league system. The Phillies chose to include Cash and Glenn in the Draft celebrations by recognizing the two players prior to their June 5, 2008

20th Century Phillies by the Numbers

game against the Cincinnati Reds at Citizens Bank Park. The Phillies presented Cash and Glenn with new Phillies jerseys while Gould and Duckett were at the MLB Draft.

The Glenside Kid Remembers ...
My step Father, Ernie Lay, grew up in the same Philly neighborhood as Roy Campanella and knew Roy well. Roy's father was Italian, his Mother African American. I heard the story many times. Ernie was a Phillies fan except when the Dodgers came to town. I recall him taking me to several games with Brooklyn where there were more than usual African Americans in the Shibe Park stands. I also had the thrill of meeting Campy before a game one Sunday – Don Newcombe was pitching for Brooklyn (I met him too), Robin Roberts for the Phils. Ernie explained that since the Negro Leagues pretty much were gone from the scene – mostly because, thanks to Jackie Robinson, the good Negro League players were now in organized ball. I was a small kid, None of it mattered to me at the time.

Philadelphia's Negro League Clubs

Team	1st Yr	Last Yr	Affiliation(s)	Notes
Bacharach Giants	1931	1942	Independent (1931–33) NNL2 (1934) Independent (1935–42)	• Based in **Philadelphia** • (Not to be confused with the Atlantic City-based team of the same name.)
Hilldale Club	1916	1932	Independent (1916–22) ECL (1923–28) ANL (1929) Independent (1930–31) EWL (1932)	• Also known as **Hilldale Daisies, Darby Daisies** • Based near **Philadelphia**
Philadelphia Pythians	1867	1887	Independent (1867–86) NCBBL (1887)	
Philadelphia Giants	1902	1916	Independent (1902–05) IL (1906) NA (1907–09) Independent (1910–16)	

294

20th Century Phillies by the Numbers

Team			
Philadelphia Stars	1933	1952	Independent (1933), NNL2 (1934–48), NAL (1949–52)
Philadelphia Tigers	1928	1928	ECL (1928)

About the Author

Recently-retired Chestnut Hill College Professor **Henry R. (Ted) Taylor** was a career educator. Ted has been a teacher, college baseball coach, administrator and athletics director. In 1989 his Philadelphia College of Textiles & Science baseball team (now Philadelphia University) made it to the NCAA Division II Final 8 and while serving as a college AD, his teams won a combined 32 championships in various sports. *(Ted is pictured here with the late Robin Roberts, a Phillies Hall of Famer. They were together at the "Babe Ruth Birthday Party" in Baltimore in the early 2000's.)*

He is a published author with eight books (counting this one) to his credit as well as three college texts. He has been a newspaper columnist and editor, magazine editor and has had countless articles published on a variety of subjects. His weekly "At Large" column still appears on the Op Ed pages of five weekly Montgomery Media newspapers and his monthly hobby column is at tedsilary.com.

He is a lifelong baseball fan, and was the founding president of The Philadelphia Athletics Historical Society that was formed in 1995 to honor the memory of Philadelphia's American League baseball team. His lectures about the A's and their amazing history over

Ted Taylor

54 years has been delivered in many venues in the tri-state area.

In May 2013 Ted returned to his first love, radio, as a disc jockey and host of the "Good Morning Show" on WRDV FM (the RDV Radio Network). Inspired by Jean Shepherd, and others, Taylor spent many years in radio and TV, a career that paralleled his time in education. He was a disc jockey, play-by-play sportscaster and talk show host on a number of Philadelphia radio stations – including the 50,000 watt WIFI FM regarded by many as one of city's pioneering rock-and-roll outlets. He served as host of a weekly nationally syndicated sports hobby talk show for a number of years and has many numerous TV appearances, including two hosting roles on Fox "In the Zone". *(Ted is pictured in 1972 with Phils sportscaster, the late, Bill Campbell who was on hand at a Kiwanis District meeting when the combined clubs honored Ted and his broadcast partners – Buzz Allen and the late Bill South as "Suburban Sportscasters of the year".)*

Ted served both Fleer and Score Board as a vice president and headed his own public relations firm for a number of years. Taylor served as vice chairman of the board of Act II Playhouse, a professional equity theatre (2000-2010) and is a member of the board of a charity 5K and helped form several area youth organizations including the Glenside Youth AC, Keystone State Football League and the Warminster Pioneers. He was first president of the Eastern Pennsylvania Sports Collectors Club.

Ted is married, the father of four and grandfather of six, great grandfather of three and lives with his wife Cindy in Abington, PA and, as frequently as he can, in Wildwood Crest NJ.

Postscript

The Phillies have fallen out of the "elite" team category for the moment and the critics all have their knickers in a bunch. Philadelphia sportswriters and internet bloggers all know what is wrong. They are clearly smarter than the people running the organization. It's obviously the fault of the general manager or the president or the scouting director or the head of the minor leagues – all of them dopes, apparently. And, you know what, maybe it is. But that really shouldn't be our worry.

Let's face facts folks. Baseball is a business. If they win they make more money (more sponsors come along, and they have our money which we happily spend with them) than if they lose. Players are given obscene salaries and why not? If I'm a player and some owner with deep pockets wants to give me a ridiculous amount of money to play a kid's game I'd be a fool not to take it. If they win they get even more fans who pay ridiculous prices for a hot dog and a beer at the ballpark and willingly allow themselves to be gouged to park in a parking lot funded, I believe, by tax money.

I've been a fan since I was a little kid. I'd go to Shibe Park/Connie Mack Stadium by train, walk over Lehigh Avenue and perch in a cheap seat, buy a hot dog, soda and a scorecard. It was because I liked it. I supported

Ted Taylor

the A's and the Phillies and, mostly, they weren't very good. I remain a fan to this day. It matters little if they win or lose – really. Think about it. When they lose nothing in your life changes, nor does it when they win. (Oh sure, you feel better, but the cost of living remains constant, you get another year older on your next birthday.)

So with this postscript that closes out this latest work of writing I'm on record as saying – win or lose, I love my team. I love baseball, most of all the pro sports. I won't die if the team loses, nor will I get healthier if it wins. It's entertainment, pure and simple. It is not the be all and end all. If you understand that you'll feel a lot better. Life will go on. At least until it doesn't.

I hope you liked this book.

The Glenside Kid

aka/Ted Taylor
2015

www.ingramcontent.com/pod-product-compliance
Lightning Source LLC
Chambersburg PA
CBHW052013070526
44584CB00016B/1727